FROM RECEPTION TO INTEGRATION OF ASYLUM SEEKERS AND REFUGEES IN POLAND

This book sheds light on the complex experiences of asylum seekers and refugees in Poland, against a local backdrop of openly anti-refugee political narratives and strong opposition to sharing the responsibility for, and burden of, asylum seekers arriving in the EU.

Through a multidimensional analysis, it highlights the processes of forced migrant admission, reception and integration in a key EU frontier country that has undergone a rapid migration status change from a transit to a host country. The book examines rich qualitative material drawn from interviews conducted with forced migrants with different legal statuses and with experts from public administration at the central and local levels, NGOs, and other institutions involved in migration governance in Poland. It discusses both opportunities for and limitations on forced migrants' adaptation in the social, economic, and political dimensions, as well as their access to healthcare, education, the labour market, and social assistance.

This book will be of particular interest to scholars, students, policymakers, and practitioners in migration and asylum studies, social policy, public policy, international relations, EU studies/European integration, law, economics, and sociology.

Karolina Sobczak-Szelc is an Assistant Professor at the Centre of Migration Research of the University of Warsaw and the Centre for Advanced Studies of Population and Religion, Cracow University of Economics, Poland.

Marta Pachocka is a Head of the Migration Policies Research Unit at the Centre of Migration Research of the University of Warsaw and an Assistant Professor in the Department of Political Studies of SGH Warsaw School of Economics, Poland.

Konrad Pędziwiatr is a Professor in the Department of International Affairs of Cracow University of Economics and a Deputy Director of the Centre for Advanced Studies of Population and Religion, Cracow University of Economics, Poland.

Justyna Szałańska is a Research Assistant at the Collegium of Socio-Economics of SGH Warsaw School of Economics and an Affiliate of the Centre of Migration Research of the University of Warsaw, Poland.

Monika Szulecka is a Research Assistant at the Institute of Law Studies, Polish Academy of Sciences and an Affiliate of the Centre of Migration Research of the University of Warsaw, Poland.

ROUTLEDGE ADVANCES IN EUROPEAN POLITICS

Electoral Politics in Crisis After the Great Recession
Change, Fluctuations and Stability in Iceland
Eva H. Önnudóttir, Agnar Freyr Helgason, Olafur Th. Hardarson and Hulda Thórisdóttir

The Pandemic Crisis and the European Union
COVID-19 and Crisis Management
Paulo Vila Maior and Isabel Camisão

Belgian Exceptionalism
Belgian Politics between Realism and Surrealism
Edited by Didier Caluwaerts and Min Reuchamps

Rethinking European Social Democracy and Socialism
The History of the Centre-Left in Northern and Southern Europe in the Late 20th Century
Edited by Alan Granadino, Stefan Nygård and Peter Stadius

From Reception to Integration of Asylum Seekers and Refugees in Poland
Karolina Sobczak-Szelc, Marta Pachocka, Konrad Pędziwiatr, Justyna Szałańska, and Monika Szulecka

For more information about this series, please visit: www.routledge.com/Routledge-Advances-in-European-Politics/book-series/AEP

FROM RECEPTION TO INTEGRATION OF ASYLUM SEEKERS AND REFUGEES IN POLAND

Karolina Sobczak-Szelc, Marta Pachocka, Konrad Pędziwiatr, Justyna Szałańska, and Monika Szulecka

Routledge
Taylor & Francis Group
LONDON AND NEW YORK

First published 2023
by Routledge
4 Park Square, Milton Park, Abingdon, Oxon OX14 4RN

and by Routledge
605 Third Avenue, New York, NY 10158

Routledge is an imprint of the Taylor & Francis Group, an informa business

British Library Cataloguing in Publication Data
A catalogue record for this book is available from the British Library

ISBN: 978-1-032-05150-5 (hbk)
ISBN: 978-1-032-05155-0 (pbk)
ISBN: 978-1-003-19632-7 (ebk)

DOI: 10.4324/9781003196327

Typeset in Bembo
by Newgen Publishing UK

CONTENTS

FIGURES

TABLES

ABOUT THE AUTHORS

Karolina Sobczak-Szelc is Assistant Professor at the Centre of Migration Research, University of Warsaw, and the Centre for Advanced Studies of Population and Religion (CASPAR), Cracow University of Economics. She combines earth science, social geography, spatial development, and sociology to study forced migrations both in countries of origin and destination. Her knowledge of this subject is supported by numerous studies conducted in Poland and countries of MENA, particularly in Egypt, Morocco, and Tunisia. She was Principal Investigator in the H2020 RESPOND Multilevel Governance of Mass Migration in EU and beyond. She is member of IMISCOE, IASFM, PERN, and EuroMedMig. Her main research interests include forced migration studies, integration of forced migrants, environmental migrations, and strategies of adaptation to environmental changes and limitations.

Marta Pachocka is Head of Migration Policies Research Unit at the Centre of Migration Research of the University of Warsaw and an Assistant Professor in the Department of Political Studies of SGH Warsaw School of Economics. She is a Ph.D. in economics. She has considerable experience as both a coordinator and a key staff member in projects funded by EU Programmes (Horizon 2020, Horizon Europe, Lifelong Learning Programme, Erasmus+, Creative Europe), and others. She is on the board of the Polish European Community Studies Association (PECSA) and Research Committee RC46 "Migration and Citizenship" of the International Political Science Association (IPSA). Her main research interests include European studies and migration studies.

Konrad Pędziwiatr is a Professor in the Department of International Affairs of the Cracow University of Economics and Deputy Director of the Center for Advanced Studies of Population and Religion. Author of numerous publications on migration, migration policy, religion and ethnicity in the processes of migration, Islam and Muslims in Europe, and the politicization of Islam in Europe and the Middle East and North Africa—including the monographs: "Muslims in Western Europe" (2007), "The New Muslim Elites in European Cities" (2010), "Polish Migration Policy" (2015), "Transformation of Islamism in Egypt and Tunisia in the shadow of the Arab Spring" (2019).

Justyna Szałańska is Research Assistant at the Collegium of Socio-Economics in SGH Warsaw School of Economics and an Affiliate of the Centre of Migration Research, University of Warsaw. She is also pursuing her Ph.D. at the University of Warsaw. Her research interests focus on European integration, identity issues in Turkey and Europe, citizenship policies and refugees and asylum seekers protection policies. She has been a key staff member of the two Horizon 2020 projects: RESPOND Multilevel Governance of Mass Migration in Europe and Beyond (2017–2021) and "Investing in 'Welcoming Spaces' in Europe: revitalizing shrinking areas by hosting non-EU migrants (2020–2024)".

Monika Szulecka is Research Assistant at the Institute of Law Studies, Polish Academy of Sciences (member of the Criminology Department and the Migration Law Research Centre), an Affiliate at the Centre of Migration Research, University of Warsaw. A criminologist, political scientist, and migration researcher. Author of publications devoted to migration policy and migration control, immigration and asylum law in action, economic adaptation of migrants and the phenomenon of irregular migration.

ACKNOWLEDGEMENTS

This book is based on the research results achieved within the project "RESPOND: Multilevel Governance of Mass Migration in Europe and Beyond" that has received funding from the European Union's Horizon 2020 Research and Innovation Programme under grant agreement No 770564.

Open access for this book was financed from the following sources:

- the project "RESPOND: Multilevel Governance of Mass Migration in Europe and Beyond";
- the Program "Excellence Initiative—Research University" at the University of Warsaw from the funds of the minister responsible for higher education and science;
- the Cracow University of Economics' funds.

The proofreading of this book was financed by the SGH Warsaw School of Economics within KES/DB/21:2. Development of the regional staff (2.).

ABBREVIATIONS

ABBREVIATION	*FULL NAME*	*ENGLISH TRANSLATION (if applicable)*
AIDA	Asylum Information Database	
AMIF	Asylum, Migration and Integration Fund	
BRPO	Biuro Rzecznika Praw Obywatelskich	Office of the Commissioner for Human Rights (in Poland)
CBS	Central Bureau of Statistics [Statistics Netherlands]	
CEE	Central and Eastern Europe	
CEECs	Central and Eastern European Countries	
CJEU	Court of Justice of the European Union	
CMR	Centre of Migration Research	
CoE	The Council of Europe	
COVID-19	Coronavirus disease 2019	
EACEA	Education, Audiovisual and Culture Executive Agency	
ECtHR	European Court of Human Rights	
EEA	European Economic Area	
EMN	European Migration Network	
EU	European Union	
GUS	Główny Urząd Statystyczny	Central Statistical Office (in Poland)
ICCPR	International Covenant on Civil and Political Rights	

ABBREVIATION	*FULL NAME*	*ENGLISH TRANSLATION (if applicable)*
ICESCR	International Covenant on Economic, Social and Cultural Rights	
IDPs	Internally Displaced Persons	
IIP	Individual Integration Programme	
ILO	International Labour Organization	
IMF	International Monetary Fund	
INSEE	National Institute of Statistics and Economic Studies of France	
IOM	International Organization for Migration	
ISIS	Islamic State of Iraq and Syria	
KORWIN	Koalicja Odnowy Rzeczypospolitej Wolność i Nadzieja	Coalition for the Renewal of the Republic – Liberty and Hope
MEN	Ministerstwo Edukacji Narodowej	Ministry of National Education (in Poland)
MENA	Middle East and North Africa	
MGN	Migration Governance Network Migration Governance Network	
MIPEX	Migrant Integration Policy Index	
MLG	Multi-Level Governance	
MSWiA	Ministerstwo Spraw Wewnętrznych i Administracji	Ministry of the Interior and Administration (in Poland)
MZ	Ministerstwo Zdrowia	Ministry of Health (in Poland)
NGO	Non-Governmental Organisation	
NFZ	Narodowy Fundusz Zdrowia	National Health Fund (in Poland)
NIK	Najwyższa Izba Kontroli	Supreme Audit Office (in Poland)
NLI	National Labour Inspectorate (in Poland)	
OECD	Organisation for Economic Co-operation and Development	
OF	Office for Foreigners (in Poland)	
PIP	Państwowa Inspekcja Pracy	National Labour Inspectorate (in Poland)
PiS	Prawo i Sprawiedliwość	Law and Justice
PO	Platforma Obywatelska	Civic Platform
PSL	Polskie Stronnictwo Ludowe	Polish People's Party
PTSD	Post-traumatic Stress Disorder	
PZPR	Polska Zjednoczona Partia Robotnicza	Polish United Workers' Party
RESPOND	H2020 project entitled 'Multilevel Governance of Mass Migration in Europe and Beyond'	

ABBREVIATION	*FULL NAME*	*ENGLISH TRANSLATION (if applicable)*
TFEU	Treaty on the Functioning of the European Union	
TVP	Telewizja Polska	Polish Public Television
UK	United Kingdom	
UNHCR	United Nations High Commissioner for Refugees	
USSR	Union of Soviet Socialist Republics	
V4	Visegrad Group	
WFSC	Warsaw Family Support Centre	

1
INTRODUCTION

The fall of communism in 1989, followed by the deep political and socioeconomic transformations in the early 1990s, led to the opening of the Polish borders and increased mobility from and to Poland. For almost the two–and-a-half decades that followed, most of the economic migrants and asylum seekers arriving in Poland treated the latter as a transit country on their way to Western Europe, rather than a destination country. However, recent years have brought a change in the migration status of Poland, which is undergoing a transformation from an emigration to an emigration-immigration country, or even an immigration country (Okólski, 2021), mostly characterised by the so-called "Ukrainisation" of economic immigration (Górny and Kindler, 2018, p. 221). Despite the changes in migration status, Poland is still perceived as a state that cannot develop an effective and coherent migration and asylum policy strategy. Since 2015, this condition has been ascribed mostly to the fact that the country itself was going through a serious internal crisis (political and institutional, democracy and the rule of law), following the change of government at the end of that year.

The percentage of foreigners among the country's population is increasing. Ukrainian citizens predominate in the foreign population, but the latter is becoming more diversified, due to a large extent of the recruitment of migrant workers from countries other than the neighbouring states, in particular from South Asia. The growing migrant population is the result of a mix of internal pull factors such as economic growth and labour market needs in Poland, and external push factors such as increasing political, humanitarian, and socioeconomic instability in third countries.

Among the latter factors, the complex situation in Ukraine, with which Poland borders in the east, deserves special attention. The dynamic increase in Ukrainian migration to Poland (both voluntary and forced) was initially associated with the outbreak of the Russian-Ukrainian war in 2014 (after Russia's military intervention

DOI: 10.4324/9781003196327-1

in the Crimean Peninsula and eastern Ukraine). This mobility has been facilitated by various legal instruments linked, however, to economic migration or in connection with the Polish nation rather than asylum-seeking. Legal and institutional steps to support Ukrainians fleeing conflict in Ukraine were introduced only at the end of February 2022 after the Russian full-scale invasion of Ukrainian territory. The latter will definitely affect the population of asylum seekers in Poland. Until 2020, it was predominated by Russian citizens of Chechen origin. In mid-2020, Belarussians became the main group applying for international protection in Poland. They remained the key addressees of asylum policy in Poland in 2021. In that year, however, the events in Afghanistan and the evacuation of Afghan citizens by Poland changed the trends in both the receiving of asylum applicants and in granting international protection to them.

Another external factor in recent years, important in the political dimension and with reference to government activities, was the migration and refugee management crisis in Europe in 2015–2016. Although Poland did not directly experience an increased inflow of asylum seekers at that time, the intensive debates on how to respond to the phenomenon at the EU level contributed to a change in Poland's approach towards immigrants in general and asylum seekers in particular. These factors also led to the consolidation of reluctant practices towards forced migrants. Together with Hungary and the Czech Republic, Poland was a major opponent of the mechanisms for sharing the burdens and responsibilities for asylum seekers in the European Union during the refugee crisis. Despite all this, however, Poland remained a destination for asylum seekers, originating mostly from the Caucasus, or an "unwanted destination" for those returned from other EU countries in line with the Dublin regulations.

This book focuses on the complex situation of forced migrants in Poland, one of the Central and Eastern European (CEE) Member States of the European Union since 2004 and a Schengen zone member since 2007. This specific case study is particularly important given that the country's eastern border serves as the EU external frontier and hence is prone to the inflow of forced and irregular migrants from third countries, although from the early 2000s until 2021 both categories of migrants were not a real challenge for the Polish authorities. For the purposes of this publication, we focus on forced migrants, by which we mean people seeking asylum, wishing to submit or having already submitted an application for international protection in Poland (regardless of the outcome of the asylum procedure), as well as those already granted international protection. The latter are considered beneficiaries of international protection and include people granted refugee status or subsidiary protection. Therefore, the term "forced migrants" encompasses both asylum applicants and beneficiaries of international protection, as well as those who, for various reasons, seek asylum but were denied the opportunity to apply for it or their asylum claims were rejected.

Since 2015, the situation of asylum seekers and refugees in Poland has been of great interest to politicians, media, the wider public, and scholars, but still many misconceptions have arisen or been reinforced regarding the reasons for their arrival, circumstances of applying for international protection, their functioning during the reception procedure, the potential change in their situation when they receive protection status, and their (un)willingness to remain in Poland afterwards. This book aims not only to draw attention to the situation of forced migrants during all stages of the asylum procedure and integration process but also to show how forced migrants and other actors involved in the reception and integration of this group in Poland respond to the changing political, institutional, and social environment after 2011.

The Arab Spring of 2011 contributed to a radical change in asylum realities of some EU states and intensified debates about the possible response to a mass influx of forced migrants in every EU country. To shed light on the roots of the legal, institutional, and organisational framework of forced migrants' admission, reception, and integration, we refer also to the preceding two decades. The development of asylum policy in post-communist Poland is elaborated against the background of the transformations of the asylum system in the EU. We pay special attention, however, to the most recent determinants of asylum policies and practices, namely since 2015 when many processes affecting forced migration governance started. These concerned both the external dimension, such as building cooperation with other CEE countries aimed at elaborating response mechanisms to higher migration pressures and to mechanisms other than those proposed at the EU level. Also, at the end of 2015, along with the change of political power in Poland, we could observe the beginning of an intensive debate about Poland's capacity and readiness to admit asylum seekers in the context of the presumed higher risks to security and public order. All these facts constituted the circumstances in which the forced migrants that eventually reached Poland could execute their right to asylum and enjoy assistance offered to asylum seekers and refugees.

Poland is a country that in recent years has been characterised by anti-refugee and anti-European narratives, especially in 2015–2017 in connection with the implementation of the temporary EU relocation mechanism for asylum seekers from Italy and Greece during the migration and refugee management crisis in Europe. It is a country that in spite of promises (Pędziwiatr and Legut, 2016), together with Hungary and the Czech Republic, did not implement this mechanism. At the same time, the admission of asylum seekers was implemented within the regular framework of national legislation. Poland is a country of contrasts. It represents actual openness to economic and educational migration from countries perceived as culturally and linguistically close, bearing in mind the country's demographic and socioeconomic interests (depopulation, ageing of the society, decline in the number of students, and the need to increase the internationalisation of universities, the labour market needs, etc.). But it also represents reluctance declared and publicly communicated by the central government to accept forced and irregular migrants from Middle East countries, often identified as Muslim countries (see, e.g., Klaus, 2020). Poland is also a country with a growing role and involvement in migration management and the implementation of immigration and integration policies at the subnational level, which can be seen in the actions, practices, and policies of local authorities in regions, cities, and communes (including those in rural areas), non-governmental organisations (NGOs) and immigrant organisations, and local communities and grassroots initiatives.

Forced Migration: The Terminological Challenge

Research into migration reveals various typologies of the phenomenon that translate into identifying specific categories (types) of migrants. One of the well-known classifications is based on the degree of freedom of movement of an individual or a group, divided into migration as voluntary (also referred to as spontaneous) and involuntary (also referred to as forced). These classifications overlap with the division of migration movements by main motive (cause): some movements coincide more often with voluntary reasons, for example, settlement, labour, or family migration, while others are typical of forced migration, such as seeking refuge or escaping a sudden environmental event. The division into voluntary or forced migration is definitely descriptive and serves to systematise part of the migration reality. However, the causes of migration often occur in various combinations, which in most cases makes it impossible to identify one case as exclusively voluntary or forced (Pachocka and Sobczak-Szelc, 2018, p. 335).

What do we mean by forced mobility or displacement, or the more common concept of forced migration? These terms have been used for a long time in the migration literature, but also by international organisations such as UNHCR, IOM, or the EU and scientific associations and research networks such as the International Association for the Study of Forced Migration (Klaus and Pachocka, 2019).

So far though, as is often the case in migration research, no universally accepted definition has been developed in the area in question, resulting in many concepts, interpretations, and contexts of their use. This applies to both the legal and working definitions. The status of a forced migrant in international law is not specified, and there is no single standard definition in the methodology of the most important international entities collecting data on international migration, which translates into incompleteness and estimation in international statistics on the phenomenon of forced migration (Pachocka and Sobczak-Szelc, 2018, pp. 335–336). This applies not only to global data but also to European data. However, data on forced migrants at the EU level can be approximated by data on the number of people applying for international protection in the Member States and the number of beneficiaries of different forms of this protection (Pachocka and Wach, 2018).

The IOM's Glossary on Migration is a common definition reference source for international comparisons. Its most recent edition, from 2019, does not define forced mobility at all but explains "forced migration" and "displacement" (IOM, 2019, pp. 55–56, p. 77). The first term, that is "forced migration", denotes "A migratory movement which, although the drivers can be diverse, involves force, compulsion, or coercion", and is followed by an additional comment stating that:

> the [w]hile not an international legal concept, this term has been used to describe the movements of refugees, displaced persons (including those displaced by disasters or development projects), and, in some instances, victims of trafficking. At the international level, the use of this term is debated because of the widespread recognition that a continuum of agency exists rather than a voluntary/forced dichotomy and that it might undermine the existing legal international protection regime.
>
> *IOM, 2019, p. 77*

Then, "displacement" is understood as

> [t]he movement of persons who have been forced or obliged to flee or to leave their homes or places of habitual residence, in particular as a result of or in order to avoid the effects of armed conflict, situations of generalized violence, violations of human rights or natural or human-made disasters.
>
> *IOM, 2019, pp. 55–56*[1]

As a result, in the most general approach, a forced migrant, which is not defined *per se*, can be understood as a person who migrates due to the occurrence of some form of coercion of various nature and scope, and the most frequently mentioned among them are refugees and internally displaced persons (Pachocka and Sobczak-Szelc, 2018, p. 336). Since the post-war years, UNHCR has remained the leading international agency with global reach, collecting data on people belonging to the group broadly understood as forced migrants. Although it does not explicitly use the collective category of forced migrants, it provides detailed statistics on, among other things, asylum seekers, refugees, people in refugee-like situations, internally displaced persons (IDPs), returnees (refugees and IDPs), stateless persons, and other persons of concern to the UNHCR (Pachocka and Sobczak-Szelc, 2018, pp. 339–341; UNHCR, 2017, pp. 56–57, pp. 60–71).[2] This, to some extent, is an indication of who may be considered a forced migrant.

Theoretical Inspirations

Among the theoretical inspirations for our research in this book, the concept of multi-level governance (MLG) constitutes the main framework of the analysis. On the one hand, it is a concept widely used in migration research in the European academic tradition and literature (see, e.g., Zincone and Caponio, 2006; Scholten and Penninx, 2016). On the other hand, it is criticised (see, e.g., Caponio and Jones-Correa, 2018; Campomori and Ambrosini, 2020), and modifications of it and alternatives are proposed (the concept of "battleground", see Campomori and Ambrosini, 2020, p. 3; Ambrosini, 2018, and the concept of "multilevel playing field", see Lahav and Guiraudon, 2006, p. 208). Nevertheless, we found it suitable to frame our analysis, implementing, however, a critical approach to using it, as was done in the comparative studies within which we gathered empirical data referred to in the book (see Federico and Pannia, 2021, pp. 16–17).

Using an MLG-based approach (Scholten, 2013a; 2013b), we seek to understand the relations between various levels of migration and integration governance in Poland. In efforts to decipher types of configurations of relations between government levels, we also look at non-governmental actors and their role in the reception and integration of forced migrants. Since the book focuses to a large extent on reception and integration processes, the indicators of integration proposed by Ager and Strang (2004) constitute the conceptual framework for analysing forced migrants' access to the labour market, healthcare, education, and housing. In line with the same framework and with regard to all the above-mentioned indicators, the book analyses also the social connections between the migrants and the host society as well as various groups within it (e.g., ethnic and religious minorities) seen as playing a crucial role in the process of their integration at the local level. Particular attention is paid to barriers and facilitators, where Ager and Strang (2004) identified two major areas of existence: (1) language and cultural knowledge and (2) safety and security. In addition, we look at the rights of refugees versus the rights of citizens to have a holistic view of the integration process from both perspectives.

In addition to MLG, another key concept for our book is integration, which can be understood both as a process and a field of public policy. Previous considerations on this subject in the Polish context, based on the empirical data referred to in this book (see Sobczak-Szelc et al., 2021), led us to the conclusion that despite rich literature on the subject, there is no single commonly used definition of integration or integration policy. Among the definitions of integration, we constantly find the one proposed by Rinnus Penninx (Penninx, 2005, 2007, 2013; Penninx and Garcés-Mascareñas, 2016) to be the most useful and which assumes that integration is "the process of becoming an accepted part of society" (Penninx and Garcés-Mascareñas, 2016, p. 14). Integration, as conceptualised by Penninx and others, refers to three dimensions of society—political-legal, socioeconomic, and cultural-religious. This corresponds, respectively, to the institutions of the state, the market, and the nation (Entzinger, 2000; Penninx and Garcés-Mascareñas, 2016 p. 14). These dimensions are complementary and interdependent, and the time factor cannot be neglected in analysing integration. Integration is embedded in the space of interactions between the two parties involved (immigrants and the receiving society) within the three mentioned areas. The exchanges also take place on three different levels: (1) the individual one (migrants and natives), (2) the collective level (entities like NGOs and trade unions), and (3) the institutional level (general public institutions and group-specific institutions) (see Sobczak-Szelc et al., 2021, pp. 277–278; Penninx and Garcés-Mascareñas, 2016, pp. 16–19).

Following the understanding of integration presented above, we claim that forced migrants, as people who involuntarily left their homes, where they often had lacked a sense of safety and sometimes also the possibility to satisfy basic needs, deserve the most attention. This relates to both persons seeking asylum and those already granted a form of international protection with the reservation that in the case of asylum seekers, we can rather speak about pre-integration activities. If we look at this issue from a country and institutional perspective, in Poland integration seems to apply only to beneficiaries of international protection—there is no overarching, coherent integration policy towards migrants residing in Poland. It is instead a narrow and specialised policy targeting persons granted refugee status or subsidiary protection (Sobczak-Szelc et al., 2021, pp. 277–278). In applying a concept of integration broader than the scope of domestic integration policy, in our analysis we go beyond special programmes offered by the states and take into account all other initiatives (undertaken at various levels and by various actors, including forced migrants themselves) aimed at the acceptance of asylum seekers and refugees in the host societies.

Finally, to explain forced migration governance in the Polish context, we also apply the theoretical approach of "push out-push back" (Klaus and Pachocka, 2019) proposed to study the policies of the Global North countries in the area of the (re) admission of forced migrants. This approach is an adaptation of the popular concept of push and pull factors (Lee, 1966) to the realities of admission and deterrence of asylum seekers. It assumes the existence of "push out" factors forcing migrants to leave either their countries of origin or the countries where they are staying temporarily, together with "push back" factors aimed at keeping forced migrants away from the territory of a given state (Klaus and Pachocka, 2019). In particular, we apply this concept in the analysis of forced migrants' experiences in accessing the asylum procedure in Poland, as well as in benefitting from the accessible forms of assistance and rights. We provide examples of the "push out" and "push back" factors through accounts of forced migrants having trouble submitting asylum claims in Poland and being subjected to additional control measures, such as detention. We also point to policies and practices indicated by various actors involved in forced migration governance that can be interpreted as "push out" and "push back" factors in the Polish context. Thus, we contribute to the studies focused on either the deterrence or admission of forced migrants in Poland (Białas et al., 2019; Klaus, 2017; Kulesa, 2021; Szczepanik, 2018; Szulecka, 2022).

Methodology and Sources

Data analysed for the purpose of this book and the applied theoretical and methodological approaches and sources used in the course of work on it are inspired by a common framework and guidelines adopted for the implementation of the H2020 project RESPOND–*Multilevel Governance of Mass Migration in Europe and Beyond*. The project encompassed several interdisciplinary research activities implemented by an international consortium of 14 institutions (from academia and NGO sector) from 11 countries coordinated by the University of Uppsala in Sweden.[3] It was implemented between 2017 and 2021. Data collection regarding Poland as well as analysis of the Polish case (also from a comparative perspective) were conducted by the Centre of Migration Research (CMR) of the University of Warsaw. The main focus of the project was on forced migration governance in mainly (but not only) the countries adjacent to the so-called Eastern Mediterranean migration route since 2011, with an emphasis on the situation related to the migration and refugee management crisis in Europe in 2015–2016 (see Barthoma and Çetrez, 2021, pp. 1–12).

The results presented in this book are based on the data obtained thanks to mixed research methods (Brannen, 2005), with a prevailing qualitative approach. The first stage, desk research, included the analysis of the legal, institutional, and policy framework in the field of migration, asylum, and integration from 2011 to 2020, although, where necessary, we also considered its development since the early 1990s and the most recent changes from 2021. The analysis encompassed legal acts and other official documents, reports, and works published by international organisations and NGOs, as well as the academic literature and other important sources. Discursive frame analysis (Foucault, 1969; Goffman, 1974; Entman, 1993; Ensink and Sauer, 2003; Korkut and Eslen-Ziya, 2018) was used to present the production of security discourses towards asylum seekers and refugees. In addition, we analysed the statistical data regarding migration, international protection, and integration in Poland in a wider European context, referring to national (Central Statistical Office in Poland, Office for Foreigners, data from ministries) and international databases (Eurostat). An empirical legal approach (Baldwin and Davis, 2005; Cane and Kritzer, 2012; Epstein and Martin, 2014; Kubal, 2019) has been applied to study the provisions concerning the investigated processes of admission, reception, and integration of forced migrants "in action", based on the interviews collected in the fieldwork.

The second—and core—stage of our research activities in Poland was fieldwork carried out between July 2018 and November 2020. The fieldwork data involved: (1) 30 interviews with forced migrants having different legal statuses (called micro-level interviews); (2) 17 expert interviews (meso-level interviews) with representatives of public administration at the central and local levels, individuals from NGOs, and practitioners dealing with immigration, asylum and integration-related issues; and (3) material from three roundtable discussions of the RESPOND Migration Governance Network (MGN) in Poland held from 2018 to 2020. We applied deliberate sampling in the selection of the meso- and micro-level respondents as well as participants of the MGN roundtable discussions. The objective was to approach persons with certain experiences of either implementing asylum policies or being subjected to them to obtain opinions on the qualitative aspects of how asylum, reception, and integration policies and practices function and how forced migrants perceive them.

The micro-level interviewees (Table 1.1) were selected with consideration of the gender, age, and ethnic structure of the asylum seekers and beneficiaries of international protection in Poland between 2011 and 2017.[4] We also considered such variables as migrants' year of arrival in Poland, place of residence, and legal status. Therefore, the majority of our respondents were from four countries of origin, namely the Russian Federation (15), Syria (5), Ukraine (4), and Iraq (3). Individual

TABLE 1.1 Sample of micro-level interviews in Poland with codes

No.	*Code*	*Nationality*	*Gender*	*Age group*	*Legal status*	*Time of arrival***
1	PLMICh01	Russian/Chechen*	Female	27–50	Under subsidiary protection	2011–2014
2	PLMICh02	Russian/Chechen*	Female	27–50	Asylum applicant	2015–2017
3	PLMICh03	Russian/Chechen*	Female	27–50	Asylum applicant	2015–2017
4	PLMICh04	Russian/Chechen*	Female	27–50	Under subsidiary protection	2015–2017
5	PLMICh05	Russian/Chechen*	Female	27–50	Asylum applicant	2015–2017
6	PLMICh06	Russian/Chechen*	Female	27–50	Asylum applicant	2015–2017
7	PLMICh07	Russian/Chechen*	Female	27–50	Under subsidiary protection	2015–2017
8	PLMICh08	Russian/Chechen*	Female	27–50	Other or no legal status	2015–2017
9	PLMICh09	Russian/Chechen*	Male	>50	Under subsidiary protection	2015–2017
10	PLMICh10	Russian/Chechen*	Male	27–50	Under subsidiary protection	2011–2014
11	PLMICh11	Russian/Chechen*	Male	27–50	Under subsidiary protection	2011–2014
12	PLMICh12	Russian/Chechen*	Male	18–26	Other or no legal status	2015–2017
13	PLMICh13	Russian/Chechen*	Male	27–50	Asylum applicant	2015–2017
14	PLMICh14	Russian/Chechen*	Male	27–50	Under subsidiary protection	2015–2017
15	PLMICh15	Russian/Chechen*	Male	27–50	Asylum applicant	2015–2017
16	PLMIUk16	Georgian/ Ossetian	Male	27–50	Under subsidiary protection	2011–2014
17	PLMIUk17	Ukrainian	Male	18–26	Asylum applicant	2015–2017
18	PLMIUk18	Ukrainian	Male	27–50	Asylum applicant	2011–2014
19	PLMIUk19	Ukrainian	Female	27–50	Under subsidiary protection	2011–2014
20	PLMIUk20	Ukrainian	Female	27–50	Under subsidiary protection	2011–2014
21	PLMISy21	Syrian	Male	27–50	Refugee status	2011–2014
22	PLMISy22	Syrian	Male	18–26	Refugee status	2015–2017
23	PLMISy23	Syrian	Male	27–50	Refugee status	2015–2017
24	PLMISy24	Syrian	Male	>50	Asylum applicant	2015–2017
25	PLMISy25	Syrian	Female	18–26	Other or no legal status	2015–2017
26	PLMIIr26	Iraqi	Male	27–50	Refugee status	2015–2017
27	PLMIIr27	Iraqi	Male	27–50	Asylum applicant	2015–2017
28	PLMIIr28	Iraqi	Female	>50	Refugee status	2011–2014
29	PLMIJe29	Yemeni	Male	27–50	Under subsidiary protection	2015–2017
30	PLMIKa30	Kazakh	Female	27–50	Asylum applicant	2015–2017

* "Chechen" means a Russian citizen with Chechen nationality.
** at the moment of the interview.
Source: Own elaboration by the RESPOND team in Poland.

responders came from Kazakhstan, Georgia, and Yemen. As a result, the interviews were carried out with interviewees differentiated by:

- age—children under the age of 18 were excluded from the research,
- gender—the inflow from Russia, specifically Chechnya,[5] and Ukraine was dominated by families, while for other national groups males prevailed,
- year of arrival—before and after 2015,[6]
- place of residence (cities and small towns or villages)—based on the number of beneficiaries of international protection as well as major availability of assistance services and offices of relevant authorities; both the micro- and

TABLE 1.2 Sample of meso-level interviews in Poland with codes

No.	*Code*	*Type of stakeholder*
1	PLMZBG1	Border Guard
2	PLMZOF1	Office for Foreigners
3	PLMZOF2	Office for Foreigners
4	PLMZOF3/4	Office for Foreigners (two respondents)
5	PLMZP1	Practitioner
6	PLMZP2	Practitioner
7	PLMZP3	Practitioner
8	PLMZLG1	Local governor
9	PLMZLG2	Local governor
10	PLMZSO1	Social organisation
11	PLMZSO2	Social organisation
12	PLMZSO3	Social organisation
13	PLMZSO4	Social organisation
14	PLMZSO5/6	Social organisation (two respondents)
15	PLMZSO7	Social organisation

Source: Own elaboration by the RESPOND team in Poland.

meso-level interviews were carried in the two voivodeships (provinces)[7] of Mazovian and Lubelskie,

- legal status—out of 30 respondents, 11 were under the asylum procedure, 16 had already received a positive decision (5 with refugee status, 11 with subsidiary protection status), and 3 declared other legal status (including irregular one).

Meso-level interviews were conducted with 17 experts from public administration at the central and local levels, NGOs, and other practitioners dealing with immigration issues (Table 1.2). The aim of those interviews was to explore local-level practices and to understand how policies are received and implemented in different localities, how different civic (social) actors fill the gaps where government policies have failed to deliver the needed services, and how policymaking is influenced at various levels through diverse governance practices.

We also base our analysis on the voices expressed by experts participating in the group discussions organised within the MGN (in December 2018, January 2020, and November 2020). Each meeting was attended by about 20 experts representing different institutions and organisations, including the Office of the Polish Commissioner for Human Rights, the Office for Foreigners, the Border Guard, governmental and local institutions involved in integration programmes for persons granted refugee status or subsidiary protection, non-governmental and international organisations, local authorities, and academia.

The micro-level interviews were conducted in Russian, Arabic, Polish, and English. All of them were first transcribed and then translated into English. The meso-level interviews were carried out and transcribed into Polish. The group discussions within the MGN were also held in Polish. Both the micro- and meso-level interviews and transcripts from the group discussions were coded and analysed with NVivo or Maxqda software. In line with the triangulation technique, the empirical data gathered through the application of sociological methods, such as in-depth interviews with forced migrants and semi-structured interviews with experts in migration and asylum governance, were juxtaposed with the observed facts, decisions, and behaviours and with the respective laws in the books. Whenever other methods were used it is stated in the particular chapters of this book. The above-mentioned methodology is well-reflected in the content of the book, discussed below. The primary results of the analysis of empirical data, the law, and other analysed sources (such as media accounts or reports from parliamentary debates) were already published in comprehensive and detailed reports focused on areas such as the legal and policy framework of migration governance, border management and migration controls, asylum policy, reception policy, integration policy and discourses on refugees in Poland (see Szulecka et al., 2018; Szulecka, 2019; Pachocka and Sobczak-Szelc, 2020; Pachocka et al., 2020; Sobczak-Szelc et al., 2020; Szałańska, 2020). We draw on these findings and refer to them. However, for the purpose of the analysis presented in the book, we applied a broader perspective than just a description of experiences. Our ambition is to give voice to forced migrants and people directly involved in forced migration governance when discussing laws, practices, and discourses on the country and regional levels.

Structure of the Book

Our book consists of 11 chapters. It begins with an introduction, Chapter 1, which sheds light on the need to better understand the context of the functioning of the phenomenon of forced migration in Poland, which is both one of the newer EU Member States and a Visegrad Group (V4) country. It is also geopolitically a part of Europe known as the CEE, associated with a specific history after Second World War. The introduction signals the geopolitical aspects and other macro-level conditions that have to be taken into account to study the current policies and practices towards asylum seekers and how they may be both received and interpreted by forced migrants themselves and professional actors involved in forced migration governance. The first chapter also introduces the main theoretical and methodological framework of the analysis presented in subsequent chapters of the book.

The main part of the book includes nine thematic chapters that present the migration situation of Poland in the context of Europe, the EU, and the V4, in the historical perspective after 1989 and the present, and with an emphasis on the 21st century. This is to outline the background and to show the conditions of the functioning of the phenomenon of forced migration in this country (also in the context of political and media discourses) and public policies concerning forced migrants, that is, asylum, reception, and integration policies in relation to the legal and institutional frameworks of the Polish asylum system (international protection of refugees), education system, housing, labour market, healthcare, and citizenship opportunities.

Chapter 2 aims to shed light on the geopolitical circumstances in which the system of admitting asylum seekers to Poland developed after 1989. It requires a broader perspective than simply the state level since asylum-seeking is not only about crossing borders and asking for protection but also about commitments accepted or denied by the states in the area of providing various kinds of assistance to persons who flee conflict, violence, and persecution. The latter relates to international agreements, among which the UN-level Geneva Convention of 1951 and the New York Protocol of 1967 are keystones. European Union legislation and policies regarding migration and asylum are also crucial points of reference. Therefore, this chapter is organised around two main issues. The first one is a description of Poland as a post-communist country joining an international community committed to providing international protection to persons fleeing persecution, symbolically confirmed in 1991 along with the signing of the 1951 Geneva Convention by Poland. This part is aimed at presenting both the phenomena and developments in international and EU law that influence the creation of Poland's system of forced migration governance. The second part focuses on the scale of forced migration to Poland after 1989, considering the EU and Visegrad Group contexts. Data on this subject were approximated by selected indicators from Eurostat asylum statistics for 2008–2021.

Chapter 3 shows how securitisation of forced migration in Poland started in 2015 as a result of the refugee and migration management crisis, which coincided with the electoral campaigns before the presidential and parliamentary elections in Poland held the same year. The potential arrival of refugees to Poland was successfully presented as a major "security threat" that led to a shift in Polish society's attitudes towards asylum seekers and refugees. The chapter examines how forced migrants (both asylum seekers and refugees) have been framed by politicians and media as a security issue in Poland since 2015, and the consequences of that framing on the public opinion of forced migrants. This presentation of the main discourses on forced migration in Poland produced by politicians and reproduced by media also depicts the socio-political atmosphere of the reception and integration policies of the country. In addition, it enquires about stakeholders' reactions and opinions on these discourses and whether they have been internalised by Polish public opinion. To achieve the mentioned aims, a three-step analysis of forced migration discourses in Poland was conducted: political speech analysis, media analysis, and stakeholder discussion analysis.

Two chapters on foreigners' access to the asylum system in Poland follow. Due to the complexity of the problem of foreigners' access to protection on the territory of the Republic of Poland, our attention is focused on the access to forms of international protection provided for in the Polish legal order, disregarding national protection. Chapter 4 presents the legal framework for admitting asylum seekers and providing them with necessary assistance, as well as providing protection to recognised refugees. The overview covers the decade 2011–2021 and aims to present the stable elements of the asylum system and explain important changes introduced in this period. The presentation of the legal framework is preceded by a mapping of the institutional actors involved in implementing asylum policy as widely understood in Poland. The overview of the domestic legislation is structured along the course of applying for asylum from the perspective of forced migrants. First, we describe the provisions related to accessing the asylum procedure (at the border and within the territory of Poland), second we present the rules of processing asylum claims, and finally, we reflect on the provisions determining the possible outcomes of the asylum procedure, that is, granting international protection or denying it. Special attention was also given to legislation referring to selected spheres of forced migrants' adaptation, that is, access to the labour market, education, housing, and healthcare, which aims to offer the legal context of the empirical analysis presented in other chapters of the book.

The institutional and legal context examined in the previous chapter is enriched by Chapter 5 in which we discuss the outcomes of the empirical analyses dedicated to asylum seekers' and refugees' experiences with exercising their rights attached to seeking asylum in the Polish context. This chapter focuses on the issue of requesting protection and obtaining or being denied it, as reflected by asylum seekers and representatives of organisations and institutions involved in forced migration governance. It precedes more specific analyses focused on the economic adaptation of asylum seekers and refugees, their access to education, housing and healthcare, as well as their aspirations in civic participation. Describing the very access to the asylum procedure and access to protection in the Polish context, we refer to statements shared with us by migrant interviewees and observations from experts involved in implementing asylum policy in Poland. This issue is presented against the more general background encompassing the reasons for forced mobility revealed by persons seeking asylum in Poland (or in the EU) and the phenomenon of onward mobility, frequently associated with the Polish asylum reality.

The objective of Chapter 6 is to present the legal and institutional aspects of the integration of asylum seekers and refugees in the domain of education and examine the actual practices of integration in one chosen area, namely Polish language learning. The focus is put on adult asylum seekers' and refugees' access to Polish language courses, together with their effectiveness and participants' motivations for starting and continuing their learning, in order to see what facilitations and barriers there are in host country language acquisition by applicants and beneficiaries of international protection. The chapter also seeks to investigate whether the practices of language education at each step of the integration process (reception during the asylum procedure and actual integration after being granted protection status) are coherent. In addition, by presenting the actual practices of Polish language learning by refugees, the shortcomings and good practices in this area are identified.

Chapter 7 reveals how important housing is as one of the most basic needs that all persons claiming asylum must be provided with or satisfy individually. Housing quality has a crucial influence on the pace of the foreigners' integration into the new socio-cultural conditions of the host country, as well as on the psychophysical condition of the individuals and entire families that are escaping war or various types of persecution in their home countries. This part of the book sheds light on the housing conditions of persons seeking asylum in Poland, as well as on those who have been granted international protection. It analyses statistical information about the provision of accommodation for asylum seekers in the existing centres for foreigners in Poland as well as outside them and evaluates key problems linked with the provision of housing and allowances. Foreigners granted international protection must leave these "refugee centres" within two months from the moment of receiving the decision. While analysing the experiences of persons with international protection with access to housing, we also evaluate their transition from being provided with some form of shelter or very modest housing allowances during the application procedure to the situation when they might be deprived of such assistance.

Another important area of the functioning of forced migrants in the host country, regardless of their legal status, is economic integration into the labour market. This is elaborated in Chapter 8. It explores the situation of forced migrants—both asylum seekers and beneficiaries of international protection (refugees and persons with subsidiary protection)—in the Polish labour market after 2011. The main research question is how the change of legal status from an applicant for international protection to a refugee (or a person with subsidiary protection) affects the situation of these people in the labour market, both according to law and practice. The chapter includes an overview of provisions related to access to the labour market for asylum seekers and refugees. It discusses the challenges and facilitations that influence the labour market integration process and how asylum seekers and refugees respond to these factors. It refers to the results of the analysis of research material from individual in-depth interviews at the micro-level (asylum seekers and refugees) and meso-level (among others, NGOs local authorities and practitioners) carried out in Poland.

Chapter 9 outlines the importance of the provision of medical services to forced migrants in the receiving country. We explain how asylum seekers are provided with these services by a healthcare provider selected by the Office for Foreigners (currently the private company Petra Medica) both in the centres for foreigners and outside them. The chapter also provides some statistical information on the provision and evaluates the practice, its perception, as well as key problems linked with access to healthcare, pointed out by the interviewed asylum seekers. Then, it evaluates the experiences of the beneficiaries of international protection while accessing medical services. We analyse their perception of the transition from medical care provided by the selected medical care institution (during the asylum procedure) to the situation when they are covered by the general healthcare system or the National Health Fund.

Finally, Chapter 10 leads us to a discussion on the fundamental role of rights and citizenship to the successful integration of refugees. The numbers of naturalisation of refugees in Poland are low since, considering the statistics of granting international protection, 10 times more people have been entitled to apply for citizenship than actually acquire it. However, even without citizenship, refugees engage in various civic participation in the host communities. The chapter aims to present two important domains of integration, namely the fundamental principles of citizenship and rights, and belonging and civic participation as forms of social connection. It outlines the legal framework of access to citizenship and other rights for beneficiaries of international protection in Poland. It also contains an overview of the refugee naturalisation statistics in Poland. Furthermore, it brings the findings of the RESPOND empirical research and sheds light on the experiences and perceptions of asylum seekers and beneficiaries of international protection towards acquiring citizenship, belonging, and their participation in the political, social, and cultural life of Poland.

The book ends with conclusions, Chapter 11, in which we summarise our considerations important for decision-makers and experts dealing with the issues of the refugee system in Poland, reception, and integration policies, which we have developed as a result of our research. We also emphasise the interdisciplinary nature of our research in this book and the wide possibilities of its use in teaching, research, and disseminating knowledge about migration processes and accompanying policies for various audiences in Europe and beyond.

The content of this book is solely the responsibility of the authors. However, it is the result of continuous works that were partly published in a variety of working papers. Therefore, we are very grateful to all those from whom we have received very valuable support during this continuous work. We would like to especially thank the leaders of the RESPOND project, Andreas Önver Cetrez and Soner Barthoma from the Uppsala University, all WP leaders, Naures Atto from the University of Cambridge, Veronica Federico from Universita Degli Studi Di Firenze, N. Ela Gökalp-Aras from the Swedish Research Institute in Istanbul, Sabine Hess and Alexander-Kenneth Nagel from the University of Göttingen, Ayhan Kaya from Istanbul Bilgi University, Umut Korkut and Lena Karamanidou from the Glasgow Caledonian University, Electra Petracou from the University of the Aegean, Ursula Reeger from Austrian Academy of Science, and Susan Rottmann from Ozyegin University and other team members in this project. We express also our appreciation to the external reviewers of our reports representing various institutions involved in the research on the processes of border management, reception and integration of forced migrants and asylum governance: Jacek Białas (Helsinki Foundation for Human Rights), Piotr Bystrianin (Ocalenie Foundation), Marcin Gońda (University of Łódź, CMR of the University of Warsaw), Marta Górczyńska (Helsinki Foundation for Human Rights), Agata Górny (CMR of the University of Warsaw), Anna Górska (Institute of Public Affairs), Jan Grzymski (CMR of the University of Warsaw), Paweł Kubicki (SGH Warsaw School of Economics), Jan Misiuna (SGH Warsaw School of Economics), Katarzyna Przybysławska (Halina Nieć Legal Aid Centre), Renata Stefańska (CMR of the University of Warsaw), and Dominik Wach (Warsaw Family Support Centre and CMR of the University of Warsaw). To this end, it is important to emphasise that the accomplishment of this book—firmly based on the qualitative research material from interviews—would not have been possible without the involvement of members of the Polish team of the RESPOND project, who were responsible, inter alia, for reaching respondents, conducting meso- and micro-level interviews, and their translation, transcription, and coding. These were Karolina Sobczak-Szelc, Marta Pachocka, Justyna Szałańska, Monika Szulecka, Konrad Pędziwiatr, Gagik Grigoryan, and Feras Daboul. Our sincere thanks go also to the other members of the Polish team who were more involved in the quantitative research in the project, that is: Anita Brzozowska, Agata Górny, and Barbara Jancewicz. We would also like to acknowledge the support in language editing provided by Brien Barnett and technical editing provided by Julia Nurzyńska.

Last but not least, we wish to thank all of the forced migrants who shared their experiences with us. We are very grateful for their trust and openness. We are aware that speaking about personal experiences in such complex circumstances as fleeing the country of origin, crossing national borders, and starting "new" lives in other countries brings about emotional costs. We guarantee that we applied all measures to prevent all harms that could be potentially caused by the research activities and appreciate very much all the voices of forced migrants we could collect. We also thank all participants representing NGOs or public institutions involved in forced migration governance. Their expertise enriched our analysis and inspired many questions that we have already posed and tried to address in this book or in future studies.

Notes

1 Glossary informs this definition as "adapted from Guiding Principles on Internal Displacement, annexed to United Nations Commission on Human Rights, Report of the Representative of the Secretary-General, Mr Francis M. Deng, Submitted Pursuant to Commission Resolution 1997/39, Addendum (11 February 1998) UN Doc. E/CN.4/1998/53/Add.2, para. 2 of the introduction".

2 UNHCR (2017). Global Trends. Forced Displacement in 2016. Geneva: United Nations High Commissioner for Refugees: 56–57, 60–71, www.unhcr.org/statistics/unhcrstats/5943e8a34/global-trends-forced-displacement-2016.html.

3 This project has received funding from the European Union's Horizon 2020 Research and Innovation Programme (grant agreement No 770564). For more information about the RESPOND project, see: https://respondmigration.com/.

4 The encountered limitations, reflections on ethical awareness, and principles stemming from the RESPOND consortium's code of ethics, adjusted for the national context, are described in detail in the three country research reports from the RESPOND project (Pachocka and Sobczak-Szelc, 2020; Pachocka et al., 2020; Sobczak-Szelc et al., 2020).

5 "Chechnya is a republic in southwestern Russia, situated on the northern flank of the Greater Caucasus range. Chechnya is bordered by Russia proper on the north, Dagestan Republic on the east and southeast, the country of Georgia on the southwest, and Ingushetiya Republic on the west. In the early 21st century, more than a decade of bitter conflict had devastated the republic, forced the mass exodus of refugees, and brought the economy to a standstill" (Brittanica.com).

6 In other countries studied within the RESPOND project, justification of this division is strictly linked to the so-called refugee and migrant management crisis that affected asylum

statistics in many European countries in 2015. In Poland, this cut-off point was adjusted to relate to the refugee crisis, but as much as possible we aimed to reflect the situation in Poland as well, which was influenced by the outbreak of the military conflict between Ukraine and Russia in 2014.

7 Poland is administratively divided into 16 voivodeships (regions).

References

Ager, A., Strang, A., 2004. *Indicators of Integration: Final Report. Home Office Development and Practice Report 28.* Home Office, London.

Ambrosini, M., 2018. *Irregular Immigration in Southern Europe: Actors, Dynamics and Governance.* Springer, Cham.

Baldwin, J., Davis, G., 2005. Empirical research in law. in: Tushnet M., Cane P. (Eds.), *The Oxford Handbook of Legal Studies.* Oxford University Press, Oxford.

Barthoma, S., Cetrez, Ö.A., 2021. *RESPONDing to Migration: A Holistic Perspective on Migration Governance.* pp. 1–12. http://urn.kb.se/resolve?urn=urn:nbn:se:uu:diva-449097.

Białas, J., Górczyńska, M., Witko, D., 2019. *Access to Asylum Procedure at Poland's External Borders. Current Situation and Challenges for the Future.* Helsinki Foundation for Human Rights, Warsaw.

Brannen, J., 2005. Mixing methods: the entry of qualitative and quantitative approaches into the research process, *International Journal of Social Research Methodology*, 8(3), pp. 173–184. DOI: 10.1080/13645570500154642.

Campomori, F., Ambrosini, M., 2020. Multilevel governance in trouble: the implementation of asylum seekers' reception in Italy as a battleground, *CMS* 8(22), https://doi.org/10.1186/s40878-020-00178-1.

Cane, P., Kritzer, H., 2012. *The Oxford Handbook of Empirical Legal Research.* OUP, Oxford.

Caponio, T., Jones-Correa, M., 2018. Theorising migration policy in multilevel states: the multilevel governance perspective, *Journal of Ethnic and Migration Studies*, 44(12), 1995–2010, DOI: 10.1080/1369183X.2017.1341705.

Ensink, T., Sauer, C. (Eds.). 2003. *Framing and perspectivising in discourse* (Vol. 111). John Benjamins Publishing.

Entman, R.M. (1993), Framing: Toward Clarification of a Fractured Paradigm, *Journal of Communication*, 43, 51–58. https://doi.org/10.1111/j.1460-2466.1993.tb01304.x.

Epstein, L., Martin, A. D., 2014. *An Introduction to Empirical Legal Research.* OUP, Oxford.

Federico, V., Pannia, P., 2021. The Ever-Changing Picture of the Legal Framework 15 of Migration: A Comparative Analysis of Common Trends in Europe and Beyond, in: Barthoma, S., Cetrez, Ö. (Eds.), *RESPONDing to Migration: A Holistic Perspective on Migration Governance.* Acta Universitatis Upsaliensis, Uppsala, pp. 16–17.

Foucault, M., 1969. *Archaeology of Knowledge* (2nd ed.). Routledge. https://doi.org/10.4324/9780203604168.

Goffman, E., 1974. *Frame analysis: An essay on the organization of experience.* HUP, Harvard.

Górny, A., Kindler, M., 2018. Cudzoziemcy w Polsce na przełomie XX i XXI wieku, in: Lesińska, M., Okólski, M. (Eds.), *25 wykładów o migracjach.* Scholar, Warszawa, p. 221.

IOM, 2019. Glossary on Migration, https://publications.iom.int/system/files/pdf/iml_34_glossary.pdf.

Klaus, W., 2017. Security First: The New Right-Wing Government in Poland and its Policy towards Immigrants and Refugees. Surveillance and the Global Turn to Authoritarianism, *Surveillance & Society*, 15(3/4), 523–528. DOI: https-//doi.org/10.2307/2060063.

Klaus, W., 2020. How Does Crimmigration Unfold in Poland? Between Securitisation Introduced to Polish Migration Policy by its Europeanisation and Polish Xenophobia, in: Koulish, R., van der Woude, M. A. H. (Eds.), *Crimmigrant Nations: Resurgent Nationalism and the Closing of Borders.* Fordham University Press, New York.

Klaus, W., Pachocka, M., 2019. Examining the global north migration policies: a "Push Out – Push Back" approach to forced migration, *International Migration*, 57, 280–293. DOI: https://doi.org/10.1111/imig.12575.

Korkut, U., Eslen-Ziya, H., 2018. *Politics and Gender Identity in Turkey: Centralised Islam for Socio-Economic Control.* Routledge, London and New York.

Kubal, A., 2019. *Immigration and Refugee Law in Russia: Socio-Legal Perspectives (Law in Context).* Cambridge University Press, Cambridge, DOI:10.1017/9781108283656.

Kulesa, A., 2021. *The Polish Asylum System since 2015. A hostage to domestic politics, Asylum Challenges, Debates and Reforms How Germany, Poland, Portugal and Sweden Have Developed Their Asylum Systems since 2015.* Bertelsmann Stiftung, Gutersloh, pp. 58–98.

Lahav, G., Guiraudon, V., 2006. Actors and venues in immigration control: Closing the gap between political demands and policy outcomes, *West European Politics*, 29(2), 208, DOI: 10.1080/01402380500512551.

Lee, E. S., 1966. A Theory of Migration, *Demography*, 3(1), 47–57. DOI: https://doi.org/10.2307/2060063.

Nabil, A., Korkut, U., Eslen-Ziya, H., 2018. *Politics and Gender Identity in Turkey: Centralised Islam for Socio-Economic Control.* New York: Routledge.

Okólski, M., 2021. The migration transition in Poland, *Central and Eastern European Migration Review,* 10(2), 151–169. DOI: 10.17467/CEEMR.2021.16.

Pachocka, M., Pędziwiatr, K., Sobczak-Szelc, K., Szałańska, J., 2020. Reception Policies, Practices and Responses. Poland – Country Report, "Working Paper Series. Global Migration: Consequences and Responses", no. 2020/45. DOI: 10.5281/zenodo.3727093.

Pachocka, M, Sobczak-Szelc, K., 2018. Migracje przymusowe, in: Lesińska, M., Okólski, M. (Eds.), *25 wykładów o migracjach.* Scholar, Warszawa, pp. 335–341.

Pachocka, M., Sobczak-Szelc K., 2020. Refugee Protection Poland – Country Report, "Working Paper Series. Global Migration: Consequences and Responses", no. 2020/35. DOI: 10.5281/zenodo.3632827.

Pachocka, M., Wach, D., 2018. Migracja a integracja (imigrantów) w Unii Europejskiej – w poszukiwaniu rozwiązania, in: Latoszek E., Proczek M., Szczerba-Zawada A., Masłoń-Oracz A., Zajączkowski K. (Eds.), *Unia Europejska: istota, szanse, wyzwania.* CeDeWu, Warszawa, pp. 127–160.

Penninx, R., 2005. Integration of Migrants: Economic, Social, Cultural and Political Dimensions, in: Macura M., MacDonald A.L., Haug W. (Eds.), *The New Demographic Regime Population Challenges and Policy Responses.* United Nations, New York, Geneva: 137–152.

Penninx, R., 2007. Integration processes of migrants: Research findings and policy challenges, *Migracijske I Etničke Teme,* 23(1–2), 7–32.

Penninx, R., 2013. *Research on Migration and Integration in Europe: Achievements and Lessons.* Amsterdam University Press, Amsterdam.

Penninx, R., Garcés-Mascareñas, B., 2016. The Concept of Integration as an Analytical Tool and as a Policy Concept, in: Penninx, R., Garcés-Mascareñas, B. (Eds.), *Integration Processes and Policies in Europe.* Contexts, Levels and Actors, Springer, Heidelberg, pp. 16–19.

Pędziwiatr, K., Legutn, A., 2016. Polskie rządy wobec unijnej strategii na rzecz przeciwdziałania kryzysowi migracyjnemu, in: Wojtaszczyk, K.A., Szymańska, J. (Eds.), *Uchodźcy w Europie – Uwarunkowania, Istota, Następstwa.* Wydawnictwo Uniwersytetu Warszawskiego, Warszawa.

Scholten, P., 2013a. Agenda dynamics and the multi-level governance of migrant integration. The case of Dutch migrant integration policies, *Policy Sciences,* 46, 217–236.
Scholten, P., 2013b. The multi-level governance of migrant integration: a multi-level governance perspective on Dutch migrant integration policies, in: Korkut, A.O. (Ed.), *The Politics of Migration in Europe. The role of language, discourse and political parties.* Palgrave, Rotterdam.
Scholten, P., Penninx, R., 2016. The Multilevel Governance of Migration and Integration. In: Garcés-Mascareñas, B., Penninx, R. (Eds.), *Integration Processes and Policies in Europe. IMISCOE Research Series.* Springer, Cham. DOI: https://doi.org/10.1007/978-3-319-21674-4_6.
Sobczak-Szelc, K., Pachocka M., Pędziwiatr K., Szałańska J., 2020. Integration Policies, Practices and Experiences – Poland Country Report, "Working Paper Series. Global Migration: Consequences and Responses", no. 2020/63. DOI: 10.5281/zenodo.4008666.
Sobczak-Szelc, K., Szałańska, J., Pachocka, M., 2021. *The integration of asylum seekers and refugees in the field of education and labour market Comparative thematic report, Global Migration: Consequences and Responses – RESPOND Working Paper Series.* University of Warsaw, Uppsala.
Szałańska, J., 2020. Conflicting Conceptualisation of Europeanisation – Poland Country Report "Working Paper Series. Global Migration: Consequences and Responses", no. 2020/68. DOI: https://doi.org/10.5281/zenodo.4153036
Szczepanik, M., 2018. Border politics and practices of resistance on the eastern side of "Fortress Europe": the case of Chechen asylum seekers at the Belarusian–Polish border. *Central and Eastern European Migration Review,* 7, 69–89. DOI: https://doi.org/10.17467/ceemr.2018.08.
Szulecka, M., 2019. *Border Management and Migration Controls in Poland.* "Working Paper Series. Global Migration: Consequences and Responses", no. 2019/24. DOI: https://doi.org/10.5281/zenodo.3385242
Szulecka, M., 2022. The undermined role of (domestic) case law in shaping the practice of admitting asylum seekers in Poland. *European Journal of Legal Studies,* 14(SI), 171–209 http://hdl.handle.net/1814/74464
Szulecka, M., Pachocka M., Sobczak-Szelc K., 2018. Poland – Country Report: Legal and Policy Framework of Migration Governance, "Working Paper Series. Global Migration: Consequences and Responses", no. 2018/09. DOI: 10.5281/zenodo.1418583.
UNHCR, 2017. Global Report 2017, www.unhcr.org/publications/fundraising/5b4c89bf17/unhcr-global-report-2017.html.
Zincone, G., Caponio, T., 2006. The Multilevel Governance of Migration, in: Penninx, R., Berger, M., Kraal, K., (Eds.), *The Dynamics of International Migration and Settlement in Europe.* Amsterdam University Press, Amsterdam.

2

POLAND'S POSITION ON THE MAP OF FORCED MOBILITY IN THE EUROPEAN CONTEXT

Introduction

This chapter aims to shed light on the geographical, historical, and political background in which the system of admitting asylum seekers to Poland has developed. It requires a broader perspective than simply the state level since asylum-seeking is not only about crossing borders and asking for protection but also about commitments accepted or denied by the state in the area of providing various kinds of assistance to persons who flee conflicts, violence, and persecution. The latter is connected to international agreements, among which the UN Geneva Convention of 1951 with the New York Protocol of 1967 are crucial, accompanied later by European Union legislation. To present this picture, it is necessary to return to the beginning of the 1990s, when the political and socioeconomic transition started in Central and Eastern Europe. This shaped political and societal approaches towards outward and inward mobility in this region and in particular states.

This chapter is organised around two main issues. The first and prevailing one is the description of Poland as a post-communist country joining an international community committed to providing international protection to persons fleeing persecution, confirmed in 1991 along with the signing of the 1951 Geneva Convention by Poland. This part aims to present the critical phenomena and developments in international and EU law that influenced the creation and development of Poland's asylum regime. The second part focuses on the scale of forced migration to Poland after 1989, considering the EU and Visegrad Group (V4) contexts. Data on this subject were approximated by selected indicators from Eurostat asylum statistics for 2008–2021. For the purposes of this chapter, the acts of international, European, and national law in the area of migration, asylum, and human rights were overviewed, introducing the reader to the in-depth analysis of domestic legislation presented in other parts of the book (see Chapter 4).

DOI: 10.4324/9781003196327-2

The Creation of Poland's System of Forced Migration Governance in the International and EU Context

The discussion of Poland against the background of other European countries must be placed appropriately and contextualised, especially bearing in mind the country's historical and political contexts. After the Second World War, the Iron Curtain divided Europe into two areas, one covering Western-aligned countries and one grouping the countries of the Eastern Bloc, which included the Union of Soviet Socialist Republics (USSR) and Soviet-aligned countries. Of course, this division did not exhaust the list of all European countries, among which were those outside this division of power and influence, such as Yugoslavia, or neutral countries, such as Finland and Switzerland. At that time, Poland, like Czechoslovakia, Hungary, Bulgaria, Romania, and East Germany, was included in the Eastern Bloc, being Soviet satellite state. They cooperated with the USSR through the Warsaw Pact[1] and Comecon.[2] These satellite states in Europe shared the same fate during the communist era, being *de facto* people's republics politically, militarily, and socioeconomically dependent on the USSR. These were countries with limited involvement in international cooperation and thus in international migration. Despite the general closure to international migration and the restrictive policy of border control during the communist regime, the approach of the Polish People's Republic,[3] strongly based on a no-exit rule, evolved in the second half of the 20th century "from static immobility to movement on a massive scale and from an initial policy of isolation toward the gradual removal of restrictions and the adoption of policies encouraging labour migrations" (Stola, 2010, p. 472).

Poland is also often discussed through the prism of its belonging to a region known as Central and Eastern Europe (CEE), the scope of which is not commonly agreed upon. Various international organisations still use different methodologies and definitions, taking geographic, historical, and political contexts into account. According to the definition of the Organisation for Economic Co-operation and Development (OECD), often quoted in the literature on the subject, the Central and Eastern European Countries (CEECs) include Albania, Bulgaria, Croatia, the Czech Republic, Hungary, Poland, Romania, the Slovak Republic, Slovenia, Estonia, Latvia, and Lithuania. This is a comprehensive understanding of the CEE, including the Balkan states and three Baltic states.[4] In its classification of various country groups, the International Monetary Fund (IMF) describes the Czech Republic, Hungary, Poland, Slovak Republic, and Slovenia as CEE (IMF, 2016).[5] For the purposes of its statistical analyses, the National Institute of Statistics and Economic Studies of France (INSEE) uses the concept of CEE, which encompasses countries such as Bulgaria, Croatia, Estonia, Hungary, Latvia, Lithuania, Poland, Romania, Slovenia, Slovakia, and the Czech Republic.[6] In turn, the Dutch Central Bureau of Statistics (known as Statistics Netherlands, CBS) references CEE countries and understands it to include Bulgaria, the Czech Republic, Estonia, Hungary, Lithuania, Latvia, Poland, Romania, Slovenia, and Slovakia as EU Member States that were part of the former Eastern Bloc.[7] Moving on to the level of European official statistics and its methodology for collecting data in the EU, Eurostat, in its statistical portrait of EU regions in 2009, did not use the term "Central and Eastern Europe" as a proper name but referred to "the central and eastern European countries that joined the EU in 2004 or 2007" (Eurostat, 2019, pp. 15–16), including Poland, Hungary, the Czech Republic, Slovakia, Slovenia, Bulgaria, and Romania. According to Eurostat's glossary, Estonia, Latvia, and Lithuania are among what are called the EU Baltic Member States.[8] The presented brief overview of the approaches to the classification of CEE countries clearly shows no consensus in this regard, and international organisations and national statistical institutes adopt their own approach as presented in the data collection methodology.

In this chapter, and especially in the part concerning the statistical profile of Poland in the area of forced migration, the concept of CEE refers to the four former Eastern Bloc countries that joined the EU in May 2004 and at the same time have been cooperating since the 1990s within the Visegrad Group.[9] These are countries with a similar historical trajectory after the Second World War and which experienced a systemic transformation at the turn of the 1980s and 1990s and then became the new EU Member States at the beginning of the 21st century. Their common path to accession to the EU and the effects of further membership in its structures are of crucial importance here, as they required adjustment of the legal and institutional frameworks in these countries to the European legal order, also in the area of the migration-management system, and then joint participation in the development and implementation of EU policy on border management, asylum, and immigration.

From the time of the partitions of Poland at the end of the 18th century and subsequent national uprisings, through the period of two world wars and the Polish People's Republic in the 20th century, until the beginning of the 21st century, Poland was primarily a country of emigrants, many of whom considered themselves refugees (Ząbek and Łodziński, 2008, p. 73). Poland accepted immigrants, including forced ones, on a very small scale, mainly due to political and ideological reasons. Pursuant to Article 75 (and since 1976 Article 88[10]) of the Constitution of 1952, the People's Republic of Poland granted asylum to citizens of foreign countries, persecuted for defending the interests of the working masses, fighting for social progress, acting in defence of peace, the national liberation struggle, or scientific activity. Thus, mainly refugees with communist views and beliefs were eligible for support. The two most frequently cited examples of people granted political asylum in Poland are the Greeks and Macedonians in 1948–1954 and Chileans in 1973, some of whom later left the country (Ząbek and Łodziński, 2008, pp. 74–76). After the Second World War, the migration situation in Czechoslovakia and Hungary, which also belonged to the Eastern Bloc, was similar to that in Poland. Apart from movements of people after the end of war hostilities, changes in the course of interstate borders and a new division of influence between the West and the East (e.g., forced displacement of Germans from Czechoslovakia, voluntary outflows of Jews from Poland and Czechoslovakia to the newly created state of Israel), these countries were closed to international migration, ensuring the tightness of their borders and pursuing an emigration policy similar to the Soviet one (e.g., refusal to issue passports to their own citizens). At the same time, they were rather countries of origin of political refugees who did not support the communist regime and tried to oppose the repressive authority and implement political changes (e.g., developments in Hungary in 1956, Czechoslovakia in 1968, Poland in 1980–1981) or simply did not want to live in totalitarian countries. The inhabitants of these CEE states fled from behind the Iron Curtain to Western Europe and even to the U.S., Canada, and Australia (Slany, 1995, pp. 74–109). In such political circumstances, it was difficult to perceive the CEE countries belonging to the Warsaw Pact as safe countries with a developed and internationalised asylum regime that would receive refugees.

Development of Forced Migration Governance in Contemporary Poland

A decade ago, Polish researchers of migration divided the development of Polish migration policy after 1989 into three stages: institutionalisation (1989–2001), Europeanisation (2001–2004), and stabilisation (from 2004 to 2010, which was the last year covered by the authors). Such phases could be distinguished in the development of migration policies also in other CEE states (Lesińska, Stefańska, Szulecka, 2010, pp. 262–264). The Polish literature on the subject clearly indicates the critical role of preparations for Poland's accession to the EU (2004) and the Schengen area (2007) and subsequent membership in these structures in terms of adjusting the Polish legal system to the EU acquis, including the asylum regime (see, e.g., Ząbek and Łodziński, 2008; Weinar, 2006; Górny et al., 2010; Okólski and Wach, 2020).

Newer analyses of the development of migration governance in Poland also distinguish an important phase of the legal and political changes following the 2015 "refugee crisis" and ambivalent response of EU states and EU institutions to it. The latter may be seen in the near future as a crucial phase of adjusting migration law and policies to the increased scale of forced mobility and other challenges related to it. In their periodisation, Łodziński and Szonert (2017, p. 47) distinguished four periods of development of this policy: 1989–1997, related to the commencement of democratic political changes in the country and the adoption of the new Law on Foreigners in 1997; 1998–2004, years regarding the preparations for Poland's accession to the EU; 2005 to mid-2015, a period of "maturity" of this policy; and from mid-2015 to 2017, a time of changes related to the response to the "migration-management crisis" in Europe. In a newer analysis of migration policy development in Poland, Stefańska and Szulecka, referring to the dominant direction of developing laws and practices regarding migration, proposed to distinguish the following phases: opening of the borders; regulation of migration; controlled opening; and revision of policy (Stefańska and Szulecka, 2018, pp. 2–5). The last phase may be equated with the phase of responding to the "migration-management crisis", as proposed by Łodziński and Szonert (2017). Indeed, the necessity to revise relatively liberal ("open") laws and policies was presented by the Polish government as an inevitable step to prevent uncontrolled migration and a migration crisis in the Polish context (see also Skiba et al., 2016).

Before asylum and migration policy achieved "maturity" or became "institutionalised", the early 1990s witnessed significant political and socio-economic changes in the CEE region due to the fall of communism in 1989. This opened up the borders to international migration flows, which did not mean the abolition of border controls, but less restrictiveness of the rules concerning their crossing. As a result, Poland became a transit country for various groups of migrants, some of whom were asylum seekers heading to Western Europe and Scandinavia, often assisted by networks of smugglers (Okólski and Wach, 2020, p. 150). It was also the beginning of the shaping of the foundations of Poland's modern migration policy in terms of law, institutions, and practice, including asylum policy (Łodziński and Szonert, 2017).

Poland found itself in a situation in 1990 when it had to accept several hundred people (including Somalis, Ethiopians, Libyans, Iraqis, and Syrians) who had been returned from Sweden where they were seeking asylum. At that time, Sweden was already burdened with a large number of refugees. Through this move, it minimised the forced migration pressure in the country and recognised Poland as a safe country for asylum seekers. In the same year, the Polish government adopted the first national institutional solutions at the central level, which took over the coordination of refugee cases from the Polish Red Cross. Contacts were also established with UNHCR, which opened the door for Poland to enter into the framework of international refugee law (Ząbek and Łodziński, 2008, pp. 77–80). Therefore, the first steps on the way to entering the European asylum system and applying relevant policies were made "spontaneously" due to Poland's ongoing political transition and external developments.

The symbolic date of Poland's declaration to participate in the international refugee protection system was 1991 when the Polish government, third after Hungary and Czechoslovakia, signed the Geneva Convention on the Status of Refugees of 1951 and the New York Protocol of 1967.[11] This event initiated the formal process of establishing an asylum regime in Poland, which was directly influenced by such factors as the development of a legal framework regarding the reception of asylum seekers by the EU Member States, the characteristics and routes of forced mobility to and through Europe, and the changing geopolitical position of Poland. Furthermore, 1991 was also crucial for another reason, as Poland signed an agreement on readmission with Schengen countries, which meant the introduction of a visa-free regime between Poland and the Schengen countries (Stefańska and Szulecka, 2018).[12]

Another important act of international law that concerned the treatment of refugees and foreigners, ratified by Poland in 1993, was the European Convention for the Protection of Human Rights and Fundamental Freedoms of 4 November 1950.[13] It should be emphasised that Poland had ratified two other key acts of international human rights law essential for the protection of refugees rights much earlier, in the times of the People's Republic of Poland. These were the 1966 International Covenant on Civil and Political Rights (ICCPR)[14] and the 1966 International Covenant on Economic, Social and Cultural Rights (ICESCR), both ratified in March 1977 (Ząbek and Łodziński, 2008, p. 81).[15]

Stronger ties between domestic law and the international legal framework resulted in changes to the Polish legal system relating to foreigners, including forced migrants and the Polish asylum regime, in the 1990s and the first two decades of the 20th century. Furthermore, the development of the Polish asylum system was significantly related to international cooperation with various organisations such as UNHCR (see also Chapter 4) and the Europeanisation of Polish migration policy, encompassing an asylum one.

The changes were numerous, with varying degrees of detail and scope. Several changes deserve attention. The amendment to the Law on Foreigners of 1963 in September 1991[16] resulted in the introduction of the institution of "refugee status" into the Polish legal system and the necessity to apply the provisions of the 1951 Convention and the 1967 Protocol. This allowed Poland to accept applications for international protection legally, dissect them on their own, and issue legally binding decisions (Ząbek and Łodziński, 2008, p. 82). Another critical moment ending the initial period of building the asylum system in Poland was the adoption of new legal acts, including the Constitution of the Republic of Poland of 1997 (with Article 56 as the basis for national and international protection; see also Chapter 4), and the new Law on Foreigners of 1997[17] specifying the rules of granting refugee status (Chapter 5 of this Law) and the national form of protection (Chapter 6 of this Law). The provisions related to protection under the 1951 Geneva Convention relating to the Status of Refugees (included in the mentioned Chapter 5 of the Law on Foreigners of 1997) were fundamental because they detailed the procedures concerning foreigners applying for refugee status and its beneficiaries, indicating the scope of social assistance for people awaiting a decision in the asylum procedure (Ząbek and Łodziński, 2008, pp. 87–88).

The new law was aimed at a gradual adjustment of Polish legislation to EU requirements, becoming part of the process of the Europeanisation of Polish law and politics in connection with preparations for Poland's membership in the EU (Ząbek and Łodziński, 2008, p. 93; Weinar, 2006, pp. 86–95). The culmination of preparing Poland's legislation regarding international protection to the EU requirements was the adoption of a new law devoted entirely to asylum-related issues in 2003.[18] Within the scope of its regulation, the Law on Protection implemented two crucial asylum-related Directives of the European Communities: (1) Council Directive 2001/55/EC on Temporary Protection[19] and (2) Council Directive 2003/9/EC of 27 January 2003 on Reception.[20] An essential amendment to the Law on Protection took place in 2008, extending the catalogue of forms of international protection in Poland by so-called subsidiary protection, which modified the protection in the form of tolerated stay (a national instrument). This amendment also implemented into the Polish asylum law two EU Directives, one on Qualification[21] and a second on Procedures[22] (Ząbek and Łodziński, 2008, pp. 97–98).

The vital framework of international law dealing with migration and asylum and binding on Poland includes also the Convention for the Protection of Human Rights and Fundamental Freedoms, 4 November 1950, Rome, and Protocol No. 7 to the Convention for the Protection of Human Rights and Fundamental Freedoms, 22 November 1984, Strasbourg; Convention on the Rights of the Child, 20 November 1989, New York, that set standards for the human rights protection and guarantees for children's rights in the international forced-mobility context. Other legal acts that can be mentioned with respect to forced migration governance in Poland are international agreements: the European Agreement on the Abolition ofVisas for Refugees, 3 September 1960, Strasbourg, and the European Agreement on Transfer of Responsibility for Refugees, 16 October 1980, Strasbourg.[23]

Asylum Law in Poland as an EU Member State

The asylum law in Poland must be consistent with the European framework, which in turn is related to the EU asylum policy. This one, along with immigration policy and border control policy, is one of the three specific/sectoral EU policies in the area of international migration management (Pachocka, and Wach, 2018; Gońda et al., 2020). They are all part of the policy area of freedom, security, and justice, which is subject to shared competencies between the EU and the Member States (Article 4 (2)(j) TFEU) in that both "may legislate and adopt legally binding acts in that area" (Article 2(2) TFEU). Furthermore, as stipulated in Article 67(1)(2) TFEU:

1. The Union shall constitute an area of freedom, security and justice with respect for fundamental rights and the different legal systems and traditions of the Member States.
2. It shall ensure the absence of internal border controls for persons and shall frame a common policy on asylum, immigration and external border control, based on solidarity between Member States, which is fair towards third-country nationals. For the purpose of this Title, stateless persons shall be treated as third-country nationals.

The legal basis for the EU's asylum policy under primary law is constituted by Articles 67(2), 78, and 80 TFEU and Article 18 of the EU Charter of Fundamental Rights.[24] Detailed legal provisions are provided by secondary law and supplementary sources such as unilateral acts of law (e.g., directives, regulations), international agreements and case law of the Court of Justice of the EU. Article 78(1)(2) TFEU provides for three basic forms of international protection at the EU level and in its Member States, which include a uniform status of asylum (in other words, refugee status) and subsidiary protection for third-country nationals as well as a common system of temporary protection of displaced persons in the event of their massive inflow. This is being developed under the Common European Asylum System (Article 78(2) TFEU). What is important, EU asylum policy must be in accordance with the 1951 Geneva Convention and the 1967 New York Protocol relating to the Status of Refugees, and other relevant treaties, which is explicitly stated in Article 78(1) TFEU.

As of late 2021, the crucial EU Directives related to the asylum procedure and providing international protection, that is, the Qualification Directive (recast), Reception Conditions Directive (recast), and Asylum Procedure Directive (recast), were transposed into Polish legislation (see also Chapter 4). The key EU Regulation deserving attention as part of forced migration governance in Poland, applied directly, is Regulation (EU) No. 604/2013 establishing the criteria and mechanisms for determining the Member State responsible for examining an application for international protection (Dublin Regulation).[25]

In 2015, at the height of the migration-management crisis in Europe, Article 78(3) TFEU turned out to be of crucial importance, stating that:

> In the event of one or more Member States being confronted by an emergency situation characterised by a sudden inflow of nationals of third countries, the Council, on a proposal from the Commission, may adopt provisional measures for the benefit of the Member State(s) concerned. It shall act after consulting the European Parliament.

It was the legal basis for the emergency relocation mechanism for asylum seekers proposed by the European Commission in May 2015 in its communication on European Agenda on Migration.[26] It was made more specific in EU secondary law under two Council Decisions adopted in September 2015 (2015/1523 and 2015/1601)[27] on the temporary relocation of applicants for international protection from Italy and Greece. The two-year relocation mechanism was expected to cover a total of upto 160,000 people from 2015 to 2017. Relocation to other EU countries was to take place based on a specific distribution key, which some EU countries did not agree to. Ultimately, Poland, Hungary, and the Czech Republic—all members of the Visegrad Group—did not implement relocation, for which the European Commission initiated a Treaty-infringement procedure in July 2016 and referred these EU Member States to the Court of Justice of the EU (CJEU).[28] As stated in the judgement of the Court (Third Chamber) of 2 April 2020,[29] Poland, Hungary, and the Czech Republic failed to fulfil their obligations under the specific stipulations of the above-mentioned Council Decisions (EU) 2015/1523 and 2015/1601.

In general, the years of the 2015–2016 migration-management crisis were marked by a strengthening of political cooperation between the Visegrad Group countries, including the development of a common position on migration and asylum policy at the EU forum. Among the four members of this CEE regional grouping composed of Poland, Hungary, the Czech Republic, and Slovakia, only Hungary was significantly affected by the crisis as the Western Balkans migration route ran through its territory. Hungary could have been included in the relocation mechanism along with Italy and Greece but refused. The other V4 countries were neither the main transit nor destination countries for forced or irregular migrants during the crisis years (Pachocka, 2016).

In the case of Poland, however, these years were marked by strong politicisation and mediatisation of the topic of migration and refugees and demonising the EU as unjustifiably imposing solutions in the field of migration and asylum policy on "sovereign" Poland (e.g., relocation).[30] This was related to the accession to power of the Law and Justice (*Prawo i Sprawiedliwość,* PiS) political party in the presidential and parliamentary elections in 2015. Considered right-wing, conservative, and populist, PiS launched anti-refugee and anti-European political and media discourses in the country (Pachocka and Sobczak-Szelc, 2020; Molęda-Zdziech et al., 2021; Górak-Sosnowska and Pachocka, 2019) (see Chapter 3). This translated into negative, even hostile, public attitudes towards receiving asylum seekers and refugees in Poland, especially those adhering to the Muslim religion (Klaus, 2017; Pachocka and Sobczak-Szelc, 2020; Molęda-Zdziech et al., 2021, and see more in Chapter 3).

The first years of the rule of Law and Justice also marked an unfavourable political climate for NGOs providing support to migrants. The Ministry of the Interior and Administration significantly changed the rules for financing projects from EU money through the Asylum, Migration and Integration Fund (AMIF), which limited the activities of many NGOs specialising in legal assistance for asylum seekers and refugees in Poland. From 2015/2016, the situation on Poland's eastern border, being part of the EU's external border, was complex. Border Guard officers made access to the territory of the Republic of Poland difficult for people declaring their willingness to apply for international protection. They practised multiple pushbacks, mainly at the Brest-Terespol railway border crossing (see, e.g., Chrzanowska et al., 2016; Górczyńska and Szczepanik, 2016; Szczepanik, 2018; Szulecka, 2019; see, Chapter 5). As a result, in Poland, the Commissioner for Human Rights (Ombudsman) and the Commissioner for Children's Rights, some NGOs (such as the Association for Legal Intervention or the Helsinki Foundation for Human Rights) and individual lawyers (in particular, from the Warsaw Bar Association) became involved in the situation at the Polish-Belarusian border in different ways, such as monitoring visits, interventions, and actions at border crossings, publications of reports, as well as initiating appeals against the refusals of entry issued to persons willing to apply for asylum (Białas et al., 2019; Pachocka and Sobczak-Szelc, 2020, pp. 82–83; Szulecka, 2022). Under the pretext of the migration-management crisis in Europe and the worsening international situation (e.g., the growing threat of terrorism), the government initiated laws and practices that in fact gave priority to protecting the national borders and ensuring internal security (see also Chapter 4), rather than providing asylum to third-country nationals in compliance with European and international refugee law and human rights standards (see more Szulecka, 2022). As mentioned above, the post-2015 period of migration and asylum policy development could be characterised as a phase of revision, extending control and selective openness towards migrants, with a welcoming approach mainly towards certain migrant workers and a reluctance towards asylum seekers.

The Scale of the Phenomenon of Forced Migration in Poland after 1989 in the EU/CEE Contexts

Between 1992 and 2007, as stated by Ząbek and Łodziński (2008, p. 107), Poland accepted applications for granting refugee status from more than 60,000 people. Refugee status was granted to more than 2,000 applicants. In addition, there were more beneficiaries of the national status of "tolerated stay", introduced into Polish law in 2003 as a legal institution dedicated to persons not eligible to obtain international protection but whose return to the country of origin could not be executed (because it would pose a threat to their life, safety, freedom from torture or forced labour, among others). This status was granted to about 7,600 people by 2007. Thus, in 2004–2007, over 30% of the people applying for protection in Poland received some kind of legal protection; however, only about 3% were recognised with refugee status. The rest were allowed to stay in Poland despite the refusal to grant them refugee status and were in fact protected from deportation or the obligation to leave Poland.

The number of asylum seekers and the structure of their population by nationality/country of origin changed over the years. In 1992–1993, most applicants for refugee status came from the former Yugoslavia (because of the war in Croatia and Bosnia and Herzegovina), but there were also people from Ethiopia, Armenia, Iraq, and Lebanon. The following years were characterised by the domination of one or several nationalities among the applicants: in 1994, they were mainly Armenians; in 1995–1996, they came mostly from South Asia (India, Pakistan, Afghanistan, Sri Lanka, and Bangladesh); in 1997, from Somalia and Armenia; and in 1998, from Bulgaria and Romania (Ząbek and Łodziński, 2008, pp. 83–86). Even though the scale of forced migration to Poland grew in the 1990s, it was still a country of temporary stay for most of these arrivals due to difficulties in access to housing and the labour market and the low economic attractiveness of Poland compared to Western European countries. An interesting tendency from the end of the 1990s was related to the growth in the number of Armenians, Roma from Romania and Bulgaria, and Vietnamese among those applying for protection, who were seen as quickly adapting to the new society and arriving with entrepreneurial abilities and, at the same time, reaching for refugee procedures as a way to legalise their stay in Poland as a last resort. After 1998, the number of applicants for refugee status increased to about 4,000 people a year, and after 2003 there was another jump to about 6,000–7,000 people annually. A clearly noticeable and later dominant group of applicants was forced migrants from Chechnya, who formally were Russian Federation citizens (Ząbek and Łodziński, 2008, pp. 90–91). Apart from Chechens, at the beginning of the 2000s, more and more Belarusians, Pakistanis, and Ukrainians applied for international protection, while other Asian and African nationalities were quite diverse but fractional (Ząbek and Łodziński, 2008, p. 94).

For years, the influx of asylum applicants was a marginal phenomenon compared to migration driven by economic motives. The latter type of migration has been a distinctive feature of Poland since 2016 when the country became the leader among OECD countries in admitting temporary migrant workers.[31] That year was also the first year when Poland recorded a slightly positive migration balance, as Poland's Central Statistical Office reported.[32] This confirms that this CEE country was transforming from a net emigration country to a net immigration country, in other words, from a traditional emigration country to a new immigration country (Górny et al., 2010, Okólski, 2021; Pędziwiatr et al., 2019). The end of the second decade of the 21st century brought about the "Ukrainisation" of – in vast majority economically driven – immigration to Poland—Ukrainian citizens have comprised the most numerous group of foreigners among permanent and temporary residents and foreign students (Górny and Kindler, 2018, pp. 221–222). In the first quarter of 2022, Ukrainian nationals quickly became the main group of forced migrants in Poland, fleeing because of Russia's full-scale invasion that began on 24 February. The number of people arriving since then have exceeded all the reported numbers of asylum seekers in Poland for the previous three decades. According to UNHCR, as of mid-April 2022, out of the 5 million recorded Ukrainian forced migrants, about 2.8 million had gone to Poland (UNHCR Operational Data Portal, 2022). Such a scale of forced mobility posed new challenges on the national and EU authorities and soon led to the introduction of legal and institutional solutions—ones that vary from those described in this book and targeting asylum seekers reaching Poland or the CEE region and EU up to 2021.

Referring to asylum realities prior to 2022, it is important to understand the context of the characteristics of forced migration to Poland in recent years compared to the EU and other CEE countries, especially Visegrad Group countries. According to the provisions of Regulation (EC) No. 862/2007 regarding migration data in the EU,[33] Eurostat collects statistics on international migration and international protection from the EU Member States. Therefore, an approximation of the scale of forced migration in the EU might be the number of non-EU citizens (including both third-country nationals and stateless persons) applying for international protection (people having submitted an application for international protection or having been included in such an application as a family member). They are also often referred to as asylum applicants. According to Eurostat data,[34] the total number of asylum applicants in the EU-27[35] grew to over 1.2 million in 2015 and 2016, which were the peak years of the migration-management crisis in Europe. The following years are characterised by a downward trend until 2021, with a fluctuating number of asylum applicants every year.

Asylum applicants in the four Visegrad states, including first-time applicants, represented 9% of the total for the EU in 2014 and 15% one year later (Table 2.1). In the following years, however, it was minimal, from 1% to 4%. The year 2015 was an exception due to the large influx of forced migrants to Hungary, a country located on the Western Balkan migration route. Between 2008 and 2021, the most applications for international protection in a single year submitted in Poland (more than 15,000) was in 2013, that is before the migration-management crisis. At the peak of the crisis in 2015–2016, Poland registered more than 12,000 applications

TABLE 2.1 Non-EU asylum applicants in EU and V4 countries in 2008–2021

Year	*2008*	*2009*	*2010*	*2011*	*2012*	*2013*	*2014*	*2015*	*2016*	*2017*	*2018*	*2019*	*2020*	*2021*
EU-27 countries (from 2020)	n/a	n/a	n/a	n/a	n/a	n/a	594,180	1,282,690	1,221,185	677,470	625,575	698,760	472,395	630,550
Czech Rep.	1,645	1,235	775	750	740	695	1,145	1,515	1,475	1,445	1,690	1,915	1,160	1,405
Hungary	3,175	4,665	2,095	1,690	2,155	18,895	42,775	177,135	29,430	3,390	670	500	115	40
Poland	8,515	10,590	6,540	6,885	10,750	15,240	8,020	12,190	12,305	5,045	4,110	4,070	2,785	7,795
Slovakia	895	805	540	490	730	440	330	330	145	160	175	230	280	370
% V4 to total EU							9%	15%	4%	1%	1%	1%	1%	2%

n/a - not available

Source: Own elaboration by the RESPOND team in Poland based on: Eurostat, Asylum applicants by type of applicant, citizenship, age and sex, annual aggregated data (rounded) [MIGR_ASYAPPCTZA__custom_2527461] (last visited 18.04.2022).

TABLE 2.2 Recognition rate (%) in EU and V4 countries in 2008–2021

Year	*2008* (%)	*2009* (%)	*2010* (%)	*2011* (%)	*2012* (%)	*2013* (%)	*2014* (%)	*2015* (%)	*2016* (%)	*2017* (%)	*2018* (%)	*2019* (%)	*2020* (%)	*2021* (%)
EU-27 countries (from 2020)	27	27	25	25	32	34	46	53	62	46	37	38	41	n/a
Czech Rep.	15	19	35	47	24	38	38	34	33	12	11	10	11	28
Hungary	44	22	25	17	32	8	9	13	8	31	38	8	27	67
Poland	65	38	12	15	21	24	27	18	12	20	15	13	19	67
Slovakia	24	57	31	53	43	37	61	62	84	67	56	39	50	35

n/a – not available

Source: Own elaboration by the RESPOND team in Poland based on: Eurostat, First-instance decisions on applications by citizenship, age and sex, annual aggregated data (rounded) [MIGR_ASYDCFSTA__custom_2527630] (last visited 18.04.2022).

annually. The following years saw a significant drop to about 2,800–5,000 applicants a year. A new increase to almost 8,000 was recorded in 2021 (UdSC, 2022).

Another critical indicator in the asylum statistics is the recognition rate, understood as a share of the total positive decisions (in other words, the granting of one of the following forms of international protection to asylum applicants: refugee status, subsidiary protection, or non-EU harmonised protection, which usually translates into a permit for stay due to humanitarian reasons) in the total of first-instance decisions in a given country (Table 2.2). The recognition rate was quite variable between 2008 and 2020, not only for each V4 country but also for the entire EU-27. In the case of the EU, the period with the most positive decisions compared to all decisions (over 50%) was in 2015–2016, that is, during the migration-management crisis. At the same time, Poland and Hungary had significantly lower recognition rates than Slovakia and the Czech Republic. Refugee status related to the Geneva Convention of 1951 and subsidiary protection (which are forms of international protection) prevailed over non-EU harmonised forms of protection among all the beneficiaries of protection status in the EU and Visegrad countries (including Poland[36]).

It is worth noting that in the case of Poland, after nearly 20 years of migration dominated by Russian citizens (mainly Chechens) among people applying for international protection, 2021 marked a significant change because of new migration challenges in Europe and its neighbourhood. The top three nationalities among asylum seekers in 2021 included Belarusians (fleeing increasing political instability in that country), Afghans (mainly evacuated at the turn of August and September from Afghanistan), and Iraq (according to the Office for Foreigners, their arrival was in connection with the Belarusian-organised irregular migration through the border with Poland) (UdSC, 2022).

Conclusions

The communist period after the Second World War and the influence of the USSR on Eastern Bloc states over many decades left their mark on Poland's migration situation and the development of its migration policy. This concerned both the management of voluntary (e.g., economic) and forced (e.g., refugee) migration. In the second half of the 20th century, Poland, then a no-exit country, experienced an influx of asylum seekers, although this phenomenon had a symbolic dimension mainly of a political and ideological nature, that is, migrants with communist views.

With the transformation of the political and socioeconomic system in the early 1990s and its consequences, Poland joined the international migration system, opening up to migration flows across its borders, cooperation with international organisations and agencies such as UNHCR, and becoming a party to various conventions in the area of refugees and human rights (e.g., 1951 Geneva Convention). Since then, Poland is most often identified in the literature as a former Eastern Bloc state, a CEE state, a newer EU Member State (since 2004), and a Visegrad Group state (since 1991).

The intensive development of forced migration governance in contemporary Poland was possible mainly due to the path of rapid preparations for Poland's membership in the EU, including the Europeanisation of the Polish acquis and asylum regimes, as well as the adoption of practices and policies common to EU members. The critical moment for Poland's management of forced migrations was 2015 when two important factors converged—one external, i.e., the migration-management crisis in Europe, and the second internal, i.e. change of political power to the government headed by Law and Justice, which pushed an anti-refugee direction of national migration policy, striving for restrictive changes in the law and implementing practices that are inconsistent with (or even against) international and EU standards, such as pushbacks on the eastern border with Belarus. The result is that Poland stepped back in the area of asylum policy to a position of strong politicisation and mediatisation of the topic of migration and refugees, especially in 2015–2016.

The following years saw new challenges in the field of forced migration governance in Poland. Although they are beyond the scope of this book, it is worth mentioning them because they already have and will continue to have a huge impact on the revision of the asylum system in Poland in terms of law, practice, and policy. It is namely about the double standard in access to the territory of the Republic of Poland and access to protection for forced migrants entering Poland through the eastern border.

On the Polish-Belarusian border, Poland has enacted a strict closed-door policy for forced migrants mainly from the Middle East and North Africa (MENA) region since mid-2021, and this situation is internationally described as a humanitarian crisis. One can observe, on the one hand, tactics such as pushbacks by the Polish Border Guard and refusals to accept applications for international protection from MENA-origin forced migrants, backed by important legal changes such as the introduction of a state of emergency in the border zone that blocked entry to the area and limited access to journalists and NGO representatives, an expulsion law, and a law allowing and funding the construction of border security measures in the form of a 6-m-tall fence. On the other hand, there is the activity of the Polish NGOs and human rights campaigners, including the informal collective Border Group, providing support to forced migrants on the border and the formation of the Researchers on the Border initiative, an inter-university, interdisciplinary, and grassroots research network specialising in eastern border situations (Pachocka, 2022).

Contrasted with the Belarusian border is the situation on the border between Poland and Ukraine after 24 February and Russia's renewed, brutal aggression against Ukraine. In less than three weeks since the start of the full-scale invasion, Poland became the primary destination for people fleeing Ukraine. Poland adopted an open-door policy for forced migrants under which the rules for crossing the border were loosened, mobility restrictions pertaining to COVID-19 were lifted, and the government adopted the "Law on assistance to Ukrainian citizens in connection with the armed conflict on the territory of the country"[37] (Pachocka, 2022).

Both of the aforementioned crises connected to the eastern border of Poland, in addition to receiving about a thousand asylum seekers from Afghanistan after their evacuation in August 2021, have forced major changes in Poland's asylum laws, practices, and policies. The coming years will be decisive in this respect, the more so that the forced migration pressure from the east will not disappear quickly.

In briefly summarising the issue of the scale of forced migration to Poland, it is worth saying that the country after 1989 was not the main destination for forced migrants, but rather a transit country. Thus, the number of applications for refugee status was small, and generally speaking, citizens of the Russian Federation—mostly of Chechen origin—prevailed. After 2004, Poland's role changed after it became an EU member and its eastern border was now part of the bloc's external border. The migration-management crisis of 2015 did not affect Poland directly in terms of numbers of migrants, but it was instrumentally treated by the PiS government to demonise refugee migration.

Poland until 2022 had been a country with not only a small number of forced migrants applying for international protection compared to the EU but also a low recognition rate. It seems that the situation will be drastically changed by the humanitarian crisis in Ukraine that began in February 2022, with more than 1.2 million forced migrants from Ukraine already having received temporary protection in Poland, which is another form of protection than the typical refugee status or subsidiary protection (UNHCR Operational Data Portal, 2022).

Notes

1 The official name of this political and military organisation was the Treaty of Friendship, Cooperation and Mutual Assistance, also known as the Warsaw Treaty Organisation. See: https://treaties.un.org/doc/Publication/UNTS/Volume%20219/volume-219-I-2962-Other.pdf.
2 The official name of this economic organisation was the Council for Mutual Economic Assistance. See: https://isap.sejm.gov.pl/isap.nsf/download.xsp/WDU19600350197/O/D19600197.pdf.
3 Poland first came under Soviet influence as early as 1944. In the years 1944 to 1952, it functioned under the name the Republic of Poland, and then in the Constitution of 1952 the name was formally changed to the Polish People's Republic, which remained until 1989.
4 OECD, Glossary of statistical terms, stats.oecd.org/glossary/detail.asp?ID=303.
5 IMF, 2016. Central, Eastern, and Southeastern Europe How to Get Back on the Fast Track, www.imf.org/external/pubs/ft/reo/2016/eur/eng/pdf/rei0516.pdf.
6 INSEE, Central and Eastern European countries, definition, www.insee.fr/en/metadonnees/definition/c2055.
7 CBS, CEE countries (CEECs), www.cbs.nl/en-gb/news/2018/31/international-road-haulage-over-4-percent-up-in-2017/cee-countries--ceecs--.
8 Eurostat, Glossary: Baltic Member States, ec.europa.eu/eurostat/statistics-explained/index.php?title=Glossary:Baltic_Member_States.
9 Visegrad Group, www.visegradgroup.eu/pl.

10 Konstytucja Rzeczypospolitej Polskiej uchwalona przez Sejm Ustawodawczy w dniu 22 lipca 1952 r. (Dz. U. Nr 33, poz. 232). (Constitution of People's Republic of Poland). In 1991, the amended Constitution of the People's Republic of Poland stipulated (in Article 88) the general right to asylum for any non-national or stateless person (Ustawa z dnia 18 października 1991 r. o zmianie Konstytucji Rzeczypospolitej Polskiej (Dz. U. Nr 119, poz. 514).

11 UNHCR, United Nations High Commissioner for Refugees, States Parties to the 1951 Convention relating to the Status of Refugees and the 1967 Protocol, www.unhcr.org/protect/PROTECTION/3b73b0d63.pdf.

12 Stefańska, R., Szulecka, M., 2018. Rozwój polityki migracyjnej Polski: otwarcie granic – regulowanie migracji – kontrolowane otwarcie – rewizja polityki, Biuletyn Migracyjny, Ośrodek Badań nad Migracjami UW, 57, pp. 2–5. http://biuletynmigracyjny.uw.edu.pl/pliki/pdf/biuletynmigracyjny57_0.pdf.

13 See Council of Europe, 1952. The European Convention on Human Rights. Strasbourg, www.echr.coe.int/documents/convention_eng.pdf.; Konwencja o Ochronie Praw Człowieka i Podstawowych Wolności sporządzona w Rzymie dnia 4 listopada 1950 r., zmieniona następnie Protokołami nr 3, 5 i 8 oraz uzupełniona Protokołem nr 2, https://isap.sejm.gov.pl/isap.nsf/DocDetails.xsp?id=wdu19930610284.

14 The Office of the High Commissioner for Human Rights, 1966. International Covenant on Civil and Political Rights, www.ohchr.org/en/instruments-mechanisms/instruments/international-covenant-civil-and-political-rights.

15 Other important publications regarding the development of the asylum regime in Poland after 1989, see e.g. Florczak, A., 2003. Uchodźcy w Polsce. Między humanitaryzmem a pragmatyzmem, Wydaw. Adam Marszałek, Toruń, http://hdl.handle.net/11320/3338; Rafalik, N., 2012. Cudzoziemcy ubiegający się o nadanie statusu uchodźcy w Polsce – teoria a rzeczywistość (praktyka) (stan prawny na dzień 31 grudnia 2011 r.). CMR Working Papers No. 55(113). Centre of Migration Research, University of Warsaw, Warszawa.

16 Ustawa z dnia 19 września 1991 r. o zmianie ustawy o cudzoziemcach (Dz. U. Nr 119, poz. 513).

17 Ustawa z dnia 25 czerwca 1997 r. o cudzoziemcach (Dz. U. Nr 114, poz. 739).

18 Ustawa z dnia 13 czerwca 2003 r. o udzielaniu cudzoziemcom ochrony na terytorium Rzeczypospolitej Polskiej (Dz. U. Nr 128, poz. 1176).

19 Council Directive 2001/55/EC of 20 July 2001 on minimum standards for giving temporary protection in the event of a mass influx of displaced persons and on measures promoting a balance of efforts between Member States in receiving such persons and bearing the consequences thereof, OJ L 212, 7.8.2001, https://eur-lex.europa.eu/legal-content/EN/TXT/?uri=celex%3A32001L0055.

20 Council Directive 2003/9/EC of 27 January 2003 laying down minimum standards for the reception of asylum seekers, OJ L 31, 6.2.2003, https://eur-lex.europa.eu/legal-content/EN/ALL/?uri=celex%3A32003L0009.

21 Directive 2011/95/EU of the European Parliament and of the Council of 13 December 2011 on standards for the qualification of third-country nationals or stateless persons as beneficiaries of international protection, for a uniform status for refugees or for persons eligible for subsidiary protection, and for the content of the protection granted (recast), OJ L 337, 20.12.2011, https://eur-lex.europa.eu/legal-content/EN/TXT/?uri=celex%3A32011L0095.

22 Directive 2013/32/EU of the European Parliament and of the Council of 26 June 2013 on common procedures for granting and withdrawing international protection, OJ L

180, 29.6.2013, https://eur-lex.europa.eu/legal-content/en/TXT/?uri=celex%3A320 13L0032.

23 UdSC: Office for Foreigners, 2019. International legal acts. [Online] Available at: https:// udsc.gov.pl/en/prawo/akty-prawa-miedzynarodowego/ (accessed 30 December 2019).

24 European Parliament, Asylum Policy, www.europarl.europa.eu/factsheets/en/sheet/ 151/polityka-azylowa.

25 Regulation (EU) No 604/2013 of the European Parliament and of the Council of 26 June 2013 establishing the criteria and mechanisms for determining the Member State responsible for examining an application for international protection lodged in one of the Member States by a third-country national or a stateless person, OJ L 180, 29.6.2013.

26 European Commission. 2019. Communication from the Commission to the European Parliament, the European Council and the Council "Progress report on the Implementationof the European Agenda on Migration". Brussels, 6.3.2019, COM (2019) 126 final, https://eur-lex.europa.eu/legal-content/EN/ALL/?uri=celex:5201 5DC0240.

27 Council Decision (EU) 2015/1523 of 14 September 2015 establishing provisional measures in the area of international protection for the benefit of Italy and of Greece (2015) OJ L 239; Council Decision (EU) 2015/1601 of 22 September 2015 establishing provisional measures in the area of international protection for the benefit of Italy and Greece (2015), OJ L 248.

28 See Cases: C-715/17 European Commission v Republic of Poland (Temporary mechanism for the relocation of applicants for international protection); C-718/17 – European v Commission v Republic of Hungary (Temporary mechanism for the relocation of applicants for international protection); C-719/17 – European Commission v Czech Republic (Temporary mechanism for the relocation of applicants for international protection) (source: InfoCuria Case-law: https://curia.europa.eu/juris/documents.jsf?oqp= &for=&mat=or&critereEcli=ECLI%253AEU%253AC%253A2019%253A917&lgrec= pl&jge=&td=%3BALL&jur=C%2CT%2CF&page=1&dates=&pcs=Oor&lg=&pro= &nat=or&cit=none%252CC%252CCJ%252CR%252C2008E%252C%252C%252C% 252C%252C%252C%252C%252C%252C%252Ctrue%252Cfalse%252Cfalse&langu age=en&avg=&cid=1138351).

29 C-715/17 – Commission v Poland (Temporary mechanism for the relocation of applicants for international protection), Judgment of the Court (Third Chamber) of 2 April 2020, European Commission v Republic of Poland and Other https://curia. europa.eu/juris/liste.jsf?oqp=&for=&mat=or&lgrec=pl&jge=&td=%3BALL&jur= C%2CT%2CF&num=C-715%252F17&page=1&dates=&pcs=Oor&lg=&pro=&nat= or&cit=none%252CC%252CCJ%252CR%252C2008E%252C%252C%252C%252C% 252C%252C%252C%252C%252C%252Ctrue%252Cfalse%252Cfalse&language= en&avg=&cid=7349999.

30 See the stance of the Polish Government on the CJEU judgement in joined cases C-715/17, C-718/17 and C-719/17: "Komunikat Centrum Informacyjnego Rządu w związku z wyrokiem TSUE w sprawie relokacji uchodźców" (Kancelaria Prezesa Rady Ministrów, 2 April 2020) <www.gov.pl/web/premier/komunikat-centrum-informacyjn ego-rzadu-w-zwiazku-z-wyrokiem-tsue-w-sprawie-relokacji-uchodzcow> (accessed 27 June 2021).

31 See OECD, 2019. International Migration Outlook 2019. OECD Publishing, https:// doi.org/10.1787/c3e35eec-en; OECD. (2020). International Migration Outlook 2020. OECD Publishing. https://read.oecd-ilibrary.org/social-issues-migration-health/intern ational-migration-outlook-2020_ec98f531-en.

32 For more information on migration and protection statistics in Poland, see Szulecka M., Pachocka M., Sobczak-Szelc K., Poland – Country Report: Legal and Policy Framework of Migration Governance, "Working Paper Series. Global Migration: Consequences and Responses" 2018, no. 2018/09, DOI: 10.5281/zenodo.1418583, pp. 11–21.

33 Regulation (EC) No 862/2007 of the European Parliament and of the Council of 11 July 2007 on Community statistics on migration and international protection and repealing Council Regulation (EEC) No 311/76 on the compilation of statistics on foreign workers (Text with EEA relevance), OJ L 199, 31.7.2007.

34 See more: Eurostat Statistics Explained. Annual asylum statistics, https://ec.europa.eu/eurostat/statistics-explained/index.php?title=Annual_asylum_statistics (accessed 18 June 2022).

35 Here we provide the most recent data from Eurostat for EU-27 which no longer include the UK.

36 In the Polish case, asylum applicants refused to be granted international protection may be granted a permit for stay due to humanitarian reasons. This kind of permit, however, is also granted to foreigners who did not participate in asylum procedures, but who meet the criteria to be protected from return to the country of origin (see more in Chapter 4).

37 Ustawa z dnia 12 marca 2022 r. o pomocy obywatelom Ukrainy w związku z konfliktem zbrojnym na terytorium tego państwa (Dz. U. poz. 583 z późn. zm.).

References

Białas, J., Górczyńska, M., Witko, D., 2019. *Access to Asylum Procedure at Poland's External Borders. Current Situation and Challenges for the Future.* Helsinki Foundation for Human Rights, Warsaw.

Chrzanowska, A., Mickiewicz, P., Słubik, K., Subko, J., Trylińska, A., 2016. *At the border. Report on monitoring of access to the procedure for granting international protection at border crossings in Terespol, Medyka, and Warszawa-Okęcie Airport.* Analyses, Reports, Evaluations No. 2/2016. Association for Legal Intervention.

Eurostat Regional Yearbook 2019. pp. 15–16, https://ec.europa.eu/eurostat/documents/3217494/10095393/KS-HA-19-001-EN-N.pdf/d434affa-99cd-4ebf-a3e3-6d4a5f10bb07?t=1574339587000.

Gońda, M., Lesińska, M., Pachocka, M. 2020. Relations between Immigration and Integration Policies in Postwar Europe, in: M. Duszczyk, M. Pachocka, D. Pszczółkowska (Eds.), *Relations between Immigration and Integration Policies in Europe: Challenges, Opportunities and Perspectives in Selected EU Member States* (1st ed.). Routledge, New York, London, pp. 24–45. DOI: https://doi.org/10.4324/9780429263736.

Górak-Sosnowska, K., Pachocka, M., 2019. Islamophobia and the quest for European identity in Poland, in: I. Zempi, I. Awan (Eds.), The *Routledge International Handbook of Islamophobia.* Routledge, London-New York, pp. 225–236.

Górczyńska, M., Szczepanik, M., 2016. *A road to nowhere. The account of a monitoring visit at the Brześć-Terespol border crossing between Poland and Belarus.* Helsinki Foundation for Human Rights, Warszawa, www.hfhr.pl/wp-content/uploads/2016/11/raport-droga-donikad-EN-web.pdf.

Górny, A., Grabowska-Lusińska, I., Lesińska, M., Okólski, M., 2010. *Transformacja nieoczywista. Polska jako kraj imigracji,* Uniwersytet Warszawski, Warszawa.

Górny, A., Kindler, M., 2018. Cudzoziemcy w Polsce na przełomie XX i XXI wieku, in: Lesińska, M., Okólski, M. (Eds.), *25 wykładów o migracjach.* Scholar, Warszawa, pp. 221–234.

IMF, 2016. Central, Eastern, and Southeastern Europe How to Get Back on the Fast Track, www.imf.org/external/pubs/ft/reo/2016/eur/eng/pdf/rei0516.pdf.

Klaus, W., 2017. *Closing Gates to Refugees: The Causes and Effects of the 2015 "Migration Crisis" on Border Management in Hungary and Poland, Yearbook of the Institute of East-Central Europe* **15**(3), pp. 11-34.

Lesińska, M., Stefańska, R., Szulecka, M., 2011. Development of migration policies of the Czech Republic, Hungary and Poland – on the way to maturity, in: Grabowska-Lusińska, I., Drbohlav, D., Hars A. (Eds.), *Immigration Puzzles.* Lap Lambert Academic Publishing, pp. 78–116.

Łodziński S., Szonert M., 2017. "Niepolityczna polityka"? Kształtowanie się polityki migracyjnej w Polsce w latach 1989–2016, CMR Working Papers, No. 90/148, www.migracje.uw.edu.pl/wp-content/uploads/2016/06/CMr_WP_90148.pdf.

Molęda-Zdziech, M., Pachocka, M., Wach, D., 2021. Immigration and Integration Policies in Poland: Institutional, Political and Social Perspectives, in: Franzke, J., Ruano de la Fuente, J.M. (Eds.), *Local Integration of Migrants Policy. Palgrave Studies in Sub-National Governance.* Palgrave Macmillan, Cham, pp. 169–199, DOI: https://doi.org/10.1007/978-3-030-50979-8_10.

Okólski M. 2021. The Migration Transition in Poland, *Central and Eastern European Migration Review,* 10(2), pp. 151–169.

Okólski, M., Wach D., 2020. Immigration and integration policies in the absence of immigrants A case study of Poland, in: Duszczyk, M., Pachocka, M., Pszczółkowska, D., (Eds.), *Relations between Immigration and Integration Policies in Europe: Challenges, Opportunities and Perspectives in Selected EU Member States* (1st ed.). Routledge, New York, London, pp. 146–172. DOI: https://doi.org/10.4324/9780429263736.

Pachocka, M., 2016. Understanding the Visegrad Group states' response to the migrant and refugee crises 2014+ in the European Union, *Yearbook of Polish European Studies,* 19, 101–132. http://cejsh.icm.edu.pl/cejsh/element/bwmeta1.element.desklight-64f1a0f0-82af-46a2-9f66-740571c18c4e.

Pachocka, M., 2022. Poland's response to the humanitarian crisis in Ukraine: actions, actors and challenges in a multi-level setting. Presentation. Roundtable on migration and humanitarian crisis in Ukraine "Continuities and Change in a Migration World", *Migration Policy Centre, EUI, Florence,* (accessed 23 May 2022), www.youtube.com/watch?v=lTIC952k3Dc.

Pachocka M., Sobczak-Szelc K., 2020. Refugee Protection Poland – Country Report, "Working Paper Series. Global Migration: Consequences and Responses", no. 2020/35, doi: 10.5281/zenodo.3632827.

Pachocka, M., Wach, D., 2018. Migracja a integracja (imigrantów) w Unii Europejskiej – w poszukiwaniu rozwiązania, in: Latoszek, E., Proczek, M., Szczerba-Zawada, A., Masłoń-Oracz, A., Zajączkowski K. (Eds.), *Unia Europejska: istota, szanse, wyzwania.* CeDeWu, Warszawa, pp. 127–160.

Pędziwiatr, K., Stonawski, M., Brzozowski J., 2019. *Imigranci w Krakowie w świetle danych rejestrowych, Centrum Zaawansowanych Badań Ludnościowych i Religijnych Uniwersytet Ekonomiczny w Krakowie,* Kraków.

Skiba, J., Stefańska, R., Szulecka, M., 2016. *"Pragmatycznie, a nie ideologicznie" – o polityce migracyjnej Polski.* Biuletyn Migracyjny, pp. 2–4.

Slany, K., 1995. *Między przymusem a wyborem: kontynentalne i zamorskie emigracje z krajów Europy Środkowo-Wschodniej, 1939–1989* (No. 295). Uniwersytet Jagielloński.

Stefańska, R., Szulecka, M., 2018. *Rozwój polityki migracyjnej Polski: otwarcie granic – regulowanie migracji – kontrolowane otwarcie – rewizja polityki* Biuletyn Migracyjny No. 57: 2–5, Ośrodek Badań nad Migracjami UW. http://biuletynmigracyjny.uw.edu.pl/pliki/pdf/biuletynmigracyjny57_0.pdf.

Stola, D., 2010. *Kraj bez wyjścia? Migracje z Polski 1949–1989.* IPN, Warszawa.

Szczepanik, M., 2018. Border politics and practices of resistance on the eastern side of "Fortress Europe": The case of Chechen asylum seekers at the Belarusian–Polish Border, *Central and Eastern European Migration Review* 7, 69–89. DOI: https://doi.org/10.17467/ceemr.2018.08.

Szulecka, M., 2019. Border Management and Migration Controls in Poland – Research Report, "Working Paper Series. Global Migration: Consequences and Responses", no. 2019/24, DOI: https://doi.org/10.5281/zenodo.3385241.

Szulecka, M., 2022. The undermined role of (domestic) case law in shaping the practice of admitting asylum seekers in Poland, *European Journal of Legal Studies*, 14, Special Issue, 171–209, http://hdl.handle.net/1814/74464.

Szulecka, M., Pachocka, M., Sobczak-Szelc, K., 2018. Poland – Legal and Policy Framework of Migration Governance, Multilevel Governance of Mass Migration in Europe and Beyond Project (#770564, Horizon2020) Report Series. Zenodo. https://doi.org/10.5281/zenodo.1418583.

UdSC, 2022. Statystyki UDSC/zestawienia roczne [WWW Document]. https://udsc.gov.pl/statystyki/raporty-okresowe/zestawienia-roczne/.

UNHCR Operational Data Portal, https://data.unhcr.org/en/situations/ukraine (accessed 18 May 2022).

Weinar, A., 2006. *Europeizacja polskiej polityki migracyjnej*, 1990-2003. Scholar, Warszawa.

Ząbek, M., Łodziński, S., 2008. *Uchodźcy w Polsce Próba spojrzenia antropologicznego*. Oficyna Wydawnicza ASPRA-JR, Warsaw.

3

SECURITISATION OF ASYLUM SEEKERS AND REFUGEES IN POLITICAL AND MEDIA DISCOURSES

Introduction

Despite a steady inflow to Poland of persons seeking asylum since the early 1990s, the phenomenon was not the subject of lively public debate, and their presence in the country and in Europe was not politicised. This situation changed in 2015 as a result of a combination of the refugee and migration-management crisis, which mainly was visible as a sharp increase in asylum seekers arriving in Europe (although not to Poland) in the aftermath of the Arab Spring, and coinciding with the electoral campaign before the parliamentary elections in Poland held on 25 October 2015. The narrative triggered at that time did not concern as much the influx of asylum seekers to Poland, which was minimal in numbers, but rather the European debate on relocation quotas of asylum applicants among the EU Member States. Although there were debates on migration, the rules governing asylum seekers' admission, and the principle of solidarity before 2015, public awareness of these issues was low. The unprecedented politicisation, securitisation, and racialisation of the forced migration in Poland since 2015 are some of the key factors that have led to a shift in Polish society's attitudes towards asylum seekers and refugees. The potential arrival of refugees in Poland was successfully presented as a major "security threat".

Since 2015, rival Polish political parties have been shaping their own narratives on migration, especially forced migration, although not all of them distinguish asylum seekers as a different category of migrants. After Law and Justice (*Prawo i Sprawiedliwość*, PiS) came to power in late 2015, the anti-refugee approach of the ruling party dominated both the political discourse on migration and the political actions and deliberate inaction of the Polish government in the areas of admission, reception, and integration of refugees.

This chapter examines how forced migrants (both asylum seekers and refugees) have been framed by politicians and media as a security issue in Poland since 2015,

DOI: 10.4324/9781003196327-3

and the consequences of that framing on the public opinion of forced migrants. This presentation of the main discourses on forced migration in Poland produced by politicians and reproduced by media also depicts the socio-political atmosphere of the reception and integration policies of the country. In addition, it enquires about stakeholders' reactions and opinions on these discourses and whether they have been internalised by Polish public opinion. To answer these questions, a three-step analysis of forced migration discourses in Poland was conducted: political speech analysis, media analysis, and finally a stakeholder discussion analysis. In each step of the analysis, respective sources were used:

- 22 speeches by the leaders of the main political parties in Poland;
- 51 news articles (opinions) selected from the three national newspapers: *Rzeczpospolita* (centrist), *Gazeta Wyborcza* (liberal), *Gazeta Polska Codziennie* (conservative, far-right);
- roundtable discussion with 17 stakeholders involved in the activity of the RESPOND Migration Governance Network in Poland.

The speeches of politicians were selected by purposive sampling (see the full list of speeches in Appendix 3.1), that is, identification of speeches by the main political parties, identification of the leaders of the parties, and search by identified keywords (e.g., "refugees", "migrants", "immigrants", "migration", "immigration") conducted via the Polish parliament's digital archive, the political parties' websites, and through the Google search engine. The main parties were selected according to their performance in the parliamentary elections in October 2015. Only those parties with registered lists of candidates to the Sejm (the lower chamber of the Polish parliament) in at least half of the constituencies that gained at least 3% of the votes in the elections were included in the analysis. Among them were the conservative, right-wing Law and Justice,[1] the liberal-centrist Civic Platform (*Platforma Obywatelska*, PO), the populist Kukiz'15, the liberal Modern (*Nowoczesna*), the United Left (*Zjednoczona Lewica*, an electoral alliance of the post-communist Left), the Polish People's Party (*Polskie Stronnictwo Ludowe*, PSL, which traditionally attracted significant votes from farmers), the libertarian KORWiN–Coalition for the Renewal of the Republic–Liberty and Hope (*Koalicja Odnowy Rzeczypospolitej Wolność i Nadzieja*), and the left-wing Together (*Razem*).

In the labelling of the above parties, it can be argued that the division between right and left cannot be easily transposed to the Polish political scene (Flis and Kwiatkowska, 2018). Following the collapse of communism in 1989, the right versus left axis was related more to the historical heritage of the parties and the roots of their members than to the parties' positions on economic and social issues. In this spirit, right-wing parties identified themselves and were perceived by the public as heirs to the Solidarity movement, whereas left-wing parties were identified as a continuation of the Polish United Workers' Party (Polska Zjednoczona Partia Robotnicza, PZPR) (Pankowski, 1997). Since the parliamentary elections in 2005, the main political struggle has been between the two parties with a post-Solidarity lineage—Civic Platform and Law and Justice, and the new ideological division has been shaped on the axis of social solidarity versus liberalism (Flis and Kwiatkowska, 2018; Jasiewicz, 2008; Markowski et al., 2015). Both PO and PiS can be labelled right-wing parties, but the main axis of their differences has been their visions of the country's development. PO generally favours more civic freedoms and greater deregulation of the economy to stimulate economic growth (liberalism), while PiS aims at reviving the national community based on tradition and values and calls for social solidarity in the economic dimension (solidarity) (Flis and Kwiatkowska, 2018; Jasiewicz, 2008; Markowski et al., 2015). Since 2005, the division between economic solidarity and liberalism has become a constant pillar of the Polish political scene and it visibly affected the parliamentary elections in 2007, 2011, 2015, and 2019.

With respect to the news articles, we focused on opinion pieces/editorials, considering this genre as debate-focused and containing deeper discussions of the issues, therefore reflecting the social and political debate in Poland. Then, using purposive sampling we selected 51 articles that thematically elaborated on the types of frames identified in Step 1. The articles were selected from three Polish nationwide newspapers: the liberal, and in some aspects left-wing, *Gazeta Wyborcza*; the centrist, with a bias towards conservatism, *Rzeczpospolita*; and the conservative and strongly far-right influenced *Gazeta Polska Codziennie*. Then we analysed how the identified security frames were debated in the newspapers across the political spectrum. Building on Dekker and Scholten's (2017, p. 208) approach in their analysis of media effects on Dutch immigration policies, we used the following analytical grid for coding:

- How were asylum seekers and refugees portrayed?
- How did the author/editor of the article interpret the security frame as presented by a politician?
- How did he/she interpret the situation as it exists?
- What was the causal narrative explaining why a particular security issue arose?
- What was the strategy for solving the issue and how is it seen by the newspaper?

To answer these questions, a discursive frame analysis was used (Ensink and Sauer, 2003; Entman, 1993; Foucault, 1972; Goffman, 1974; Korkut and Eslen-Ziya, 2018). Drawing on Foucault's work, we define discourse as a statement *(l'énoncé)* referring to social relations, describing, explaining and analysing the essence, sources, and conditions of a selected area of social reality (Foucault, 1972). "Frame" refers to the fact that discourse participants share the overall sense of the function of the discourse in the social situation (Ensink and Sauer, 2003). Frames also provide some structure for the discourse: in a way they

> define problems—determine what a causal agent is doing with what costs and benefits, usually measured in terms of common cultural values; diagnose

> causes—identify the forces creating the problem; make moral judgments—evaluate causal agents and their effects; and suggest remedies—offer and justify treatments for the problems and predict their likely effects.
>
> *Entman, 1993, p. 52*

Third, we conducted a thematic session with 17 stakeholders during the second meeting of the RESPOND Migration Governance Network in Poland held on 16 January 2020 (see Introduction). The participants of these meetings comprised representatives of social organisations (six people), public institutions (four), international organisations (one), the Catholic Church (two), and academia (four). The discussions focused on migration and refugee narratives and discourses produced and reproduced in Poland.

The time span of the analysis, and hence, the sources, was set from 2011 until 2018 (determined by the time span of the RESPOND project), although the main emphasis was put on the period between 2015 and 2018. In addition, we also used existing studies on identity, Islamophobia, discrimination, and the racism of elites in Poland in order to portray the origins of the radical shift in Polish society's attitudes towards asylum seekers and refugees. The chapter contains four parts. First, it presents the theoretical background of the politicisation and securitisation of forced migration in Poland. Then, it sheds light on the events and political situation impacting the emergence of anti-refugee discourses. The third part considers the securitisation discourses produced by politicians and reproduced by the selected print media. The fourth part displays the effects of securitisation in the form of changing attitudes towards asylum seekers, refugees, and migrants.

Politicisation and Securitisation of Forced Migration

The emergence of the refugee figure in the Polish public debate from 2015 onwards meant it had not only become part of the policy discourse but also the politics discourse (Czyżewski, Kowalski, and Piotrowski, 2010), since politicisation of migration is connected with going beyond problematising the phenomenon as a policy issue that is to be solved or alleviated through political activity and certain bureaucratic and technical practises. It also indicated adding a discursive dimension to it (Lesińska, 2016). Thus, an opportunity was created to give the phenomenon a new interpretative frame and convince the largest possible audience to accept it as a legitimate representation in order to mobilise social support and either change or reproduce the power structure.

By politicisation, we mean a process through which a specific phenomenon, issue, or theme gains a political character, is included in the political system, and becomes a subject of the political and public debate, hence drawing interest from political dissenters, mass media, and public opinion (Duszczyk and Lesińska, 2016, pp. 16–17). It is also treated as a problem that requires a state reaction, thus becoming the subject of politics (2016, pp.16–17). Although immigration had been gaining a public profile since the collapse of communism and the slow but steady inflow of immigrants to the country (Pędziwiatr, 2014), it had never before 2015 become part of an electoral campaign and treated as a key mobilisation tool. The increased inflow of asylum seekers to the EU in 2015 was successfully presented by populist nationalist politicians in Poland (and elsewhere) as a primary "security threat", and hence forced migration was strongly securitised.

As Bigo (2002, pp. 65–66) aptly noted, the securitisation of immigration has two dimensions. On the one hand,

> it emerges from the correlation between some successful speech acts of political leaders, the mobilisation they create for and against some groups of people, and the specific field of security professionals. On the other hand, it results also from a range of administrative practices such as population profiling, risk assessment, statistical calculation, category creation, proactive preparation, and what may be termed a specific *habitus* of the "security professional" with its ethos of secrecy and concern for the management of fear or unease.

Thus, insecurity as a consequence of the immigration process is both socially and politically constructed. Although this chapter focuses mainly on securitisation in the form of speech acts, it is important to remember that it is a phenomenon linking sets of discourses of unease, as well as bureaucratic and technical practises, and understandings of what constitutes security knowledge and expertise (Bigo, 2000, p. 194, Leonard, 2010, p. 235).

Securitisation of immigration, or associating the phenomenon in the public discourse with a threat to the socio-cultural cohesion of the receiving country, its labour market, and/or public order started to be observed in Western Europe already in the 1980s, both at the discursive level and later also within administrative activity. It emerged not necessarily as a response to an immediate danger but rather as a result of a discursively produced conviction that such a risk exists and is naturally bound to immigration (Buzan, Wæver, and de Wilde, 1998; Huysmans, 2000; Stephen, Ybarra, and Rios Morrison, 2009; Adamczyk, 2013). As research on the subject shows, fuelling fear of "the other" has always been an important tool for the mobilisation and consolidation of political capital. Although overtly racist, xenophobic attitudes connected to 19th-century race theories were delegitimised, largely criminalised, and as a consequence marginalised in the public discourse, new forms of racialisation and xenophobia emerged.

Today, xenophobic messaging is quite frequently nuanced and expressed only implicitly (van Dijk, 1993). This "new racism" targets, above all, immigrants and refugees. Hostility towards them is framed by references to the existence of allegedly insurmountable barriers that render integration of minority cultures impossible (Pankowski, 2006). It is not presented as the phenotypically conceived "race" but rather through categories such as culture, mentality, tradition, and religion, which are used to express new forms of contemporary racism (Barker, 1981; Gordon, 1989; Taguieff, 1988). It manifests itself, for example, powerfully in the form of Islamophobia, understood as generalised negative attitudes or feelings towards Islam and Muslims (Bleich, 2011, p. 1581). These anti-Muslim positions are a form of racism since they view Muslim "culture" in an entirely deterministic and essentialised way, making it into a functional equivalent of the biologically understood "race" (Bobako, 2014).

Pędziwiatr has convincingly shown how the year 2015, when parliamentary elections were held in the midst of the refugee and migration-management crisis, marked a significant rise in the public expression of anti-Muslim sentiments in Poland, and how 2016 saw Islamophobic views become even more mainstream, not only in politics but also in media, education, and other spheres of life. He argued that one could observe from 2015 onwards the banalisation of Islamophobia in Poland (2016, 2017). Islamophobic views became increasingly adopted in the same way as the ideas and symbols of nationhood are popularised and taken for granted in banal nationalism (Billing, 1997). If contemporary nationalism is trivialised through everyday representations of the nation, it builds a shared sense of national belonging among a given group of people. In the same way, Islamophobia has been trivialised in Poland through the near-omnipresent, unquestioned representations of Muslims as bloodthirsty, violent, aggressive, undemocratic, and upholding supposedly a radically different set of values—all taken for granted by the majority of society. As a consequence, the unquestioned, essentialist views of Muslims and Islam are being increasingly and widely held across the political spectrum, not only by right-wing elites, intellectuals, and voters but also increasingly by those who traditionally vote for more centrist or even left-wing parties (Pędziwiatr, 2016, 2017).

Numerous researchers have identified the existence of grassroots xenophobia as well as other forms of hostility towards "the other" (e.g., Bilewicz and Krzeminski, 2010; Bilewicz, Marchlewski, Soral, and Winiewski, 2014; Nowicka, 1995). Yet, less attention seems to have been paid to analysing the role of the elites, especially political elites, in initiating, channelling, and strengthening such attitudes. As van Dijk points out, elites "initiate, monitor, and control" the most influential forms of public discourse (1991, p. 4). In other words, it is the elites who have preferential access, due to their position in the social structure, to discursive resources that enable them to influence social attitudes. They are able to impose their own interpretations of events and phenomena more efficiently than other non-elite social groups, including by delegitimising and marginalising other interpretative frames, in particular those they identify as ones that could work against their interests (van Dijk, 1991, 1993).

In the case of politicians, their preferential access to the public discourse is further intensified during pre-election periods. Access to mass communication channels boosts the potential impact of their message, which, on the other hand, is not automatically internalised by recipients into their worldview but is rather subjected to processes of recontextualisation (Breeze, 201; Bielecka-Prus, 2017; Wodak and Reisigl, 2001, 2009). Also, when making a statement, politicians often take into account the expectations of their electorate. It can be assumed that between the discourse (language) and the worldview there exist a number of inter-influences, both horizontal and vertical, even though the actors involved are not on equal terms in their access to discursive resources.

What is important in the analysed case is the significant change in state-run media after the parliamentary elections in 2015. In spite of protests by the opposition and EU media watchdogs, in January 2016 the president signed controversial laws enabling the new conservative government to appoint the heads of public TV and radio, as well as civil service directors. This move was followed by the process of forcing out from state-financed media any journalists critical of PiS and strengthening the representation of voices sympathising with the ruling party. In this way, the major Polish television channels (TVP1, TVP2, TVP Info) and radio outlets (Jedynka, Dwójka, Trójka, or Radio 1, 2, 3), which have the largest broadcasting range in Poland, became key institutions normalising and thickening[2] nationalist populism in which the figure of the "Muslim refugee" played a pivotal role strengthening the narrative about refugees as "the problem" and a "security issue".

Events Impacting Anti-refugee Discourses

As mentioned, while forced migration was present sporadically in the wider Polish public debate prior to 2015, from this year the combined category of asylum seeker and refugee became important elements of political mobilisation and started to feature regularly in the public debate.

The key event that triggered this transition was the migration-management crisis followed by the refugee relocation scheme negotiations within the EU. Before 2015, asylum seekers and refugees were rarely a subject of discussion in Poland, and they were not perceived as a threat to national security. Heralding this change was the outbreak of military conflict between Russia and Ukraine in eastern Ukraine in early 2014 when the Polish government, in view of the prospective inflow of Ukrainians claiming international protection, initiated an evaluation of the prospective locations where such asylum seekers could be hosted. Interestingly, all the main political forces at that time, including the then-governing Civic Platform and the main opposition party then, Law and Justice, declared backing for the admission of prospective asylum seekers from Ukraine.

Then, in 2015, Europe experienced an inflow of more than a million forced migrants, a number not seen since the Second World War. Nearly half of those who arrived in Europe came from Syria. Smaller groups came from Afghanistan (around 20%), Iraq (9%), and other countries. Most of these migrants risked their lives by crossing the Mediterranean in order to reach Greece, Italy, or Spain. The reasons behind their decision to travel to Europe were the protracted conflicts in their countries of origin and the dire situation in transit countries, such as Turkey, Lebanon, or Jordan, where they often fled first (UNHCR, 2016). It should be noted that at the same time as the million-plus newly arrived forced migrants seemingly were overwhelming the European Union and its population of 508 million,

Turkey, a country inhabited by 77.5 million people, was hosting about 2.5 million refugees—and nearly a million of them arrived just in 2015 (UNHCR, 2016).

The increased number of forced migrants was mirrored by the rise in asylum applications in the EU. In 2015, there were 1,322,850 applications for asylum submitted to Member States, which was a 110% increase in comparison with 2014's 626,965 asylum applications. The largest number of applications was submitted in Germany (476,510), followed by Hungary (177,135) and Sweden (162,450) (Eurostat, n.d.). It needs to be highlighted that Poland did not experience an increased number of asylum seekers compared to other EU Member States. Between 2011 and 2019, the highest number of applications was submitted in 2013. That year the number of applications for international protection was 15,253. In the peak years of the refugee crisis in Europe, the number of asylum applications in Poland actually decreased to 12,325 in 2015 and 12,319 in 2016 (Eurostat, 2021; Szulecka et al., 2018).

Among the key triggers that contributed to the fierce political and public debate on refugees in Poland were two mutually interlinked developments: the EU refugee relocation scheme negotiations, which commenced in April 2015 and concluded in September 2015, and German Chancellor Angela Merkel's announcement of a policy welcoming Syrian refugees in early 2015 (Łotocki, 2019, pp. 143 151). These two external developments coincided with the election campaign in Poland before the parliamentary elections in October 2015. As a consequence, the dispute over the compulsory or voluntary admission of asylum seekers became one of the most significant topics of the election campaign. Hence, probably under pressure from opposition groups, and above all from PiS, whose representatives criticised the PO-led government for overly liberal policy towards refugees, the government of Prime Minister Ewa Kopacz (Civic Platform) turned inconsistent in its policy towards immigrants, including the number that Poland agreed to admit (Legut and Pędziwiatr, 2018; Pędziwiatr and Legut, 2016; Stolarczyk, 2017). The media debate on this matter mirrored the political discussion. While the liberal *Gazeta Wyborcza* supported Kopacz's decision to admit refugees within the Emergency Relocation System, the conservative newspapers and magazines strongly opposed the government's stance. The right-wing magazine *W Sieci* did not hesitate to link refugees with terrorism by presenting on its cover Kopacz wearing a burka and holding sticks of dynamite, together with the headline "Ewa Kopacz will arrange a hell for us at the behest of Berlin" (in Polish: "*Ewa Kopacz urządzi nam piekło na rozkaz Berlina*") (Wirtualne Media, 2015).

In September 2015, the Justice and Home Affairs Council (comprising the EU Member States' interior ministers) approved the Emergency Relocation System, a quota regime for refugee relocation (Council of the EU, 2015). It aimed at supporting the "frontline" states of Italy and Greece in the admission of asylum seekers by relocating 160,000 asylum applicants to other EU countries (Pachocka and Velez, 2019). Also significant in the Polish context was that the new system of refugee relocations was proposed by Merkel (Telegraph, 2015). Following the Chancellor's declaration of "*Wir schaffen das*" ("We can do this") with respect to the admission of asylum seekers and Germany's welcoming policy towards Syrians fleeing war, the biggest opposition party, PiS, strongly opposed the refugee relocation scheme. Nevertheless, although the Czech Republic, Hungary, Romania, and Slovakia also voted against the relocation system, Poland, then under the Kopacz government, accepted it, issuing a promise that it would accommodate 7,200 refugees in the forthcoming years (Pędziwiatr and Legut, 2016). After the October 2015 elections in which Law and Justice prevailed, the new PiS government disregarded Poland's commitments on this matter by first lowering the number of anticipated admissions of refugees to just 400 in January 2016, and then fully rescinding the plans for relocations to Poland of the first 100 refugees (65 from Greece and 35 from Italy) in May 2016 (Łotocki, 2019, pp. 176–177).

The developments depicted above comprised some of the factors leading to the production of refugee and migration discourses in Poland. The subsequent terrorist attacks in Paris (13 November 2015), Brussels (22 March 2016), Manchester (22 May 2017), and Barcelona (17 August 2017) carried out by members or supporters of the so-called Islamic State (ISIS) significantly heightened the securitisation discourses since the attacks were portrayed by the conservative and far-right outlets as the materialisation of the anticipated threat, which incited fear among public opinion and a feeling of susceptibility in an atmosphere of danger.

Securitisation of Forced Migrants in the Political Discourse

Various research has found migration to be a highly politicised topic in Europe, although the level of politicisation varies between countries. It appeared that the level of politicisation does not depend on socioeconomic factors but is attributed to party politics, competition between parties, and political conflicts within a given country (Grande et al., 2019). The latter finding was also confirmed in Poland where, despite the lack of an economic crisis, anti-refugee discourses produced by politicians found fertile ground and could make public opinion focus attention on forced migrants as a newly identified security issue.

The analysis of political leaders' speeches (see Appendix 3.1.) clearly shows the dominance of security frames associated with forced migrants, who usually were described in the much narrower category of refugees. Right-wing politicians raised issues related to forced migrants and their potential threat to security, including the difficulties with identification and security screening of asylum seekers, implying a lack of possibility to ascertain their right to asylum (confusing asylum seekers with economic migrants), their different religion (Islam), and culture as a threat to Polish identity, as well as their possible inclination to terrorism.

The first frame about the need for differentiation between asylum seekers and economic migrants was the most common and was used by politicians from the centre-right, through the right-wing and populist, to the far-right and libertarian parties. Intensification of the security factor behind this frame differed depending on the party and particular politician. The leaders of the centre-right Civic Platform often called for the need to properly identify "real" asylum seekers and differentiate them from economic migrants (PL7-2015-Kopacz, PL8-2015-Schetyna, PL10-2015-Trzaskowski) but were rather moderate in associating economic migrants with a threat to the citizens of Poland. If they referred to security, they pointed out the need to seal the EU borders in a similar way that Poland protected its eastern border.

The purported danger arising from confusing economic migrants with refugees was encapsulated by Jarosław Kaczyński, the leader of Law and Justice, when he suggested that economic migrants pretend to be asylum seekers in order to extort social benefits:

> We have to definitely distinguish refugees who are actually fleeing wars, from economic emigrants. We have to differentiate them. And who made the magnet here, great magnet, a powerful social attraction magnet for economic emigrants? Germany. And this is their problem. Here Orbán was right. This is just their problem, not ours. We can help refugees, but, I repeat, in a way that is safe for Poles.
>
> *PL6-2015-Kaczynski*

In other populist politicians' speeches, the boundary between being an asylum seeker and an economic migrant was blurred and hard to determine:

> It is difficult to call these people refugees, because according to the Geneva Convention, they would be refugees if they were in Turkey or Greece, the first country where there is no conflict. The ones who are here are certainly economic immigrants.
>
> *PL14-2015-Kukiz*

There are two probable explanations for such discourse production: politicians' ignorance of such framing (Mica et al., 2020) or intentionally fabricated framing by political leaders in order to transform the social reality, in accordance with Goffman's theory of frame analysis (Goffman, 1974). Despite left-wing politicians countering the security framings of refugees by pointing out numerous reasons behind the decision of forced migrants to flee their countries of origin, such as war, other military conflicts, or hunger (PL15-2015-Zandberg, PL18-2015-Nowacka), their voices were marginalised.

The second frame about the different religious and cultural backgrounds of forced migrants as a threat to Polish identity and values was broadly used by Kaczyński and other populist right-wing politicians who raised a public threat with visions of the Islamisation of Poland:

> The thing is not to accept the specific number of foreigners, regardless of who they are. The thing is, that there is a serious danger that the following process would be triggered: at first, the number of foreigners grows dynamically, then they do not or do not want to observe our law, our customs. And

> then, or simultaneously, they impose their sensibility and their stipulations in the public space, in different spheres of life, in a very aggressive and impetuous way. If somebody says that this is not true, he/she should look around Europe, look at least on Sweden. There are 54 zones where sharia law is binding, and there is not any state control.
>
> *PL6-2015-Kaczynski*

Another example of framing asylum seekers as Muslims threatening Polish values was presented by Jarosław Gowin, the leader of the conservative Poland Together, who called for the admission of only those "refugees, who accept principles which are a basis of our civilisation" and openly advocated for "a cultural proximity criterion" in admitting asylum seekers (PL9-2015-Gowin). In the same speech, by using the logic of cultural or even ethnic proximity, Gowin urged a reshaping of Polish migration policy in a way that would be based on Polish repatriates returning to the country (PL9-2015-Gowin). In addition to this framing, politicians deliberately used deceptive techniques such as presenting a high number of potential asylum seekers arriving in Poland despite the fact that the country reported a decrease in asylum applications in 2015–2016 (see also Chapter 2).

They used cataclysmic metaphors ("wave", "mass influx") to evoke a sense of invasion and stimulate fear in citizens' minds, and they did not refrain from disseminating disinformation targeting public opinion. The latter was mastered by Kaczyński, who cynically suggested that asylum seekers spread contagious diseases:

> After all, there are already symptoms of very dangerous diseases that have not been seen in Europe for a long time: cholera on the Greek islands, dysentery in Vienna, or, as some claim, even more dangerous diseases. And there are also differences related to geography—various types of parasites, protozoa, which are often not dangerous in the organisms of these people, can be dangerous here.
>
> *PL11-2015-Kaczynski*

In the same speech, Kaczyński misinformed the public about some agreements of which he read about in a magazine about the relocation of as many as 100,000 Muslims to Poland, confessing that he "did not know whether these news [reports] are true, but they exist" (PL11-2015-Kaczynski).

The production of this discursive frame could be explained by the Islamophobia among Polish political elites, especially right-wing parties (Pędziwiatr, 2018, 2017). "Polish Islamophobia", or the fear of the Muslim "other" paid crucial role in the country's response to EU immigration policy and how it was imposed on the Member States and against the vision of liberal modernisation realised by a united Europe. As such, it was more a "technology of power, a political instrument used for specific positioning of the national community in relation to European, liberal neocolonialism" (Bobako, 2017, p. 359).

The third identified frame, about the increased threat of terrorism related to the admission of Muslim asylum seekers, is closely related to the analysed one above. It must be underlined that in Poland's recent history there has been no terrorist attack, either successful or even thwarted one (Górak-Sosnowska and Pachocka, 2019, pp. 225–227). Despite this, right-wing politicians routinely threatened the public with this imagined threat posed by Muslim asylum seekers[3] and justified their stance towards refugees with this purported threat.

The greatest responsibility for such framing lies with the ruling Law and Justice Party and its two leaders at the time, Kaczyński and Beata Szydło, the prime minister of Poland between 2015 and 2017. Szydło used the terrorism frame when she accused the previous government of Kopacz and Civic Platform of compromising national security by accepting the refugee relocation mechanism. She defended her PiS-led government's decision not to fulfil the commitment of admitting relocated refugees, justifying it by a need to defend the state and nation:

> If you don't see that today the terrorist threat is a fact, which can take place in every country in Europe. And if you think that Poland should not defend itself, you align with those who take a weapon against Europe, against all of us. It needs to be said clearly and loudly: it is an attack on Europe, on our culture and our tradition.
>
> *PL20-2017-Szydlo*

The timing of this statement two days after the terrorist attack during a concert in Manchester was also important. Szydło made use of the attack to distinguish her party and peer politicians from the others, especially from Civic Platform, by arguing that:

> [we] will not be blackmailed and we will not succumb to political correctness [...]. There is nothing more valuable than the security of the homeland and the security of our citizens.
>
> *PL20-2017-Szydlo*

It has turned out that terrorist attacks abroad not only can instil a sense of danger among the public but also affect attitudes towards migrants in a way that this imminent fear makes people distance themselves from perceived "other" groups (Bohmelt et al., 2020). Right-wing politicians in Poland made use of this feeling of danger and directed the public's anger towards migrants, in particular Muslim asylum seekers and refugees. This framing is further proof of a kind of stereotyping of Islam and Muslims (Pędziwiatr, 2017, 2018), as well as the racialisation of refugees in general (Bobako, 2014).

Apart from the terrorist attacks in Europe between 2015 and 2017, the domestic circumstances were fertile ground for spreading the frame of refugees and terrorists as one and the same. Between 2015 and 2019, there was no party on the left in parliament, and PO, the biggest opposition party, started to adopt the securitised stance towards refugees in order not to lose electoral support. In 2015, Prime Minister Kopacz repelled accusations of an increased threat of terrorism due to the admission of refugees by saying,

> And let's remind of the '90s when Poland was a much poorer country than now, and we accepted 86,000 Chechens. Did you observe terrorists at every corner of the street? Did you witness a drop in employment? Did you notice any situations, which would threaten the security of Poles?
>
> *PL7-2015-Kopacz*

But by 2017, the new leader of Civic Platform, Grzegorz Schetyna, interviewed about his party's stance towards the admission of refugees, stated: "we will not admit illegal migrants" (PL19-2017-Schetyna).

The depicted frames show that politicians in Poland, by counting on gaining electoral support, used anti-refugee rhetoric in order to unite the public around the classical division of "us versus the others". Such instrumental treatment of refugees allowed for their securitisation, that is, linking the presence (even if prospective) of refugees to the matter of security. Paradoxically, people who had fled their countries because of war or conflict were identified as a threat to state security, and their arrival in Poland was presented as undesirable by leading politicians, including prime ministers, internal affairs ministers, and party leaders, namely Kaczyński, as the leader of PiS.

The moral panic around refugees, supposedly threatening Polish security, traditions, and values, was gradually replaced by the end of 2018 with one concerning LGBTQ+ rights, only to be revived in the context of the 2021 border crisis when Belarussian autocrat Alexander Lukashenka enabled thousands of migrants from different parts of the world to travel to Belarus on tourist visas and then try to make their way into the European Union (Pędziwiatr, Wach, and Sobczak-Szelc, 2021). In August 2021, a group of 32 Afghans (including women and children) seeking asylum were not admitted to Poland and became stuck in dire conditions on the Polish-Belarusian border. They were treated by the Polish government in a dehumanised manner, including depicting them as mere instruments of the Belarussian regime aiming at the destabilisation of Poland and the entire EU. By stating "safety is our priority. Security at the borders, just like here, and safety on the streets, so Poles can live, work and educate in peace" (Radio Bialystok, 2021), Prime Minister Mateusz Morawiecki once again used the frame of refugees threatening the safety of the Polish nation and prioritised security (even if the threat was imagined) ahead of Poland's obligations derived from international treaties, such as the 1951 Refugee Convention or European Convention of Human Rights.

Securitisation of Asylum Seekers and Refugees in Media Discourse

The politicians were not the only actors affecting Polish society's attitudes towards forced migrants. Media, especially the public TV and radio, which were taken over by Law and Justice, deepened people's feelings of fear and mistrust by reproducing all the framings mentioned above. The elites' rhetoric concerning forced migration was reproduced in the analysed media outlets, although with different severity levels of securitisation.

The frame about the need for differentiation between asylum seekers and economic migrants was most often reproduced by two out of the three analysed newspapers: by the conservative *Rzeczpospolita* and far-right *Gazeta Polska Codziennie*. The articles in *Rzeczpospolita* often pointed out the possibility of asylum seekers misleading the public institutions responsible for an examination of their applications:

> We don't know how many such people are currently looking for asylum in the EU, we don't know if those who obtained this asylum and right of residence received it by disclosing real information about themselves.
>
> *RZ_18.09.15*

The opinion also stated that the real motivation for the newcomers could be the social benefits available in the rich Western countries:

> The only question is, who are we talking about, what kind of are we going to need? Because as much as intra-EU migration does not cause major problems, the influx of newcomers from outside the EU is already problematic. And it's not a sign of some kind of specific xenophobia, but possibilities. The UN recognises this in its report by referring to the uncontrolled flow of immigrants who require healthcare and are burdening states' social assistance programmes. For this reason, Sweden, for example, may soon simply become a Third World Country and will certainly have to verify their overactive social policy soon.
>
> *RZ_02.05.15*

While the *Rzeczpospolita* framing was relatively balanced, *Gazeta Polska Codziennie* directly cited the supposed false motives of many who claimed to be refugees:

> The vast majority of immigrants who press against the borders of the Schengen area, seeking social security from wealthy EU countries, do not meet the definition of a refugee defined in international law and do not come directly from the war zone. Many of them are migrants from the Balkans or Sahel countries.
>
> *GP_25.05.2017*

The writers in the ultra-right newspaper expressed hope for the idea of establishing reception facilities outside the EU where economic migrants and asylum seekers could be differentiated:

> Opponents of mass immigration, including Poland and Hungary, have long drawn attention to the fact that only such a solution [reception facilities] may discourage those who want to enter Europe illegally. So far, just getting into one of the EU countries was tantamount to the possibility of staying in Europe because the deportation mechanisms did not work in practice.
>
> *GP_21.06.2018*

With regard to the framing of different cultural backgrounds being a threat to Polish identity, Rzeczpospolita tried to present a balanced message, although the tone depended on the writers. In general, they reiterated their appeals to admit asylum seekers of a cultural background similar to Poland's by arguing that it is a prerequisite for successful integration:

> The fact is that as of today we are not ready to accept a large mass of refugees from the Middle East, people who are from a different culture. We don't have any programmes. The Interior Ministry says they have their own plan of action for how to organise accepting refugees. But what's next? It's unclear how the integration of newcomers in Polish society would be, for example teaching the language, educating children, etc. How long would they stay in refugee centres? What's next? Who would give them a place to live and where?
>
> *RZ_11.09.15*

Without openly stating it, they were clearly delimiting the geographic area of the countries of origin of asylum seekers to Ukraine and other Eastern European countries.

The liberal *Gazeta Wyborcza* was against using the criterion of religion in admitting asylum seekers and interpreted politicians' calls for accepting only Christian asylum seekers as selfishness:

> It is true that Poland is reluctant to face the challenge of solidarity towards refugees in general, and refugees from Africa and Muslims in particular. At the moment, the most popular slogan to be used by most candidates in the recent presidential election is: "Let's take care of our own business!" This interest is understood as a so-called healthy selfishness, which has grown into a moral value.
>
> *GW_28.05.2015*

Surprisingly, in the analysed period there was no reproduction of this embedded frame by the far-right *Gazeta Polska Codziennie*, which can be explained by the newspaper's opposition to migration in general, and not only to asylum seekers of different cultural backgrounds. The only accepted form of immigration for the newspaper was repatriation, namely admitting only migrants with Polish roots (GP_10.09.2015).

Unlike the second frame, the one about the supposed threat of terrorism posed by Muslim asylum seekers was the frame most often reproduced by *Gazeta Polska Codziennie*. The newspaper in its opinion openly prioritised the security of Poland and the Polish nation and used this narrative in reacting to any terrorist attack in Europe regardless of the (non-refugee) background of the perpetrators:

> What a fool it takes to bring deadly terrorist threats upon your nation! This is what is happening in Western Europe. Today, France, Germany, Sweden, Belgium, and Spain run with the blood of innocent people through the utopian dreams of multi-culti[4] and the opening of the EU's external borders. Covering yourself with refugees is a headache. The number of real refugees fleeing war-torn Syria does not exceed 5% of all immigrants. And Europe cannot absorb the entire poor of Africa and Asia. Meanwhile, radical jihad is getting bolder, and Europeans are unable to withstand the growing aggression. Further bloodshed is inevitable. Summer is a period of mass events, but it is still safe in Poland. What kind of a fool must be someone who wants to change that?
>
> *GP_19.08.2017*

The newspaper's writers often praised PiS politicians who securitised refugees and linked them to terrorism, thanking them for countering what they saw as political correctness:

> Our country is free from extremism. There are no fanatical Muslims who blow themselves up in the name of Allah. [...] There is still common sense in Poland, free from political correctness.
>
> *GP_18.11.2015*

On the opposite pole was *Gazeta Wyborcza*, which countered the frame by depicting asylum seekers as victims of war and violence who needed assistance and protection. The *Gazeta Wyborcza* writers often blamed both Law and Justice and Civic Platform for replacing their humanitarian duty with a narrative of fears and threats:

> No rational person is in favour of opening borders completely. Ideally, there should be no refugees, but the world is not perfect. Wars, hunger, and terror are driving thousands of people out of their homes. It is a threat, but also a challenge. It forces us to answer the question of whether we want to be an open society or a closed and scared society.
>
> *GW_11.05.2017*

Gazeta Wyborcza also reminded its readers that equating asylum seekers with terrorists is against Christian morality:

> Refugees from Aleppo, whom we refuse to admit, are equated by the PiS government with terrorists. And on this particular issue, PiS politicians

> ostentatiously disregard the position of the Catholic Church and Pope Francis. This is a defeat for the evangelical mission of the Church. We are no longer a country of solidarity. We are a country of national selfishness. Not an open country, but a xenophobic one, although we consider ourselves hospitable and caress within ourselves the myth of tolerant Poland.
>
> *GW_27.06.2017*

In comparisons drawn by the writers of *Gazeta Wyborcza*, such as the issuing of work permits to 7,000 Nepalese economic migrants without references to the history of Maoist terrorism in Nepal and not admitting 7,000 Syrian refugees as agreed in the relocation scheme on the argument that there could be terrorists among them, there is clear evidence of Islamophobia among the political elites. Further, the framing of Muslim refugees as terrorists appeared to be intentionally fabricated by politicians and media in order to transform the social reality and, as a result, change attitudes in society (Goffman, 1974).

One of the side effects of the securitisation of refugees in the political and media discourses was assigning a negative meaning to the neutral words: asylum seeker, refugee, and migrant. The stakeholders of migration governance in Poland who were gathered at the second RESPOND Migration Governance Network meeting agreed that politicians' insistence on making a differentiation between economic migrants and asylum seekers/refugees had led these two terms to be associated with a negative connotation. Economic migrants who claimed a right to asylum were treated as bad because they purported to have lied about their situation in search of benefits from public assistance by pretending to be asylum seekers. Asylum seekers became equated with Muslims, who plays the role of the classic "other" in Polish culture and are all associated with negative features, including terrorism, religious fundamentalism, and disrespectful behaviour towards women.

The same identifications are reproduced by Polish media: "The image of a refugee in the Polish press or in Polish media is actually an image of a Muslim, not a refugee" (MGN2R11). While media reproduce these negative depictions of refugees, the ones who should be blamed first are the politicians who incite religious hatred. The stakeholders expressed indignation at politicians' ignorance and lack of responsibility for the hate speech they produce (MGN2R6).

An interesting initiative to counter the presented security discourses was the publication of the booklet *More knowledge, less fear. Refugees in Poland*, an action to inform the public undertaken by *Gazeta Wyborcza* in cooperation with the Office for Foreigners in 2015. The booklet presented facts about asylum seekers and refugees in Poland and was released by more than 40 media outlets (including *Gazeta Wyborcza* and *Rzeczpospolita*). Among the questions it addresses was one directly related to security: "How do the security forces check that there are no terrorists or criminals among asylum seekers in Poland?" (Czarnecki et al., 2015). Knowing the results of the October 2015 parliamentary elections, which were won by Law and Justice, and, consequently, the increasing securitisation of forced migration and deteriorating attitudes towards refugees, the booklet clearly failed to achieve its aim.

Effects of Securitisation

This analysis of Polish political leaders' speeches and newspaper articles has documented high securitisation of the issue of refugees, especially of the admission of asylum seekers and their right to seek asylum in Poland. As illustrated in Chapters 2 and 4, this securitisation has led to political decisions that have serious consequences for real people, namely asylum seekers. It has also impacted Polish society's attitudes towards migrants in general, and to asylum seekers and refugees in particular.

The attitude of Poles towards refugees has changed over the years. In 1992, the year after Poland signed the 1951 Geneva Convention, when the number of asylum seekers in the country was minimal, positive attitudes prevailed. At that time, most Poles declared their consent to either permanent or temporary settlement of refugees in Poland. Then, in the mid-1990s, there was a sharp change in attitude caused by the identification of refugees with economic migrants and fears of a big influx of the latter coming from the countries of the former Soviet Union. In 1996, 58% of Poles were in favour of readmission (deportation) of asylum seekers to their countries of origin or elsewhere. Since 2000, attitudes started normalising, and in 2008, 67% of Poles were in favour of the admission of asylum seekers and those living in Poland (Górny et al., 2017, pp. 75–76).

Between 2015 and 2017, Poles changed from being cautious supporters to decisive opponents of admitting refugees into the country. Such a change in attitude would not have happened if the anti-refugee discourses were not produced by politicians. In May 2015, nearly three-quarters of Polish society (72%) was in favour of giving refuge to asylum seekers (CBOS, 2015). By October 2015, amidst the most heated debate about refugees, the proportion of those declaring positive attitudes decreased to 54%. It reached the lowest level (33%) in October 2017 when two-thirds of Poles (67%) were against Poland admitting asylum seekers (CBOS, 2017) (see Figure 3.1). The securitisation of refugees also impacted the perception of migrants in general. According to an IOM/Ipsos opinion poll (IPSOS, 2016), nearly two-thirds of Poles had some concerns about the inflow of foreigners to Poland, regardless of whether they have had any contact with foreigners in the last year. Contradictory to the real situation, far more respondents considered the impact of migrants on the economy and labour market as negative (45%) than positive (25%). The prevailing negative attitudes towards foreigners or towards admitting refugees were reflected in a series of surveys: CBOS (2015, 2016, 2017, 2018) and IPSOS (2015, 2016).

The change in attitude towards refugees in particular, and migrants in general since 2015, was followed by an increase in racist and xenophobic incidents. According to the association Never Again (*Nigdy Więcej*), which monitors racist and xenophobic behaviour in Poland, until 2015 there had been no more than several dozen incidents a month, but by late 2015, the number had increased to several

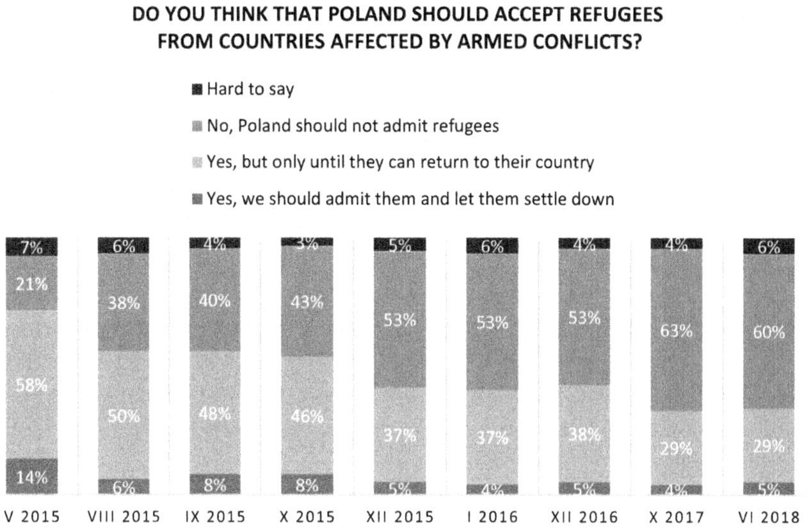

FIGURE 3.1 Results of CBOS surveys on attitudes towards refugees (2015–2018)

Source: Own compilation, based on IPSOS (2016, 2015) and CBOS (2018, 2017, 2016, 2015) surveys.

dozen a week (Kośmiński, 2017). This escalation of hate incidents against foreigners is even seen in police statistics, which showed a big increase in 2016 in the number of beatings or other physical attacks, predominantly against Muslims (22%), but also against Jews, Roma, and Black people (Kośmiński, 2017).

Surprisingly, a survey conducted by Kantar in January 2021 and ordered by the UNHCR presented far more positive attitudes towards the admission of refugees. According to the survey (2021), 77% of Poles believed that Poland should support refugees ("people who flee because of war or persecution or violation of their rights") out of humanitarian solidarity (Kantar, 2021). Furthermore, 62% of respondents believed that Poland should admit refugees because compatriots in a similar situation would want to be treated well, too (Kantar, 2021). It is difficult to ascertain to what extent the negative attitudes towards refugees have changed since 2018, due to the discontinuation of CBOS surveys on this matter and the different methodology used by the CBOS and Kantar surveys, in which different questions were asked. Nevertheless, what could be observed since autumn 2018 when local elections were held in Poland has been waning interest among politicians and media in the topic of refugees.

When the issue of refugees reappeared in the media and political debate in August 2021, it was related to the situation on the Polish-Belarusian border, when public opinion again started polarising on refugees' admission. In September 2021, 48% of Poles did not agree with admitting asylum seekers, 41% agreed, but only 9% would approve of their permanent settlement in Poland (CBOS, 2021).

Conclusions

Our research has shown that the anti-refugee discourses in Poland have led to politicisation and, consequently, to the securitisation of the issue of asylum seekers and refugees in the country. The production of such discourses would not be possible without the coexistence of specific internal processes and external factors that fuel the debate. First among them, in 2015, a key year of presidential and parliamentary elections in Poland that coincided with the refugee and migration-management crisis in Europe, the society was very vulnerable to topics of national identity, values, and security, especially when the biggest opposition party, the right-wing Law and Justice, had to distinguish itself from the ruling centre-right Civic Platform. Second, the developments in the EU and Germany with regard to policy towards asylum seekers raised the fear in Poland of a loss of sovereignty, a sentiment very easy to exploit in a country that experienced multiple partitions and later came under the controlling influence of the Soviet Union.

It turned out that the construction of the "others" by imposing imagined views of forced migrants was not only a useful tool to gain electoral support but also effective in changing attitudes towards foreigners in general, and refugees in particular. This framing with its very explicit stance towards refugees was even easier after Law and Justice came to power and took over public media, including the TV and radio stations. Acquiring the channels of communication that reach the largest area of Poland only strengthened and petrified anti-refugee sentiments in the society. Foremost, the three discursive framings depicted above: the need for differentiation between asylum seekers and economic migrants, the different religious and cultural background of forced migrants as a threat to Polish identity and values, and aligning refugees with terrorism, started to be unquestioned by numerous politicians in parliament[5] and a large part of the country's media. The tangible effect of such discourse production was an increase in attacks (both verbal and physical) against foreigners in Poland, in particular Muslims, Jews, Roma, and Black people.

After the debate about refugees calmed down somewhat in 2018, it came back to life once again in the second half of 2021 in relation to the Polish-Belarusian border crisis. However, there are many differences in comparing the current discourses with those that emerged in 2015. This time, the ruling Law and Justice Party not only criticised its biggest rival, Civic Platform, but also acted to introduce a state of emergency, adopt new laws, and send troops and security forces to the border.

The anti-refugee discourse has been produced with a different aim, namely not as a foundation for further actions but as praise of the government's quick actions and to discredit its opponents, whether politicians or civil society. This time, the security dimension has been much stronger since it directly involves tangible elements: visible, real people trying to cross the border, an actual delimited border and territory (of Poland) that needs to be defended, and recognisable officers of the Border Guard, the Polish military, and police engaged in guarding the borderland. There is also a tangible tragic dimension to the current securitisation—the suffering and deaths of migrants who try to cross the wooded border and are pushed back by the Polish security forces to the Belarusian side.

Notes

1 In the parliamentary elections of 2015, PiS also listed candidates from two other parties, Poland Together (Polska Razem, PR) and Solidarity Poland (Solidarna Polska, SP), and was actually a three-party coalition (Markowski, 2016).
2 By "thickening", we understand the term after Minkenberg as a process whereby populist ideology acquires additional features, which generates "thicker" versions. See Michael Minkenberg (ed.), Transforming the Transformation? The East European Radical Right in the Political Process (London and New York: Routledge 2015), 28.
3 Imagined, since all perpetrators behind terrorist attacks commenced in Europe between 2011 and 2018 were citizens of the countries where terrorist attacks took place. In other words, no asylum seeker or refugee organised or participated in any terrorist attack in Europe in the analysed period.
4 Right-wing slang for "multi-culturalism" connoting that the concept is cultish.
5 Especially in the 2015 elections, no left-wing party gained seats in the Sejm (the lower chamber of the Polish parliament).

References

Bielecka-Prus J., 2017. Językowe konstruowanie obcego w polskiej debacie parlamentarnej na temat uchodźców. In: Korczyński, T.M., Orla-Bukowska, A. (eds.), *Obcy w labiryncie kultur*. WWS, Warszawa.

Bigo, D., 2000. When two become one: internal and external securitizations in Europe. In: Kelstrup, M., Williams, M.C. (eds.), *International relations theory and the politics of European integration: power, security and community*. Routledge, London.

Bigo, D., 2002. Security and immigration: Toward a critique of the governmentality of unease. *Alternatives: Global, Local, Political*, 27, 63–92.

Bilewicz M., Krzemiński I., 2010. Anti-Semitism in Poland and Ukraine: The belief in Jewish control as a mechanism of scapegoating, *International Journal of Conflict and Violence*, 4 (2), 234–243.

Bilewicz M., Marchlewski M., Soral W., Winiewski, M. 2014. *Mowa nienawiści. Raport z badań sondażowych*. Fundacja im. Stefana Batorego, Warszawa.

Billig, M., 1997. *Banal Nationalism*. Sage Publications, London.

Bleich, E., 2011. What is Islamophobia and how much is there? Theorizing and measuring an emerging comparative concept, *American Behavioral Scientist*, 55(12), 1581–1600.

Bobako M. 2014. Rasa i religia. Trajektorie antysemityzmu i islamofobii. Tematy z Szewskiej. *Rasa*, 3 (13), 37–56.

Bobako, M., 2017. *Islamofobia jako technologia władzy*. Universitas, Kraków.

Bohmelt, T., Bove, V., Nussio, E., 2020. Can Terrorism Abroad Influence Migration Attitudes at Home? *American Journal of Political Science*, 64, 437–451. DOI: https://doi.org/10.1111/ajps.12494.

Breeze, R., 2011. Critical Discourse Analysis and its Critics. *Pragmatics*, 21, 493–525.

Buzan, B., Wæver, O., and de Wilde, J., eds., 1998. *Security: a new framework for analysis*. Lynne Rienner, Boulder, CO and London.

CBOS, 2015. *Polacy wobec problemu uchodźstwa (Komunikat z Badań No. 81/2015)*. Centrum Badania Opinii Społecznej, Warszawa.

CBOS, 2016. *Stosunek Polaków do przyjmowania uchodźców (Komunikat z Badań No. 24/2016).* Centrum Badania Opinii Społecznej, Warszawa.

CBOS, 2017. *Stosunek Polaków do przyjmowania uchodźców (Komunikat z Badań No. 1/2017).* Centrum Badania Opinii Społecznej, Warszawa.

CBOS, 2018. *Stosunek Polaków do przyjmowania uchodźców (Komunikat z Badań No. 87/2018).* Centrum Badania Opinii Społecznej, Warszawa.

CBOS, 2021. *Opinia publiczna wobec uchodźców i sytuacji migrantów na granicy z Białorusią (Komunikat z badań No. 111/2021).* Centrum Badania Opinii Społecznej, Warszawa.

Council of the EU, 2015. COUNCIL DECISION (EU) 2015/1601 of 22 September 2015 establishing provisional measures in the area of international protection for the benefit of Italy and Greece. *Official Journal of the European Union,* 248, 24.9.2015. Available at: https://eur-lex.europa.eu/legalcontent/EN/TXT/?uri=celex %3A32015D1601 (accessed 3 September 2021).

Czarnecki, M., Jałoszewski, M., Kwaśniewski, T., 2015. *Więcej wiedzy, mniej strachu.* Uchodźcy w Polsce. Gazeta Wyborcza.

Czyżewski M., Kowalski S., Piotrowski A. (eds.), 2010. *Rytualny chaos. Studium dyskursu publicznego.* Kraków: Wydawnictwa Akademickie i Profesjonalne, Warszawa.

Dekker, R., Scholten, P., 2017. Framing the Immigration Policy Agenda: A Qualitative Comparative Analysis of Media Effects on Dutch Immigration Policies. *The International Journal of Press/Politics,* 22, 202–222. DOI: https://doi.org/10.1177/1940161216688323.

Dijk van, T. A., 1991. *Elite Discourse and the Reproduction of Racism.* Amsterdam: Amsterdam University Press.

Dijk van, T. A., 1993. *Elite Discourse and Racism.* Sage, London.

Duszczyk, M., Lesińska, M., 2016. Upolitycznienie Procesów Demograficznych—Próba Podejścia Teoretycznego. Problemy Polityki Społecznej. *Studia i Dyskusje,* 34(3), 13–25.

Ensink, T., Sauer, C., 2003. *Framing and Perspectivising in Discourse, pbns. 111.* John Benjamins Publishing Company, Amsterdam.

Entman, R.M., 1993. Framing: Toward Clarification of a Fractured Paradigm. *Journal of Communication,* 43, 51–58. DOI: https://doi.org/10.1111/j.1460-2466.1993.tb01304.x.

Eurostat, 2021. Eurostat Database. Asylum and first time asylum applicants – monthly data (rounded), https://ec.europa.eu/eurostat/databrowser/view/tps00189/default/table?lang=en (accessed 30 November 2021).

Flis, J., Kwiatkowska, A., 2018. Polski system partyjny – idee i identyfikacje [Polish party system – ideologies and identifications], in: *Zmierzch Demokracji Liberalnej.* Instytut Europeistyki Uniwersytetu Warszawskiego, Warszawa, pp. 587–606.

Foucault, M., 1972. *The Archaeology of Knowledge.* Harper and Row, New York.

Goffman, E., 1974. *Frame analysis: An essay on the organization of experience.* Harvard University Press, Cambridge.

Górak-Sosnowska, K., Pachocka, M., 2019. Islamophobia and the quest for European identity in *Poland, in: The Routledge International Handbook of Islamophobia.* Routledge.

Gordon P. 1989. *New Right, New Racism.* Searchlight, London.

Górny, A., Grzymała-Moszczyńska, H., Klaus, W., Łodziński, S., 2017. *Uchodźcy w Polsce. Sytuacja prawna, skala napływu i integracja w społeczeństwie polskim oraz rekomendacje, Ekspertyzy Komitetu Badań nad Migracjami PAN.* Polska Akademia Nauk.

Grande, E., Schwarzbözl, T., Fatke, M., 2019. Politicizing immigration in Western Europe. *Journal of European Public Policy,* 26, 1444–1463. DOI: https://doi.org/10.1080/13501763.2018.1531909.

Huysmans J., 2000. The European Union and securitization of migration. *Journal of Common Market Studies,* 38 (5), 751–777.

IPSOS, 2015. *Badanie na temat postaw wobec cudzoziemców w Polsce.* IOM, Warszawa.

IPSOS, 2016. *Badanie na temat postaw wobec cudzoziemców w Polsce*. IOM, Warszawa.

Jasiewicz, K., 2008. The New Populism in Poland: The Usual Suspects? *Problems of Post-Communism*, 3, 7–25.

Kantar, 2021. *Postrzeganie uchodźców w Polsce*. UNHCR.

Korkut, U., Eslen-Ziya, H., 2018. *Politics and Gender Identity in Turkey: Centralised Islam for Socio-Economic Control*. Routledge, London and New York.

Kośmiński, P., 2017. *Prokuratura: Więcej przestępstw z nienawiści*. *"Gazeta Wyborcza"*, 24 April 2017.

Legut, A., Pędziwiatr, K., 2018. Sekurytyzacja migracji w polityce polskiej a zmiana postaw Polaków wobec uchodźców, in: Jończy, R. (Ed.), *Sami Swoi? Wielokulturowość We Współczesnej Europie*. Dom Współpracy Polsko-Niemieckiej, Gliwice-Opole, pp. 41–51.

Léonard, S., 2010. EU border security and migration into the European Union: FRONTEX and securitisation through practices, *European Security*, 19(2), 231–254, DOI: 10.1080/09662839.2010.526937.

Lesińska, M. 2016. Upolitycznie emigracji i diaspory. Analiza dyskursu politycznego w Polsce w latach 1991–2015, *Studia Migracyjne – Przegląd Polonijny*, 161(3), 11–30.

Łotocki, Ł., 2019. *Kryzys imigracyjny w Europie w polskim dyskursie publicznym w latach 2015–2018*. Elipsa Dom Wydawniczy, Warszawa.

Markowski, R., 2016. The Polish parliamentary election of 2015: a free and fair election that results in unfair political consequences, *West European Politics* 39, 1311–1322. DOI: https://doi.org/10.1080/01402382.2016.1177305.

Markowski, R., Cześnik, M., Kotnarowski, M., 2015. *Demokracja – gospodarka – polityka. Perspektywa polskiego wyborcy*. Wydawnictwo Scholar, Warszawa.

Mica, A., Horolets, A., Pawlak, M., & Kubicki, P. (2020). *Ignorance and Change: Anticipatory Knowledge and the European Refugee Crisis (1st ed.)*. Routledge. https://doi.org/10.4324/9781351212595.

Nowicka, E., 1995. Rom jako swój i jako obcy. Zbiorowość Romów w świadomości społeczności wiejskiej, *Lud*, 78, 357–375.

Office for Foreigners, 2018. Periodic report. [online] Available at: https://udsc.gov.pl/statystyki/raporty-okresowe/ (accessed 15 November 2021).

Pachocka M., Velez D. C., 2019. Understanding EU Member State cooperation within the asylum regime during the migration and refugee crisis from an IR perspective, in: A. Kłos, M. Pachocka, A. Adamczyk, M. (eds.), Promoting values, stability and economic prosperity in the changing world in the global context. *EU facing current challenges, opportunities, crisis & conflicts*. Dziembała, Elipsa, Warszawa, pp. 139–154.

Pankowski, K., 1997. Lewicowość–prawicowość: deklaracje polityczne Polaków 1990–1997, in: Kolarska-Bobińska, L., Markowski, Radosław (eds.), *Prognozy i Wybory – Polska Demokracja '95*. Wydawnictwo Sejmowe, Warszawa.

Pankowski, R., 2006. *Rasizm a kultura popularna*. Trio, Warszawa.

Pędziwiatr, K., 2014. Imigranci w Polsce i Wyzwania Integracyjne. *Studia BAS*, 4(40), 135–153.

Pędziwiatr, K., 2016. Islamophobia in Poland: National Report 2015, in: Bayralki, E., Hafez, F. (eds.), *European Islamophobia Report 2015*, SETA, Istanbul, pp. 423–442.

Pędziwiatr, K., 2017. Islamophobia in Poland: National Report, in: Bayralki, E., Hafez, F. (eds.), *European Islamophobia Report 2016*. SETA, Istanbul, 411–443.

Pędziwiatr, K., 2018. The Catholic Church in Poland on Muslims and Islam, *Patterns of Prejudice*, 52, pp. 461 478. DOI: https://doi.org/10.1080/0031322X.2018.1495376.

Pędziwiatr, K., Legut, A., 2016. Polskie rządy wobec unijnej strategii na rzecz przeciwdziałania kryzysowi migracyjnemu, in: Wojtaszczyk, K.A., Szymańska, J. (Eds.), *Uchodźcy w Europie – Uwarunkowania, Istota, Następstwa*. Wydawnictwo Uniwersytetu Warszawskiego, Warszawa.

Radio Bialystok, 2021. *Premier Mateusz Morawiecki z wizytą na granicy polsko-białoruskiej*, Radio Białystok, 24.08.2021, www.radio.bialystok.pl/wiadomosci/index/id/203614 (accessed 30 November 2021).

Stephan W.G., Ybarra O., Rios Morrison K., 2009. Intergroup Threat Theory, in: Nelson, T. D. (ed.) *Handbook of Prejudice,* Taylor & Francis, New York.

Stolarczyk, M., 2017. Stanowisko Polski wobec kryzysu migracyjno-uchodźczego Unii Europejskiej. *Krakowskie Studia Międzynarodowe*, (2), 15–41.

Szulecka, M., Pachocka, M., Sobczak-Szelc, K., 2018. Poland – Legal and Policy Framework of Migration Governance, Multilevel Governance of Mass Migration in Europe and Beyond Project (#770564, Horizon2020) Report Series. Zenodo. DOI: https://doi.org/10.5281/zenodo.1418583.

Taguieff, P. A., 1988. *La force du préjugé. Essai sur le racisme et ses doubles.* La Découverte, Paris.

Telegraph, 2015. Angela Merkel calls for new rules for distributing asylum seekers in Europe, 24 April 2015, www.telegraph.co.uk/news/worldnews/europe/germany/11561430/Angela-Merkel-calls-for-new-rules-for-distributing-asylum-seekers-in-Europe.html (accessed 10 October 2021).

UNHCR, 2016. *Global Trends. Forced Displacement in 2015.* Available at: www.unhcr.org/statistics/unhcrstats/576408cd7/unhcr-global-trends-2015.html (accessed 30 November 2021).

Wirtualne Media, 2015. Ewa Kopacz pozywa "W Sieci" za okładkę z burką i dynamitem, chce przeprosin i 30 tys. zł na cel charytatywny, 21 October 2015, Available at: www.wirtualnemedia.pl/artykul/ewa-kopacz-pozywa-w-sieci-za-okladke-z-burka-i-dynamitem-chce-przeprosin-i-30-tys-zl-na-cel-charytatywny (accessed 15 November 2021).

Wodak, R., Reisigl, M., 2001. *Discourse and Discrimination.* Routledge, London.

Wodak, R., Reisigl, M., 2009. The discourse-historical approach (DHA), in: Wodak R., Meyer M. (eds.), *Methods of Critical Discourse Analysis.* Sage Publications, London.

Appendix

APPENDIX 3.1 Political speeches selected to the analysis

No	*Type of speech act*	*Date*	*Politician*	*Function*	*Political party*	*Code*
1	Parliamentary speech (expose)	20.03.2013	Radoslaw Sikorski	Foreign Affairs Minister	Civic Platform (Platforma Obywatelska)	PL1-2013-Sikorski
2	Parliamentary speech	10.10.2013	Robert Biedroń	Member of Parliament	Civic Platform (Platforma Obywatelska)	PL2-2013-Biedroń
3	Parliamentary speech	19.02.2014	Donald Tusk	Prime Minister	Civic Platform (Platforma Obywatelska)	PL3-2014-Tusk
4	Speech at the celebration of the 10th anniversary of Poland joining the EU	01.05.2014	Bronisław Komorowski	President	Civic Platform (Platforma Obywatelska)	PL4-2014-Komorowski
5	Speech at the celebration of the 10th anniversary of Poland joining the EU	01.05.2014	Donald Tusk	Prime Minister	Civic Platform (Platforma Obywatelska)	PL5-2014-Tusk
6	Parliamentary speech	16.09.2015	Jarosław Kaczyński	Leader of the opposition party	Law and Justice (Prawo i Sprawiedliwość)	PL6-2015-Kaczyński
7	Parliamentary speech	16.09.2015	Ewa Kopacz	Prime Minister	Civic Platform (Platforma Obywatelska)	PL7-2015-Kopacz
8	Parliamentary speech	16.09.2015	Grzegorz Schetyna	Foreign Affairs Minister	Civic Platform (Platforma Obywatelska)	PL8-2015-Schetyna
9	Parliamentary speech	16.09.2015	Jarosław Gowin	Member of Parliament	Poland Together (Polska Razem)	PL9-2015-Gowin

(continued)

APPENDIX 3.1 Cont.

No	*Type of speech act*	*Date*	*Politician*	*Function*	*Political party*	*Code*
10	Parliamentary speech	16.09.2015	Rafał Trzaskowski	Vice Minister of Foreign Affairs	Civic Platform (Platforma Obywatelska)	PL10-2015-Trzaskowski
11	Election campaign speech (before parliamentary elections)	15.10.2015	Jarosław Kaczyński	Leader of the opposition party	Law and Justice (Prawo i Sprawiedliwość)	PL11-2015-Kaczyński
12	Political party leaders debate before the parliamentary elections	21.10.2015	Ewa Kopacz	Prime Minister, Party leader	Civic Platform (Platforma Obywatelska)	PL12-2015-Kopacz
13	Political party leaders debate before the parliamentary elections	21.10.2015	Beata Szydło	Candidate for Prime Minister from Law and Justice	Law and Justice (Prawo i Sprawiedliwość)	PL13-2015-Szydło
14	Political party leaders debate before the parliamentary elections	21.10.2015	Paweł Kukiz	Party leader	Kukiz'15	PL14-2015-Kukiz
15	Political party leaders debate before the parliamentary elections	21.10.2015	Adrian Zandberg	Party leader	Together (now Left Together) (Razem, now Lewica Razem)	PL15-2015-Zandberg
16	Political party leaders debate before the parliamentary elections	21.10.2015	Janusz Piechociński	Party leader	Polish People's Party (Polskie Stronnictwo Ludowe)	PL16-2015-Piechociński
17	Political party leaders debate before the parliamentary elections	21.10.2015	Janusz Korwin-Mikke	Party leader	KORWIN – Coalition for the Renewal of the Republic – Liberty and Hope (KORWIN – Koalicja Odnowy Rzeczypospolitej Wolność i Nadzieja)	PL17-2015-Korwin-Mikke

18	Political party leaders debate before the parliamentary elections	21.10.2015	Barbara Nowacka	Leader of United Left (Zjednoczona Lewica)	United Left (Zjednoczona Lewica)	PL18-2015-Nowacka
19	Political party leaders debate before the parliamentary elections	21.10.2015	Ryszard Petru	Party leader	Modern (Nowoczesna)	PL19-2015-Petru
20	Parliamentary speech	24.05.2017	Beata Szydło	Prime Minister	Law and Justice (Prawo i Sprawiedliwość)	PL20-2017-Szydło
21	Party convention speech	01.07.2017	Jarosław Kaczyński	Party leader	Law and Justice (Prawo i Sprawiedliwość)	PL21-2017-Kaczyński
22	Speech in the European Parliament	04.07.2018	Mateusz Morawiecki	Prime Minister	Law and Justice (Prawo i Sprawiedliwość)	PL22-2018-Morawiecki

Source: own elaboration by the RESPOND team in Poland.

4

THE INSTITUTIONAL AND LEGAL BASIS OF THE ASYLUM SYSTEM

Introduction

The analysis presented in this chapter covers the rules for granting international protection or dealing with migrants who were refused it as envisaged in Poland's domestic legislation. Therefore, some attention is paid to national forms of protection that prevent the expulsion of failed asylum applicants or other categories of migrants who cannot return to their countries of origin or cannot be sent back to other countries (e.g., transit territories). Although these regulations are to a large extent determined by the EU and international law, the latter is referred to here only when it is crucial to explain domestic regulations or assess their compliance with supranational provisions. Due to the focus on issues related to international protection, no special attention was paid to the domestic form of asylum (pl. *azyl*). The latter is separated from the asylum system in Poland and applied rather rarely.[1]

The right to asylum is envisaged in the Polish Constitution,[2] which distinguishes two forms of protection—one domestic and one international. Article 56(1) of the Constitution stipulates that: "Foreigners shall have the right of asylum in the Republic of Poland in accordance with principles specified by statute". This provision refers to a national form of asylum (pl. *azyl*) that may be granted arbitrarily by Polish authorities to any non-national. This instrument is separated from the system of granting international protection. In the context of Poland, the right to apply for international protection not only stems from international law binding in Poland[3] but also is guaranteed by the Constitution: "Foreigners who seek protection from persecution in the Republic of Poland, may be granted the status of a refugee in accordance with international agreements to which the Republic of Poland is a party" (Article 56(2)). According to the Polish Constitution, all people under the authority of the Polish State shall enjoy the freedoms and rights ensured by the Constitution (Article 37(1)), and exemptions from this principle that regard foreign

DOI: 10.4324/9781003196327-4

nationals (including asylum seekers and persons granted international protection) should be specified by statute (Article 37(2)). Therefore, non-nationals willing to exercise rights envisaged in the Polish Constitution, including the right to asylum and the right to apply for refugee status, must remain under the authority of the Polish state.[4]

As mentioned in Chapter 2, the basis of the contemporary legal and institutional system of admitting asylum seekers and providing them with necessary assistance and protection for recognised refugees is rooted in Poland's transition to a democratic state and its recognition as a safe country in the context of refugee protection. In legal terms, the state's signing of the 1951 Geneva Convention in 1991 became the starting point for building institutions responsible for the reception of asylum seekers and processing asylum claims. The aim of this chapter is to offer an overview of the asylum-related legislation binding in Poland in the decade 2011–2021. We also point out both the stable elements of the legal framework and the significant changes introduced in this period. Although the collection of empirical data showing how the law worked in practice, which is presented in Chapters 5–10, was largely completed in 2019, we also present the crucial changes in the institutional and legal frameworks observed after 2019. This approach allows us to present the most recent developments in the law affecting the admission of asylum seekers in the circumstances of the COVID-19 pandemic (2020–2021) and the increased migration pressure on the eastern border of Poland since mid-2021. These provisions may explain the asylum trends described in Chapter 2 and complement the description of the legal framework as of 2021.[5]

Presentation of the legal framework is preceded by a mapping of the institutional actors involved in implementing the widely understood asylum policy in Poland. The overview of the domestic legislation is structured along the course of applying for asylum from the perspective of forced migrants. Hence, first we describe the provisions related to accessing the asylum procedure (at the border and within the territory of Poland), second we present the rules of processing asylum claims, and last we reflect on the provisions determining the possible outcomes of the asylum procedure, that is, granting international protection or denying it. Special attention was also paid to legislation referring to selected spheres of forced migrants' adaptation, that is, access to the labour market, education, housing, and healthcare. This aims to offer the legal context of the empirical analysis presented in Chapters 5–9.

The Basis of the Institutional System of Implementing Asylum Policy in Poland

There are two main legal acts that govern migration and asylum in Poland which thus shape the competences of the institutional actors involved in implementing asylum policy:

1. The Law on granting protection on the territory of Poland of 13 June 2003 (hereinafter: Law on Protection).[6]
2. The Law on Foreigners of 12 December 2013 (hereinafter: Law on Foreigners).[7]

These acts implement EU law in the area of forced migration governance, and in particular Council Directive 2001/55/EC of 20 July 2001 (Temporary Protection Directive),[8] Directive 2013/33/EU of the European Parliament and of the Council of 26 June 2013 (Reception Directive),[9] and Directive 2011/95/EU of the European Parliament and of the Council of 13 December 2011 (Qualification Directive),[10] and Directive 2013/32/EU of the European Parliament and of the Council of 26 June 2013 (Asylum Procedure Directive).[11]

The crucial legal act shaping the asylum system is the Law on Protection of 2003. It defines the forms of protection available in Poland: refugee status, subsidiary protection, asylum (domestic form of protection), and temporary protection.[12] This legal act also specifies the asylum procedure, prerequisites for granting or withdrawing international and domestic protection status, as well as the rights and obligations of asylum applicants. The Law on Protection also stipulates the rights of beneficiaries of international protection, although these are also envisaged in other legal acts (regarding, e.g., access to labour market institutions,[13] social assistance,[14] education,[15] and public healthcare[16]). The Law on Foreigners has a more general character, but it is still very relevant in the matter of admission of asylum seekers. First of all, it describes the competences of the main institutional actors involved in asylum and migration governance. Second, it stipulates conditions of entry, prerequisites for issuing administrative decisions such as refusal of entry, a return order, and granting a permit for a tolerated stay or stay due to humanitarian reasons (e.g., for rejected asylum applicants). In general, it gives the legal basis to conduct control activities towards non-nationals both on the border and within the territory of Poland.

The main ministries responsible for implementing asylum policy are the Ministry of the Interior and Administration and the Ministry of Family and Social Policy.[17] The Ministry of the Interior and Administration supervises the Border Guard, which is responsible for border control, receiving applications for international protection (at the border and within the territory of Poland), running the guarded centres for foreigners, as well as issuing and executing return orders issued to foreigners. The Office for Foreigners is responsible for processing asylum claims and securing the social needs of asylum applicants in Poland (among others, in the form of reception centres and centres where asylum applicants stay). The Office for Foreigners also processes appeals to decisions on residence permits issued by voivodes who govern at the regional level. The Office is one of the institutions supervised by the Ministry of the Interior and Administration.

An important institution in the asylum system in Poland is the Refugee Board. It processes appeals of decisions on asylum applications issued by the Office for Foreigners. Decisions issued by the Refugee Board may be appealed before an administrative court (the Warsaw Regional Administrative Court is competent to control administrative decisions issued by public bodies with a seat in Warsaw, which is the case of the Office for Foreigners). As regards courts, matters related to asylum seekers and migrants fall mostly under the jurisdiction of administrative courts that are competent in assessing administrative conduct. Apart from administrative courts, there are also common courts competent in criminal, civil, economic, labour, and family law. As regards asylum issues, common courts play an important role in deciding on the administrative detention of asylum seekers. The decisions come on a motion by the Border Guard identifying reasons for the application of isolative measures to secure the course of the administrative procedures (asylum or return). Both the Border Guard and the common courts may also decide to apply non-isolative measures alternative to detention, having the same objective, which is securing the course of the administrative procedures.

The Ministry of Family and Social Policy[18] is responsible for providing social assistance to all citizens of Poland, as well as to foreigners who fulfil certain conditions, such as being a beneficiary of international protection. This ministry coordinates and supervises the functioning of the local (*poviat*) family support centres and local centres of social assistance, which are part of the local government. The local family support centres are involved in providing the beneficiaries of international protection with assistance as part of the individual integration programme (IIP; see more below and in Chapter 7 and Chapter 8). The Ministry of Family and Social Policy is also responsible for proposing and implementing laws concerning the employment of foreigners. It supervises local (*poviat*) and regional (*voivodeship*) labour offices, as well as departments of regional (*voivodeship*) offices (*urzędy wojewódzkie*) responsible for issuing work permits (allowing foreigners to work on a long-term basis). Permission regarding work on a short-term basis, namely seasonal work permits and employers' declarations on entrusting work to foreigners, is issued by the local labour offices. Since beneficiaries of international protection and asylum applicants are covered by other provisions on accessing the labour market in Poland than other non-nationals (see details below), the competence of labour offices related to any kind of work permit remains of little importance for migrants concerned in this book, unless they are joined by non-nationals having other migrant statuses. However, at least in theory, local labour offices may serve as facilitators in forced migrants' adaptation to the labour market, since according to the Law on Promotion of Employment the offices are responsible for registers of unemployed residents of Poland (be they Polish nationals or non-nationals), supporting unemployed in job searches, granting and paying unemployment allowances, and organising training courses and vocational training.

The Ministry of Foreign Affairs, as far as asylum issues are concerned, represents Poland in proceedings before the European Court of Human Rights (ECtHR), which is significant in light of the numerous claims submitted to ECtHR against Poland with regard to asylum-related issues.[19] Another competence of this ministry pertains to visa policy and its implementation through, for example, in very specific cases, issuing visas and organisation of work of the consulates abroad. However, in rather rare cases, asylum seekers arrive in EU territories with valid visas issued by Polish consuls (or the consuls of other EU states; see Chapter 5 for stories with examples of this). In addition to the visa-related competences of this ministry, the opinion of the minister of foreign affairs is part of the procedure of granting the domestic form of protection (*azyl*). The decision on it is issued by the Office for

Foreigners, upon the consent of the foreign minister.[20] Other ministries (such as the Ministry of Health, Ministry of Education and Science[21]) are connected to forced migration governance in areas of their competences, either setting rules for access to particular services or supervising the operation of service providers. They are also involved in the recognition of foreign diplomas, which is a task crucial for migrants' access to the Polish labour market (in particular, by specialists, such as health professionals).

Another public institution worth mentioning in the context of asylum policy and human rights protection is the Commissioner for Human Rights (Ombudsman) who, among other activities, monitors access to the asylum procedure and how the state's authorities observe the human rights of migrants (be they voluntary or forced) in various spheres: participation in the labour market, family life, and right to equal treatment. In addition to responding to individual complaints of rights holders, the Commissioner for Human Rights may also direct official and more general requests to the authorities, propose legal amendments or postulate abandoning practices that lead to human rights infringements. Regarding public bodies involved in campaigning for human rights protection, the Commissioner for Children's Rights should be mentioned, although in practice the role of this institution seemed to be less visible than the activities of the Ombudsman, which has a wider scope of competences.

The system of forced migration governance is constituted not only by public institutions on the central, regional, or local levels but also by non-governmental organisations (NGOs), which play an important role in it. In particular, they fill the institutional gap regarding the integration of forced migrants, offering various kinds of support, from language courses and vocational training, through activities facilitating adaptation in local communities, to specialised psychological aid. From the perspective of forced migrants whose legal status is to be determined (because they are within the asylum or return procedure or appealing against decisions on their asylum claims), the legal aid provided by NGOs is of particular significance. Notably, the scope and scale of support offered to migrants, including asylum seekers, depend on the financial resources or special programmes from which these organisations may benefit. The reduction of the available funding to such organisations between 2015 and 2021 (e.g., EU funds, see more in Chapter 8) posed risks to the continuity of their activities and the possibility to replicate best practices and limited the scope of the specialised assistance offered to asylum seekers or beneficiaries of international protection. Nevertheless, regardless of political or financial constraints affecting the operation of NGOs supporting forced migrants, their role has remained crucial in addressing the needs of persons seeking protection in Poland, subjected to various forms of administrative procedures or after their completion.

International organisations are also important in the governance of forced migration. The competences of the two entities are particularly relevant to the Polish context. The first one is the Polish office of the United Nations High Commissioner for Refugees (UNHCR) involved in the monitoring of various procedures to which asylum seekers are subjected (e.g., border control, detention), border crossings and reception centres, offering integration activities, and supporting people with special needs. UNHCR also offers legal aid to (the widely understood category of) refugees and provides training to frontline officers dealing with asylum seekers. The UNHCR representatives have access to foreigners and their cases during the procedure of applying for refugee status or withdrawing from it, guaranteed by the Law on Protection. UNHCR plays a significant role in observing the standards of human rights protection and campaigning for increasing them. Another organisation to be mentioned is the International Organisation for Migration (IOM). It is involved in providing information to migrants and—occasionally—in other activities aimed at increasing the knowledge of various social actors (e.g., local communities, employers). Apart from its widely recognised role in studying migration phenomena globally and regionally, the organisation is involved in organising assisted voluntary returns.[22] The latter possibility is important for persons who were refused both international and domestic forms of protection in Poland or other EU countries. As regards the organisation of forced returns of third-country nationals or assisting their voluntary returns, the role of Frontex can be mentioned, with the reservation, however, that the use of joint return flights organised by Frontex (after 2016, when the competences of Frontex were increased in this respect[23]) was not a common measure applied in Poland in the period covered by the empirical study.

The aforementioned institutional actors involved in forced migration governance cooperate with each other in various aspects and at different levels. Partially, this cooperation is determined by the law in force and has permanent character, as in the case of the Border Guard and the Office for Foreigners, all of which have certain competences with regard to the asylum procedure in Poland. Sometimes, cooperation takes an *ad hoc* character. More often, however, cooperation between various actors stems from participation in programmes or projects conducted at the international, national, or local levels. Within such projects, often coordinated by public institutions, certain tasks (such as legal aid or language courses) are entrusted to civil society actors or other specialised entities. In practice, local initiatives are often based on the collaboration of local governments with NGOs offering legal advice or integration support to asylum seekers, migrants, and refugees (such initiatives have been developed, in particular, in big cities, e.g., Warsaw, Gdańsk, Lublin, Kraków, Wrocław, and Łódź; see also Pawlak, 2018).

Legal Framework of Accessing the Asylum Procedure

Foreign nationals willing to apply for international protection in Poland must submit an application on the border during the border check, or within the territory of Poland. Detailed provisions regarding access to asylum and the asylum procedure itself are envisaged in the Law on Protection. Applications are submitted to the Office for Foreigners through the Border Guard (Article 24 of the Law on Protection[24]). The Border Guard transfers the application to the Office for Foreigners within 48 hours after its reception. According to the Dublin Regulation, the Office checks whether Poland is responsible for processing the application of the foreigner and whether the applicant has lodged applications in other countries (Article 36). If the Office for Foreigners finds that another country is responsible for processing the application, it initiates the Dublin procedure, which means that it contacts the competent bodies of that country with a request to take responsibility for processing the application (concerning the applicant and, if relevant, the other persons covered by the application). If the applicant is to be transferred to another country, the foreigner may be escorted to the border by the Border Guard (Article 37).

Applications for international protection should be lodged personally. Foreigners lodging applications at the border may be assisted, free of charge, by an international organisation or NGO providing aid to migrants upon request or with the applicant's consent to be assisted by representatives of these organisations (Article 29). Receiving the application, if necessary, the Border Guard should secure the presence of an interpreter. The officers receiving the application must confirm the identity of an applicant, check whether the foreigner possesses documents authorising them to cross the border and stay on the territory of Poland, and take photos of the person and their fingerprints. The application form includes space for crucial information about the circumstances and reasons for leaving the country of origin, seeking protection and entering the country where the application for international protection is submitted. It also contains an indication of the preferred language to be used in the asylum procedure (e.g., for hearings) as well as information on applicants' health condition. The application also contains information about previous proceedings in which the foreigner and persons covered by the application took part (Article 26(3)).

Applications for international protection may be lodged on behalf of the spouses and minors for whom the applicant is legally responsible, provided that the minor is not married (Article 25). The spouse of an applicant should be informed by the Border Guard about the consequences of lodging an application together or separately if doing so would better address the real causes of fleeing from their country of origin (Article 27). If officers receiving the application have doubts regarding the age of an applicant who claims to be a minor, they must inform him/her that his/her age can be checked by medical examination and communicate the possible consequences for the asylum procedure. If there is no possibility to determine whether the person is an adult or a minor, he/she is considered to be a minor. In cases in which the person refuses to undergo a medical examination, they are considered to be an adult (Article 32).

Foreigners staying in the guarded centres for foreigners run by the Border Guard, in a pre-trial facility, or in a prison submit an application through the Border Guard from the post located where the applicant is detained (Article 24). If the person willing to apply for asylum cannot reach the Border Guard post (e.g., due to physical disability, health condition excluding mobility, or being subjected to isolative measures), it is possible to submit a declaration of intent to apply for international protection in writing by post (regular mail or electronic). A declaration confirmed by written protocol may also be submitted to a Border Guard officer at a Border Guard post that the applicant visits personally, but the application cannot be received by the officers on that same day. In cases when a declaration of intent to apply for international protection is submitted, the application should be received as soon as possible, but no later than on the third day. In the event of a mass inflow of asylum seekers, the provisions permit the extension of this period to up to 10 days (Article 28).

People applying for international protection should be informed in writing, in a language they understand, about the procedure (what it looks like, who is responsible for issuing the decision), the applicant's rights and obligations (including the consequences of withdrawing their application), and about procedures linked to the Dublin Regulation (in particular, about the possibility of exchanging data with other countries potentially responsible for proceedings linked to an application for international protection and potential transfer to other responsible countries). The Border Guard officers should talk to applicants individually about the consequences of applying for international protection in different countries and applicants' obligation to remain on the territory of Poland until a decision is issued. Applicants should further be provided with a list of NGOs offering support for foreigners and information on the conditions for obtaining free legal support as well as the scope of social assistance and medical aid, including accommodation at the reception centres, and the possibility of getting a financial allowance for accommodation outside the centres (Article 30).

If the applicant does not provide his or her name, surname, and the country of origin, and this data cannot be obtained in the course of the control activities accompanying the reception of the asylum application, the application is not processed (Article 33(1)). From October 2021 and forward, an application also may not be processed if it was submitted by a foreigner apprehended directly after an unauthorised crossing of the external border, provided that the territory from which he/she crossed the border unlawfully did not pose a direct threat to life or safety, a direct risk of persecution, or the person did not present a justified reason to cross the border in an unlawful manner (Article 33(1a)). The new provision has been considered non-compliant with the Asylum Procedure Directive (2013/32), including the possibility to process applications submitted by persons who cross a border unlawfully in an accelerated mode or in transit or border zones.

The Office for Foreigners may consider the application inadmissible if the potential applicant has already obtained international protection in another country or a third country is considered to be the first safe country for the potential applicant and he/she may benefit from the protection provided there. It also can be deemed inadmissible when the potential applicant submits a subsequent application for international protection with no new proof or arguments relevant to their application for international protection. Another prerequisite for considering the application inadmissible is when the spouse of an applicant submits a separate application, but there are no reasons to process the application of spouses separately (Article 38).

The authorities can accelerate the proceedings following the submission of an application for international protection when the applicant's reasons for seeking protection are not due to fear of persecution because of specific types stated in the law (e.g., race, religion, and others mentioned above) or the risk of suffering serious harm caused by conflict or military actions. The proceeding may also be accelerated if information or documents provided by the applicant are false, confusing, or not reliable (i.e., when they are in contradiction to the facts determined by the responsible institutions). It is also accelerated if an applicant submits an application for the sole purpose of avoiding the execution of a return order issued against them, or if they constitute a threat to state security or public order (or were expelled from Poland for these reasons in the past) (Article 39). Regarding unaccompanied minors, the asylum proceeding is accelerated only in instances in which the person constitutes a threat to public safety and order, or if he/she was previously expelled from Poland due to these reasons (Article 63a). The duration of the accelerated procedure is limited to 30 days, and there is a seven-day period for appealing the decision.

The asylum procedure is discontinued if the applicant withdraws the application. It is also assumed that the applicant has withdrawn the application if he/she does not reach the reception centre within two days after submitting the application or after being released from a detention centre, or when he/she has been away from the reception centre for more than seven days without a justified reason.[25] The same applies to situations when applicants leave the place where they were ordered to stay during the procedure or did not report to the institution where they were ordered to report in the specified period of time. Withdrawal of the application is assumed if an applicant does not provide any address in Poland or misses a hearing and does not justify the absence within seven days. If the applicant leaves Poland, his/her asylum procedure is also discontinued. The asylum procedures as they pertain to children who became adults during the application process or to the spouse of an applicant (covered by the same application) who does not agree to take part in the procedure and leaves Poland or the reception centre without justification are discontinued. This does not affect the asylum procedure of the main applicant (Article 40). The procedure may be restarted if the applicant declares his/her interest in continuation within nine months from the decision to discontinue the procedure. Such a declaration may be submitted only once and only through the Border Guard officers to the Office for Foreigners (Article 40).

Legal Basis for Accessing International Protection in Poland

Decisions to grant protection are made by the Office for Foreigners in the first instance and by the Refugee Board in the second instance. The procedure is unified, which means that a person seeking protection applies for international protection, and the proceeding regarding this application may end with granting either refugee status or subsidiary protection. If the application covers other people assisting the applicant and the decision on granting refugee status or subsidiary protection to the applicant is positive, the positive decision also covers the other people concerned in the application. The decision will only be negative when the person covered by the application is responsible for committing acts against peace and humanity, they already benefit from protection in other countries, or they may obtain protection due to links with Polish citizenship (Articles 48 and 51). Children of foreigners granted refugee status born on the territory of Poland obtain refugee status automatically.

To get refugee status, the foreigner must experience a justified fear of persecution in the country of origin due to race, religion, nationality, or political beliefs, or belonging to a particular social group, and they cannot or do not want to benefit from the protection provided by the country of origin. The character of persecution should constitute a serious threat to human rights; an accumulation of activities constituting a threat to human rights rather than a single action. The persecution may take the form of physical, psychological, or sexual violence, a discriminatory way of applying legal, administrative, court, or police measures towards the person, disproportional or discriminatory punishment or proceedings, the lack of the possibility to appeal against the disproportional or discriminatory punishments, and punishment for refusal to serve in the army when the army is engaged in criminal activity (Article 13).

The reasons for persecution may only be associated with the applicant; it does not have to constitute an actual feature of that person. For instance, if institutions involved in persecutory activity consider the person to be a Christian and persecute them on those grounds, though the person may be Muslim, the fear of persecution is justified (Article 14). The fear of persecution or serious harm may also be justified if it concerns past events, and there is no proof that the risk of persecution or serious harm in the country of origin has ceased to exist (Article 18a).

Asylum seekers deemed not deserving of refugee status, but still seen as facing a real risk of being seriously harmed if they are returned to their country of origin, are granted subsidiary protection (Article 15). The risks taken into account when deciding about this form of protection include possibly being executed or sentenced to capital punishment, tortured or treated in an inhumane way, or experiencing a serious individual threat to their life and health due to international or internal military conflicts in which civilians are attacked (in the country of origin).

The fact that the reasons for persecution may appear after the person leaves the territory of the country of origin is recognised by Polish authorities. This means that not only asylum seekers just arriving in Poland may be considered deserving of international protection but also those who have already been in Poland, even for a longer period, especially if their actions constitute behaviour that would not be acceptable by the persecuting powers in their country of origin. Nevertheless, in deciding whether to grant international protection, the matter of whether the foreigner applied for protection as early as possible is also taken into account (Article 42). Before issuing a decision on granting international protection, the Office for Foreigners turns to the Border Guard, the head of the regional Police unit, and the head of the Agency of Internal Security (and other institutions, if necessary) to get information on potential criminal activity or threats to state security and public order that the applicant might be or might have been involved in. The information is not collected for applicants below 13 years of age (Article 45).

There are a number of reasons for negative decisions. Most important are serious suspicions of the applicant having committed a crime against peace, a war crime, or a crime against humanity, as defined in international instruments; the applicant was found guilty of behaviour not compliant with the aims and rules of the United Nations (linked to peace); or the applicant is responsible for other non-political crimes committed outside of Poland before submitting the application for international protection. If the person is considered to have encouraged others to commit crimes against peace or humanity or to have taken part in such crimes, this may also constitute a basis for denying refugee status. Refugee status is not granted when there is no justified fear of persecution in the country of origin or if the foreigner benefits from protection (other than that provided by UNHCR) in another country, where they can safely return to continue benefiting from that protection (Article 19).

Subsidiary protection is not granted if there is no risk of suffering from serious harm. Aside from foreigners accused of crimes against peace and humanity (or encouragement to commit them), those who have committed other crimes, either in Poland or in other countries, are refused this form of protection. The latter is also not granted to a person deemed a threat to state security and society. Finally, if someone's application for protection is seen as an attempt to avoid punishment for crimes committed abroad, their application for international protection will be denied (Article 20).

Depriving foreigners of refugee status may be a consequence of voluntary acceptance of the protection provided by the country of their citizenship (citizenship possessed so far or regained, or citizenship of another country that provides protection to a foreigner). Refugee status may also be revoked if a foreigner voluntarily returns to the country they left for fear of persecution, or when the fear of persecution is no longer justified and the foreigner can benefit from the protection provided by the state of origin or a previous residence. Perpetrating criminal acts against peace and humanity or acts not compliant with UN objectives, or providing false information or documents in their application for refugee status also will result in revocation of the status. An exception is implied when a foreigner who provided false or incomplete information still meets the requirements for obtaining refugee status because they experience a justified fear of persecution (Article 21). Analogous conditions lead to the withdrawal of subsidiary protection. The latter also can be withdrawn if a person commits a crime, either in Poland or outside of it. It is not revoked if the foreigner can demonstrate that the harm he/she experienced in the past may reoccur in the future upon their return to their country of origin (Article 22).

Withdrawal of refugee status or subsidiary protection is initiated by the Office for Foreigners or it follows upon a request of the Border Guard, the Police, the Internal Security Agency, or the Ministry of Justice. In cases of withdrawal, a hearing is held at which the foreigner may present information important to the decision about withdrawal of international protection status. The UNHCR may have access to the foreigner's case if they are to be deprived of international protection. The foreigner should be informed about the possibility of benefiting from free legal aid after the decision of withdrawal is issued (Articles 54a and 54b, 54d-f).

Rights and Obligations in the Course of the Asylum Procedure

Applicants for international protection get temporary confirmation of their identity, which is further used in administrative procedures following the submission of an application (Article 55). It does not allow foreigners to enter other countries or cross the border. Asylum applicants cannot leave the territory of Poland before the decision on their asylum application is issued (unless they decide to return to their country of origin) and have no right to a family reunion during the proceedings. All decisions issued to foreigners, including negative ones and decisions about transferring a person to another country, must be rendered in a language the foreigner understands and must include details on how he/she can access free legal aid.

The duration of the application processing can last from 6 to 15 months, depending on how complicated the case is, how many applications were submitted during the given period and whether the applicant performs their obligations in the asylum procedure (Article 34). If the procedure lasts longer than six months and the delay is not the result of the applicant's actions, the applicant is issued a document confirming the ongoing proceeding and authorising them to work in Poland without a work permit until a final decision is issued (Article 35; see also Chapter 8).

During the entire asylum procedure, applicants for international protection are entitled to various services and means of support, including social benefits, accommodation, access to healthcare, and free legal aid. To become eligible to obtain social assistance, asylum applicants should register at a specified time (two days) and place (reception centre) after submitting the application (Article 30). There are two reception centres (in Podkowa Leśna-Dębak and Biała Podlaska) where asylum applicants should report. These centres serve as the first places where asylum applicants are accommodated and registered before they are moved to centres for asylum seekers in other parts of Poland. Asylum applicants may, however, live independently. In such a case, to obtain social assistance they visit the contact points for foreigners benefiting from assistance outside the centres (see more in Chapter 7). Material assistance, accommodation (or financial allowance for those accommodated outside the centres), and medical care are provided to all asylum seekers during the entire period of the procedure and up to two months after the final decision on their case. If, however, an application is discontinued, assistance is offered for up to 14 days after that decision becomes final.

Asylum applicants have access to medical aid. Its scope is the same as for Polish citizens, with the exception of sanatorium treatment and sanatorium rehabilitation.

The provision of medical care starts when a given asylum seeker arrives at one of the centres for foreigners, except in special situations related to threat to the life or health of the foreigner. Upon submitting an application, asylum seekers with life-threatening health problems receive emergency health care either at the border, on the way to a reception centre, or after registering at a reception centre. During the asylum procedure, asylum applicants obtain medical services from healthcare units contracted by the Office for Foreigners, which creates a parallel healthcare system for asylum seekers (see more in Chapter 9). Foreigners placed in the centres for foreigners are provided with, among other things, tickets for transport in order to attend medical examinations or prophylactic vaccinations or in other particularly justified cases.

Polish legislation includes several provisions envisaging the need to address the special needs of vulnerable groups.[26] Such people receive special procedural guarantees in the course of the asylum procedure,[27] including conditions adapted to their mental and physical state, the presence of a psychologist or doctor during the hearing, or the possibility to be heard at one's place of residence (including, e.g., a hospital as a temporary place of residence, Article 69). Vulnerable groups are to be provided with the necessary medical and psychological treatment.

A specific category of vulnerable persons is unaccompanied foreign minors. Their declaration of intent to apply for international protection should be prioritised by the Border Guard. Border Guard employees are obliged to register this declaration, to immediately turn to the regional custodial court to establish a legal representative for the underage applicant (a special guardian – *kurator*)[28] and to place the applicant in foster care. The legal representative is responsible for representing the minor's interests in applying for international protection and other procedures: transferring to another Member State based on the Dublin Regulation, getting social assistance, participating in the IIP, as well as getting support for voluntary return to the country of origin (Article 61). The Border Guard also turns to the custodial court in cases of unaccompanied minors being transferred from other Member States based on the Dublin Regulation, having no legal representative or having not been placed in foster care previously. If it turns out that the person covered by the application is an unaccompanied minor in the course of the asylum procedure, the Office for Foreigners submits a motion to the custodial court to place the minor in foster care. Special needs of minors are also guaranteed in the course of passing information to the minor and organising the hearing. During the asylum procedure, information is passed to the minor by the legal representative. The hearing should be conducted in a language and manner understandable to the minor and adjusted according to his/her age. The guardian should be present at the hearing. Also, a psychologist or education specialist should take part in the hearing with the aim of preparing an assessment of the child's physical and psychological condition (Article 65).

Asylum applicants have the right to free communication with representatives of UNHCR, representatives of international organisations, and civil society organisations ensuring assistance to foreigners, including legal aid. They also have the right to free legal information given by employees of the Office for Foreigners (in the course of the asylum procedure). They may enjoy free legal assistance relating to appeals against negative decisions on an application, the transfer of an applicant to another Member State, the discontinuance of the procedure, the refusal to consider a foreigners' declaration of intent to apply for international protection, the treatment of an application as inadmissible, and the deprivation of international protection. Making use of such free legal assistance requires that foreigners give power of attorney in writing.

Asylum applicants are entitled to free Polish language lessons and education for children. The right to education is a provision in the Polish Constitution (Article 70(1)). The law determining forced migrants' access to education corresponds to the main EU Directives in this respect (see more in Chapter 6). It implements Article 14(1) of Directive 2013/33/EU of the European Parliament and of the Council[29] providing that children of asylum seekers and minor asylum seekers should be granted access to the education system "under similar conditions as nationals of the host Member State"; and Article 14(2) of this Directive requiring that children entering a Member State should be included in education within three months and that "preparatory classes, including language classes, shall be provided to minors where it is necessary to facilitate their access to and participation in the education system". Polish legislation is also compliant with Article 27 of the Directive 2011/95/EU[30] stipulating that minors granted refugee or subsidiary protection status should have access to education "under the same conditions as nationals" and providing that adults granted international protection should be allowed access to the general education system, further training or retraining, under the same conditions as legally resident third-country nationals.

Asylum-seeking children have the right to education in Poland. Adult asylum applicants have access to education in public schools for adults, public post-secondary schools, public art schools, public institutions and colleges of social service employees, and vocational qualification courses under conditions applicable to Polish citizens (Article 165(3) of the Law on School Education). If asylum seekers want to begin or continue their studies, they have to pay tuition.

The Scope of International Protection

Foreigners granted refugee status and subsidiary protection have access to:

1. the labour market and economic activity (they can work or run their own business on the same basis as Polish citizens);
2. social assistance on the same basis as Polish citizens;
3. individual integration programmes (IIP);
4. healthcare financed by the state;
5. housing sponsored by the state (available to all residents of Poland in difficult situations);
6. public education (compulsory for children);

7. professional training financed by the state, within programmes of professional development;
8. family reunion.

Access to the labour market and the economy for the beneficiaries of international protection may be limited only in the case of professions that require special certificates (see more in Chapter 8). Foreigners granted international protection are entitled to an IIP that is based on an agreement between the beneficiary and the local family support centre. The scope of support depends on the condition of the foreigner and his/her family. The family support centre should provide assistance in enabling the foreigner to establish contacts with the local community and contacting the local centre for social assistance. The centre should also provide assistance in finding housing (preferably a flat; see more in Chapter 7). The programme at the individual level is coordinated by a particular employee of the family support centre. It is assumed that during the programme beneficiaries are registered at local labour offices and actively looking for jobs and taking part in language courses (to learn Polish if they do not know it already). They should contact the person responsible for the programme at least twice a month. The programme is financed by the voivodes, but its functioning is delegated to the family support centre at the local level. The cost of the programme is paid for on an individual basis (Article 93 of the Law on Social Assistance).

Beneficiaries of international protection and members of their families are subject to the same rules as residents of Poland in accessing healthcare, based on public health insurance. Being "insured" usually is related to the age and economic activity of the people (e.g., those under 18 years old, lawfully employed or retired, or registered as an unemployed person). Beneficiaries of international protection and members of their families who have temporary residence permits are directly included on the list of persons authorised to access public healthcare services if they are not "insured", provided that their income meets the criterion specified in the Law on Social Assistance. Beneficiaries of refugee status or subsidiary protection obtained in Poland covered by an IIP are "insured" under the programme (except when they are insured for another reason).

Minor and adult beneficiaries of international protection have access to public primary, secondary, and post-secondary education. The obligation to attend school applies to children under 18. With respect to higher education, refugees and subsidiary or temporary protection beneficiaries have free access to it under the conditions applicable to Polish citizens (Article 324(2) of the Law on Higher Education). To study in Poland, they must have completed secondary level education and hold a maturity certificate confirming eligibility to apply to university. By virtue of law, the lack of such a document in the case of refugees does not constitute an obstacle to study since there is an administrative recognition procedure intended especially for them.

According to the Law on Education System of 1991, foreign school certificates, diplomas, or other educational documents may be recognised in Poland either automatically or through an administrative recognition procedure conducted by a province education superintendent. Regarding the latter, the Mazovian Educational Superintendent (*Mazowiecki Kurator Oświaty*) may confirm the level of educational qualifications obtained abroad by a refugee or a beneficiary of subsidiary protection in Poland in case of significant difficulties with the provision of an original (or duplicate) certificate or the authentication of such certificate. The procedure of administrative decision can be used to confirm the primary, lower secondary, basic vocational, or upper secondary level of educational qualifications and the entitlement to continue one's education in Poland, including the entitlement to apply for admission to a higher education programme (Article 93a of the Law on Education System).

With regard to recognition of foreign higher education degrees in Poland, the general rule is that a foreign degree giving access to further studies or the right to start doctoral proceedings in the country where it was awarded gives its holder access to second-cycle studies, postgraduate studies, third-cycle/doctoral studies, or the right to start doctoral proceedings in Poland. A foreign degree may also be recognised for the purpose of further education on the basis of an international agreement. If the obtained degree does not give access to further studies in a country where it was obtained, in order to continue education in Poland there is a need to confirm or recognise the degree. Confirmation of the degree is a procedure stipulated in the Law on Higher Education for refugees and beneficiaries of subsidiary protection (and members of their families with a temporary residence permit) who graduated from universities but do not have a diploma. Recognition is a process of acknowledging a foreign diploma as equivalent to a Polish diploma. The competent authorities to conduct the confirmation or recognition procedure with regard to higher education diplomas (university degrees) are higher education institutions authorised to grant the academic degree of a doctor (PhD) in a given field of science or art (Article 327 of the Law on Higher Education). A diploma of completion of studies abroad may be recognised as equivalent to the relevant Polish diploma and professional title on the basis of an international agreement determining equivalence.

The Status of Rejected Asylum Applicants

Rejected asylum applicants having no authorisation to stay in Poland may take advantage of assistance with voluntary returns (provided by IOM or the Office for Foreigners). Persons who were rejected international protection should leave the territory of Poland within 30 days from the day when the negative decision on their asylum application became final. Ignoring this obligation may result in the issuance of a return order by the Border Guard, since overstaying the period of obligatory departure from the country after it does not grant international protection is one of the premises of issuing a return order to foreign nationals (Article 302 of the Law on Foreigners). Execution of the return order may be independent of the state's authorities (when a foreigner leaves the country voluntarily within a specified period of 15 to 30 days) or with the deployment of law enforcement (in case of forced return assisted by the Border Guard, executed immediately). Detention is applied in cases in which there is a risk that the foreigner will not leave the territory of Poland voluntarily or that the foreigner constitutes a threat to state security and public order (394–407 of the Law on Foreigners).

The return procedure is initiated by the Border Guard, which decides about possible barriers to issuing a return order. In the course of the return procedure (i.e., investigating whether a breach of the conditions of stay should lead to the issuance of a return order), the officers examine whether the person is willing to apply for international protection and whether there are reasons preventing their return to the home country. There are two categories of reasons why a return order should not be issued (described in Chapter 3 of Part VIII of the Law on Foreigners). The first one pertains to humanitarian reasons, and in particular threats to the fundamental rights of migrants, family and private life, children's rights, the risk of being tortured or forced to work, or the potential of being deprived of the right to a fair trial after return. The discovery of such risks should lead to the issuance of a permit for stay due to humanitarian reasons. The permit is not issued if the foreigner committed a serious crime in Poland or another country or if he/she constitutes a threat to state security or public order. It may be withdrawn if it is discovered that the documents upon which the decision to issue the permit was based were false or if other grounds that would normally disqualify a candidate from receiving this kind of permit are discovered after the permit has already been issued.

The second set of reasons preventing the issuance of a return order is related to either technical obstacles to organise return travel or to get travel documents for the foreigner concerned, or the lack of cooperation with the authorities of the third country. Such obstacles should result in issuing a permit for tolerated stay. This permit is also granted to persons who are under threat to life, threat of torture or being forced to work in the country where the foreigner would be sent, but who committed crimes or constitute a threat to state security or public order, which means that they are not eligible to obtain a permit for stay due to humanitarian reasons.

Holders of the above-mentioned permits have reduced access to social assistance, including shelter, food, necessary clothing, and financial (goal-oriented) benefits. They may work in Poland or run their own business, but they cannot access any support in terms of integration or adaptation to the Polish labour market, enjoyed by beneficiaries of international protection. The permits are valid for two years. They may be prolonged if there are still reasons to protect the foreigner from being returned to his/her country of origin. Whereas the permit for stay due to humanitarian reasons allows the holder to cross borders, crossing borders is not possible with a permit for a tolerated stay. The protective dimension of these permits should be mostly understood as preventing foreigners from having to return to their country of origin, since their return could cause harm to their rights and those of their family, including children's rights.

Post-2015 Changes to the Legal Framework of Accessing International Protection in Poland

In the post-2015 context of forced migration governance, till mid-2021 we could observe mostly a change in practices rather than significant changes in the legal framework. Between 2017 and 2019 there were, however, announcements about changes that would visibly affect the administrative conduct towards forced migrants. The most important of these was a proposal for a border procedure applying detention towards specified categories of asylum applicants and processing their applications in a short period of time (28 days). Eventually, the work on these amendments to the law was abandoned after two years (Ministerstwo Spraw Wewnętrznych i Administracji, 2019; Rządowe Centrum Legislacji, 2017; see also Szulecka, 2019, 2017). As of February 2022, Polish legislation did not envisage provisions for processing asylum applications within the border procedure, although the introduction of it was expected due to the New Pact on Migration and Asylum (*Communication from the Commission on a New Pact on Migration and Asylum*, 2020).

The crucial legal changes regarding forced migration governance came along with the COVID-19 pandemic and the increased migration pressure on the border with Belarus (in 2020 and 2021). First came the restrictions on cross-border mobility to prevent the spread of COVID-19 in March 2020, which unintentionally restricted access to the asylum procedure at the border. Many international connections were suspended, some border checkpoints were closed, and importantly people seeking asylum were not included in the list of categories of persons authorised to cross the border and enter Polish territory during the time when the provisions restricting cross-border mobility were in force.[31] Further in August 2021, in response to the increasing number of arrivals through the "green border" (outside the border checkpoints at the land border, but in an unauthorised place), the pandemic-related provisions were changed to stipulate the immediate return of any person detected after crossing the border in an unauthorised manner (through a closed checkpoint or outside of checkpoints). This effectively excluded the possibility of applying for asylum in such circumstances, after an unauthorised border crossing. This law did not exclude the right to apply for asylum, but it provided a legal basis for turning people back ("pushbacks").

In October 2021, provisions allowing the authorities to "push back" migrants to the neighbouring country were included in the main act on migration governance, that is, Law on Foreigners[32] (see also Baranowska, 2021, Klaus ed, 2021). As already mentioned, in October 2021 a new law was introduced allowing the authorities to leave an asylum application without examination in cases when an applicant was apprehended directly after an unlawful border crossing. The new laws were implemented in practice despite international criticism and even an international court decision to prevent turning away forced migrants stranded at the border with Belarus (see, e.g., *R.A. and Others v. Poland*).[33] Instead, the government introduced a state of emergency in the border region and denied access to persons other than residents and law enforcement.[34] Journalists, professional lawyers supporting migrants, and activists offering humanitarian and medical aid were "pushed out" from the border area. Thus, the Polish authorities contributed to the vulnerable position of foreign nationals and infringements of crucial principles, such as the right to life and safety of all those remaining under the authority of the Polish state, as well as the right to asylum and freedom from inhuman and degrading treatment.

Conclusion

The legislation stipulating the right to ask for asylum, the course of the asylum procedure, and the scope of protection granted in Poland could be seen as compliant with both international and EU laws (in particular the 1951 Geneva Convention and EU Directives). In the following chapter, we demonstrate, however, that the legislation, while not raising legal concerns (until mid-2021), may be either abused or infringed in practice, thus leading to a breach of the fundamental rights of forced migrants. This concerns first and foremost a lack of access to the asylum procedure at the border checkpoints, as reported by human rights defenders (see, e.g., Białas et al., 2019) as well as our interviewees (see Chapter 5). Practices aimed at denying access to the asylum procedure remain in breach of a crucial principle of asylum law, that is, non-refoulment. In this context, the newest amendments to the asylum and immigration law, giving bases for returning migrants (including asylum seekers) to the border line, in case their unlawful border crossing is immediately detected, bring additional serious concerns about forced migrants' access to protection or even right to apply for this if legal routes to enter Polish territory are not accessible.

The execution of provisions related to forced migrants' access to healthcare, housing, education, or the labour market depends very much on the resources (including human, social, and financial capital) of forced migrants, their legal status, and the resources and capacities of local institutions and organisations involved in either forced migration governance or adaptation of asylum seekers and beneficiaries of international protection (see more in Chapters 6–9). The general framework of accessing accommodation, education, language courses, medical services, and social assistance does not offer solutions to the particular problems or special needs of forced migrants. To some extent, this relates to deficiencies of social policy in practice in Poland, as in the case of reduced access to state-sponsored housing, or shortcomings of the healthcare system in Poland, experienced by both Polish and foreign nationals (see more in Chapter 9).

Notes

1 For instance, in 2020 there were 31 applications for the national form of protection, azyl, and only four of them ended up with a positive decision (Urząd do Spraw Cudzoziemców, 2021).
2 Konstytucja Rzeczypospolitej Polskiej z dnia 2 kwietnia 1997 r. (Dz.U. 1997 nr 78 poz. 483) [Polish Constitution].
3 Convention Relating to the Status of Refugees, 28 July 1951, United Nations, Treaty Series, vol. 189, p. 137.

4 In practice, it means a presence on Polish territory, but there have been situations in which Polish authorities denied responsibility for persons physically present on the territory of Poland being refused the possibility to enter Poland at the border checkpoint (see case MK and Others v Poland, para 236) or persons present at the border line (Ministry of the Interior and Administration, 2021).

5 The last year covered by the desk research analysis conducted for the purpose of this book.

6 Ustawa z dnia 13 czerwca 2003 r. o udzielaniu cudzoziemcom ochrony na terytorium Rzeczypospolitej Polskiej (t.j. Dz. U. z 2021 r. poz. 1108 z późn. zm.) [Law on Protection].

7 Ustawa z dnia 12 grudnia 2013 r. o cudzoziemcach (t.j. Dz. U. z 2021 r. poz. 2354 z późn. zm.) [Law on Foreigners].

8 Council Directive 2001/55/EC of 20 July 2001 on minimum standards for giving temporary protection in the event of a mass influx of displaced persons and on measures promoting a balance of efforts between Member States in receiving such persons and bearing the consequences thereof (OJ L 212, 7.8.2001, pp. 12–23).

9 Directive 2013/33/EU of the European Parliament and of the Council of 26 June 2013 laying down standards for the reception of applicants for international protection (recast) (OJ L 180, 29.6.2013, pp. 96–116) that repealed Council Directive 2003/9/EC of 27 January 2003 laying down minimum standards for the reception of asylum seekers (OJ L 31, 6.2.2003, pp. 18–25).

10 Directive 2011/95/EU of the European Parliament and of the Council of 13 December 2011 on standards for the qualification of third-country nationals or stateless persons as beneficiaries of international protection, for a uniform status for refugees or for persons eligible for subsidiary protection, and for the content of the protection granted (recast) (OJ L 337, 20.12.2011, pp. 9–26).

11 Directive 2013/32/EU of the European Parliament and of the Council of 26 June 2013 on common procedures for granting and withdrawing international protection (OJ L 180, 29.6.2013, pp. 60–95).

12 Until the end of 2021, the provisions on temporary protection had not been applied.

13 Ustawa z dnia 20 kwietnia 2004 r. o promocji zatrudnienia i instytucjach rynku pracy (t.j. Dz. U. z 2021 r. poz. 1100 z późn. zm.) [Law on Promotion of Employment].

14 Ustawa z dnia 12 marca 2004 r. o pomocy społecznej (t.j. Dz. U. z 2021 r. poz. 2268 z późn. zm.). [Law on Social Assistance].

15 Ustawa z dnia 14 grudnia 2016 r. – Prawo oświatowe (t.j. Dz. U. z 2021 r. poz. 1082 z późn. zm.). [Law on Education].

16 Ustawa z dnia 27 sierpnia 2004 r. o świadczeniach opieki zdrowotnej finansowanych ze środków publicznych (t.j. Dz. U. z 2021 r. poz. 1285 z późn. zm.) [Law on Public Healthcare].

17 As of January 2022. In the studied period, the competences and names of the ministries were changing relatively often. However, the role of ministers responsible for social policy, labour market policy and internal affairs in the area of forced migration governance remained unchanged.

18 At the moment of gathering empirical data—Ministry of Family, Labour and Social Policy.

19 See, e.g., cases DA and Others v Poland App no 51246/17 (ECtHR, 8 July 2021), MK and Others v Poland App nos 40503/17, 42902/17, 43643/17 (ECtHR, 23 July 2020), Sherov v Poland and 3 Other Applications App no 54029/17 (ECtHR, 11 January 2021), RA and Others v Poland App no 42120/21 (ECtHR, 25 August 2021).

20 Provisions related to granting or withdrawing the domestic form of protection, azyl: Articles 90–96 of the Law on Protection.

21 At the time of collecting empirical data, there were two ministries, one responsible for national education and one for science and higher education.

22 Based on the Agreement between the Minister of the Interior and Administration of the Republic of Poland and the International Organisation for Migration on cooperation in the field of voluntary returns of foreigners leaving the territory of the Republic of Poland, 12 July 2005, Warsaw.

23 See Article 27 of Regulation (EU) 2016/1624 of the European Parliament and of the Council of 14 September 2016 on the European Border and Coast Guard and amending Regulation (EU) 2016/399 of the European Parliament and of the Council and repealing Regulation (EC) No 863/2007 of the European Parliament and of the Council, Council Regulation (EC) No 2007/2004 and Council Decision 2005/267/EC (OJ L 251, 16.9.2016, pp. 1–76), repealed by Regulation (EU) 2019/1896 of the European Parliament and of the Council of 13 November 2019 on the European Border and Coast Guard and repealing Regulations (EU) No 1052/2013 and (EU) 2016/1624 (OJ L 295, 14.11.2019, pp. 1–131).

24 If not stated otherwise, the articles mentioned in the next paragraphs concern the Law on Protection.

25 See the asylum statistics, including the scale of decisions on discontinuance between 2011 and 2017 (e.g., Szulecka et al., 2018).

26 Minors, disabled persons, elderly persons, pregnant women, single parents, victims of human trafficking, seriously ill persons, mentally disordered persons, victims of torture, victims of psychological, physical and sexual violence as well as violence due to gender, sexual orientation, and gender identity (Article 68 of the Law on Protection).

27 For instance, in February 2018, the Border Guard was obliged to guarantee food and transport to the reception centre for vulnerable groups who declare their will to continue their procedure after they are transferred within the Dublin Procedure from other countries (Article 40a of the Law on Protection).

28 In practice, the Border Guard uses a list of NGOs whose representatives are willing to become guardians for unaccompanied minors since the law requires that such guardians have experience working with unaccompanied minors (HFHR, 2021).

29 Directive 2013/33/EU of the European Parliament and of the Council of 26 June 2013 laying down standards for the reception of applicants for international protection (recast) (OJ L 180, 29.6.2013, pp. 96–116).

30 Directive 2011/95/EU of the European Parliament and of the Council of 13 December 2011 on standards for the qualification of third-country nationals or stateless persons as beneficiaries of international protection, for a uniform status for refugees or for persons eligible for subsidiary protection, and for the content of the protection granted (recast) (OJ L 337, 20.12.2011, pp. 9–26).

31 Rozporządzenie Ministra Spraw Wewnętrznych i Administracji z dnia 13 marca 2020 r w sprawie czasowego zawieszenia lub ograniczenia ruchu granicznego na określonych przejściach granicznych (Dz U poz 435 z późn zm) [Ordinance of the Minister of Interior and Administration of 13 March 2020 on temporary suspension or reduction of border traffic in selected border crossing points]. See also the intervention of the Commissioner for Human Rights regarding practices of border check during the pandemic (Rzecznik Praw Obywatelskich 2020).

32 Ustawa z dnia 14 października 2021 r. o zmianie ustawy o cudzoziemcach oraz niektórych innych ustaw (Dz. U. poz. 1918) [Amendment of 14 October 2021 to the Act on Foreigners]; Rozporządzenie Ministra Spraw Wewnętrznych i Administracji z dnia 20 sierpnia 2021 r. zmieniające rozporządzenie w sprawie czasowego zawieszenia lub ograniczenia ruchu granicznego na określonych przejściach granicznych (Dz. U. poz.

1536) [Ordinance of the Minister of Interior and Administration of 20 August 2021 changing the Ordinance on temporary suspension or reduction of border traffic in selected border crossing points].

33 RA and Others v Poland App no. 42120/21 (ECtHR, 25 August 2021).

34 Rozporządzenie Rady Ministrów z dnia 2 września 2021 r w sprawie ograniczeń wolności i praw w związku z obowiązywaniem stanu wyjątkowego (Dz U poz 1613 z późn zm) [Ordinance of the Council of Ministers of 2 September 2021 on the reduction of freedoms and rights due to the enforcement of the state of emergency]. The state of emergency has been revoked and replaced with provisions banning access to the border zone from 1 December 2021 (based on Rozporządzenie Ministra Spraw Wewnętrznych i Administracji z dnia 30 listopada 2021 r. w sprawie wprowadzenia czasowego zakazu przebywania na określonym obszarze w strefie nadgranicznej przyległej do granicy państwowej z Republiką Białorusi (Dz. U. poz. 2193) [The Ordinance of the Minister of Interior and Administration of 30 November 2021 on temporary ban of stay in the indicated area of the border zone near the border with Belarus].

References

Białas, J., Górczyńska, M., Witko, D., 2019. *Access to asylum procedure at Poland's external borders. Current situation and challenges for the future.* Helsinki Foundation for Human Rights, Warsaw.

European Commission, 2020. *Communicate from the Commission to the European Parliament, The Council, The European Economic and Social Committee and the Committee of the Regions on a New Pact on Migration and Asylum*, EC, Brussels, 23.9.2020 COM (2020) 609 final.

Ministerstwo Spraw Wewnętrznych i Administracji, 2019. Projekt ustawy o zmianie ustawy o udzielaniu cudzoziemcom ochrony na terytorium Rzeczypospolitej Polskiej oraz niektórych innych ustaw.

Ministry of the Interior and Administration, 2021. *Poland provided the ECHR with its position on the order for interim measures [WWW Document].* Ministry of the Interior and Administration. www.gov.pl/web/mswia-en/poland-provided-the-echr-with-its-position-on-the-order-for-interim-measures (accessed 27 October 2021).

Pawlak, M., 2018. Polityki publiczne wobec migracji, in: Kwaśniewski, J. (Ed.), *Nauki o polityce publicznej: Monografia dyscypliny.* IPSIR UW, Warszawa, pp. 288–311.

Rządowe Centrum Legislacji, 2017. Projekt ustawy o zmianie ustawy o udzielaniu cudzoziemcom ochrony na terytorium Rzeczypospolitej Polskiej oraz niektórych innych ustaw.

Rzecznik Praw Obywatelskich, 2021, *Koronawirus a prawa cudzoziemców szukających ochrony przed prześladowaniami.* RPO pyta Straż Graniczną o obecne procedury na granicy wschodniej [WWW document] https://bip.brpo.gov.pl/pl/content/koronawirus-granice-ochrona-miedzynarodowa-w-Polsce (accessed 29 July 2021).

Szulecka, M., 2019. Border Management and Migration Controls in Poland (RESPOND Working Paper Series No. 2019/24).

Szulecka, M., 2017. *Zapowiedź dużych zmian w prawie azylowym.* Biuletyn Migracyjny, pp. 1–2.

Szulecka, M., Pachocka, M., Sobczak-Szelc, K., 2018. *Poland – Country Report: Legal and Policy Framework of Migration Governance.*

Urząd do Spraw Cudzoziemców, 2021. Statystyki UDSC/zestawienia roczne [WWW Document]. https://udsc.gov.pl/statystyki/raporty-okresowe/zestawienia-roczne/ (accessed 4 June 2021).

Legal acts

Agreement between the Minister of the Interior and Administration of the Republic of Poland and the International Organisation for Migration on cooperation in the field of voluntary returns of foreigners leaving the territory of the Republic of Poland, 12 July 2005, Warsaw.

Convention Relating to the Status of Refugees, 28 July 1951, United Nations, Treaty Series, vol. 189, p. 137.

Council Directive 2001/55/EC of 20 July 2001 on minimum standards for giving temporary protection in the event of a mass influx of displaced persons and on measures promoting a balance of efforts between Member States in receiving such persons and bearing the consequences thereof (OJ L 212, 7.8.2001, pp. 12–23).

Council Directive 2003/9/EC of 27 January 2003 laying down minimum standards for the reception of asylum seekers (OJ L 31, 6.2.2003, pp. 18–25).

DA and Others v Poland App no 51246/17, ECtHR, 8 July 2021.

Directive 2011/95/EU of the European Parliament and of the Council of 13 December 2011 on standards for the qualification of third-country nationals or stateless persons as beneficiaries of international protection, for a uniform status for refugees or for persons eligible for subsidiary protection, and for the content of the protection granted (recast) (OJ L 337, 20.12.2011, pp. 9–26).

Directive 2013/32/EU of the European Parliament and of the Council of 26 June 2013 on common procedures for granting and withdrawing international protection (OJ L 180, 29.6.2013, pp. 60–95).

Directive 2013/33/EU of the European Parliament and of the Council of 26 June 2013 laying down standards for the reception of applicants for international protection (recast) (OJ L 180, 29.6.2013, pp. 96–116).

Konstytucja Rzeczypospolitej Polskiej z dnia 2 kwietnia 1997 r. (Dz.U. 1997 nr 78 poz. 483) [Polish Constitution].

MK and Others v Poland App nos 40503/17, 42902/17, 43643/17, ECtHR, 23 July 2020

RA and Others v Poland App no 42120/21, ECtHR, 25 August 2021.

Regulation (EU) 2016/1624 of the European Parliament and of the Council of 14 September 2016 on the European Border and Coast Guard and amending Regulation (EU) 2016/399 of the European Parliament and of the Council and repealing Regulation (EC) No 863/2007 of the European Parliament and of the Council, Council Regulation (EC) No 2007/2004 and Council Decision 2005/267/EC (OJ L 251, 16.9.2016, pp. 1–76).

Regulation (EU) 2019/1896 of the European Parliament and of the Council of 13 November 2019 on the European Border and Coast Guard and repealing Regulations (EU) No 1052/2013 and (EU) 2016/1624 (OJ L 295, 14.11.2019, pp. 1–131).

Rozporządzenie Ministra Spraw Wewnętrznych i Administracji z dnia 13 marca 2020 r w sprawie czasowego zawieszenia lub ograniczenia ruchu granicznego na określonych przejściach granicznych (Dz U poz 435 z późn zm).

Rozporządzenie Ministra Spraw Wewnętrznych i Administracji z dnia 20 sierpnia 2021 r. zmieniające rozporządzenie w sprawie czasowego zawieszenia lub ograniczenia ruchu granicznego na określonych przejściach granicznych (Dz. U. poz. 1536).

Rozporządzenie Rady Ministrów z dnia 2 września 2021 r w sprawie ograniczeń wolności i praw w związku z obowiązywaniem stanu wyjątkowego (Dz U poz 1613 z późn zm).

Rozporządzenie Ministra Spraw Wewnętrznych i Administracji z dnia 30 listopada 2021 r. w sprawie wprowadzenia czasowego zakazu przebywania na określonym obszarze w strefie nadgranicznej przyległej do granicy państwowej z Republiką Białorusi (Dz. U. poz. 2193).

Sherov v Poland and 3 Other Applications App no 54029/17, ECtHR, 11 January 2021.

Ustawa z dnia 13 czerwca 2003 r. o udzielaniu cudzoziemcom ochrony na terytorium Rzeczypospolitej Polskiej (t.j. Dz. U. z 2021 r. poz. 1108 z późn. zm.) [Law on Protection].

Ustawa z dnia 12 marca 2004 r. o pomocy społecznej (t.j. Dz. U. z 2021 r. poz. 2268 z późn. zm.). [Law on Social Assistance].

Ustawa z dnia 20 kwietnia 2004 r. o promocji zatrudnienia i instytucjach rynku pracy (t.j. Dz. U. z 2021 r. poz. 1100 z późn. zm.) [Law on Promotion of Employment].

Ustawa z dnia 27 sierpnia 2004 r. o świadczeniach opieki zdrowotnej finansowanych ze środków publicznych (t.j. Dz. U. z 2021 r. poz. 1285 z późn. zm.) [Law on Public Healthcare].

Ustawa z dnia 12 grudnia 2013 r. o cudzoziemcach (t.j. Dz. U. z 2021 r. poz. 2354 z późn. zm.) [Law on Foreigners].

Ustawa z dnia 14 grudnia 2016 r. – Prawo oświatowe (t.j. Dz. U. z 2021 r. poz. 1082 z późn. zm.). [Law on Education].

Ustawa z dnia 14 października 2021 r. o zmianie ustawy o cudzoziemcach oraz niektórych innych ustaw (Dz. U. poz. 1918).

5

EXPERIENCES IN ACCESSING INTERNATIONAL PROTECTION

Introduction

This chapter presents the outcomes of empirical analyses dedicated to asylum seekers' and refugees' experiences with exercising their rights attached to seeking asylum in the context of Poland. The chapter focuses on the very issue of requesting protection and obtaining or being denied it. It precedes more specific analyses focused on the economic adaptation of forced migrants, their access to education, housing, and healthcare, as well as their aspirations towards civic participation. Describing the very access to the asylum procedure in the context of Poland, we refer to statements shared with us by migrant interviewees and observations from experts involved in implementing asylum policy in the country. This issue is presented against the more general background encompassing the reasons for forced mobility revealed by persons seeking asylum in Poland (or in the EU) and the phenomenon of onward mobility, frequently associated with the asylum reality in the country (Górny et al., 2019, p. 97; Rafalik, 2012; Stummer, 2016; Szulecka, 2019). The chapter also aims to analyse the course of the asylum procedure, its discontinuance or renewal as reflected in the accounts of forced migrants, and the institutional or social actors dealing with them in various contexts. Since one of the common experiences reflected by asylum seekers was linked to leaving Poland for other EU states (mainly Germany), followed by the usually undesirable transfer back to Poland under the Dublin Regulation, we also analyse these experiences. We believe these issues constitute important factors determining both the state's practices towards forced migrants and feelings of the latter about the accessibility and scope of international protection offered by Poland.

This chapter, like the other empirical ones, is based on the analysis of qualitative data gathered between 2018 and 2019, that is, 30 interviews with persons seeking asylum in Poland (16 of whom obtained a positive decision) and 12 interviews[1]

DOI: 10.4324/9781003196327-5

with professionals involved in forced migration governance, including non-profit activity in this respect. The analysis also refers to the outcomes of one of the three expert group discussions[2] organised within the Migration Governance Network. The following analysis takes into account the discussion on the practices in Poland of admitting asylum seekers, with the provision of support and assistance in the course of the asylum procedure taken into account.

Need for In-depth Reflection on the Reasons for Fleeing and Onward Mobility

Before discussing the reasons why people flee their homes and start usually difficult journeys that culminate in requesting asylum in a safe destination, we have to admit that we are aware that Poland is usually not the preferred destination for asylum seekers.[3] However, its geopolitical position as part of the EU and in the Schengen zone, as well as its location at the bloc's external border, makes it an attractive country to apply for international protection, with the perspective of onward mobility to preferred destinations within the EU. Therefore, when analysing the reasons why people seek asylum in Poland (as reflected on by our migrant and expert interviewees), we take into account that Poland is not necessarily the first choice, but as a part of the EU, it remains the preferred solution if the alternative means staying in unsafe or poor environments where the prospects for improving one's safety or living conditions are very low.

Despite this acknowledgement, we must also emphasise the significance of studying in an in-depth manner the reasons why people leave their (sometimes temporary and substandard) homes and why they try various means to avoid returns to countries where they had previously lived. Such analysis backed by the accounts of forced migrants is of particular value when the authorities' perception of forced migrants is reduced to portraying them as bogus asylum seekers. As already stated (in Chapter 3), asylum seekers approaching Poland have been very often seen by Polish politicians and the administration as economic migrants instrumentally making use of asylum procedures just to enter EU territory. Even if the statement that asylum seekers approaching Poland want to reach other EU countries or want to improve their living conditions is partially true, this does not encompass the full characteristics of the drivers of forced mobility. The latter can be approached by evoking forced migrants' voices, that is, the experiences shared with researchers during the migrants' stay outside their home country, often contested by the asylum state's authorities when forced migrants exercised their right to asylum.

Reasons for Seeking Asylum in Poland

Experience with Armed Conflict and Its Consequences

As regards the factors revealed in our empirical study that pushed forced migrants from their countries of origin, the majority of migrant interviewees indicated conflict or war as the reason for their departure (15 respondents of various nationalities) and other traumatic events related to persecution because of political views or family situation (11 respondents). The latter concerned women who were brutally treated by their husbands and other members of their close family. Indeed, people interviewed within the project were from regions that were afflicted by different conflicts, political instability, or violence towards certain social groups (such as women or religious minorities). In some regions, there were ongoing armed conflicts, such as the civil war in Syria since 2011 or in the Ukrainian Donbas region since 2014. Others were from places where the conflicts had ended (before the period of interviews with the forced migrants), for example, the wars in Iraq (2003–2011, 2013–2017) or the wars in Chechnya (1994–1996, 1999–2009).

Asylum seekers' accounts confirmed that war or armed conflict is not only a direct threat to the life of inhabitants but also causes a significant deterioration of their living conditions and results in a lack of basic resources. One interviewee, a Syrian man over 50 years old, reflected on how the events related to the war affected the status of his family:

> When the events [war] started in Syria, everything got messed up, life got messed up, relations, safety. There was no more safety. One was not able to go around, goods became scarce [...] And the lack of basic needs for living, nourishment goods. The majority of them were lost due to the events; services, water and electricity, flammable goods [fuels]—they were not available. These are all things which all were in great supply before the events, and especially with our social status, our high educational status, which led to having good jobs. Our economic situation was very good [...] so everything was available for us. After the events began, all of this was lost, even if we had money. And later, after I managed to get my children out, our economic situation became bad because we paid a lot of money to help them leave.
>
> *PLMISy24*

In this quote above, like in other conversations, a sense of constant danger and uncertainty was mentioned by the asylum seeker.

A young female refugee briefly described the daily concerns she had had when staying in Syria:

> You don't know when you are going to your work or your university whether you will come back home or not.
>
> *PLMISy25*

Ukrainian interviewees also described war circumstances as triggers of their migration decisions, even among people who had never thought about migration before. The experiences of a man who used to live with his family 15 km from the centre of Ukrainian Donetsk can serve as an example. The man claimed that he did not want to leave Ukraine and all the time had hoped to be able to stay there and live undisturbed by fears or the effects of the war. He admitted that this period of hoping for changes for good eventually contributed to his family's worsening condition:

> [I thought] Maybe tomorrow it will be better than today. I'll wait a bit more … Maybe tomorrow, maybe the day after tomorrow, in a month, maybe after half a year. But when I was coming home after work and I was looking at my children who didn't have an appetite, I couldn't sleep … And it had an impact on my wife's mental state because it was visible that something was wrong with them [the children], something was going the wrong way […] It has been happening since they [twin children] were born. […] It was an everyday struggle. We used to see tanks, people with guns, etc. Then I was thinking "Well, we need to go somewhere where we can wait. Maybe in a year, half a year, something will change and we will come back". And we decided that we would go to Poland.
>
> *PLMIUk16*

The ongoing daily fighting and uneasiness of his wife and young children prompted this family to migrate to Poland to seek asylum. As the interviewee admitted, the situation was difficult, and not only in the areas affected directly by violent activities. Also in other parts of Ukraine, citizens from the eastern regions afflicted by the conflict did not feel welcome since they were associated with pro-Russia separatists and accused of instigating the fighting in Donetsk and Lugansk. This sheds light on the scale of the problem, and we should indicate the number of internally displaced persons in Ukraine as a result of Russia's forced annexation of Crimea and military intervention in Donbas. As many as 1.5 million people from the affected areas left their homes and tried to find a safe place in other parts of Ukraine (IOM, 2021, p. 9). However, as the Ukrainian interviewee stated, even people fleeing Donbas and trying to adapt to life in other parts of Ukraine were viewed with suspicion:

> (…) You could hear and be said to your face [accusations of initiating the conflict in Donbas], or if you were looking for a job and you were about to sign the papers, they would open the passport and see where you came from, and someone would say "No, maybe next time". So, the atmosphere was not good, a lot of aggression was happening.
>
> *PLMIUk16*

In some cases, the war made people follow their thoughts they had before the conflict started, as in the case of a young male Ukrainian asylum applicant who planned to go to work abroad even before the conflict, but eventually he decided to leave Ukraine when he directly witnessed war-related events (PLMIUk17). A similar situation was described by a young refugee from Syria who always wanted to leave the country, but the start of the civil war in Syria prompted him to act on it (PLMISy23).

As the accounts of Chechen asylum seekers confirm, war-related reasons may still push people to leave their country of origin years after the conflict has ended. In this case, it is because of the persecution of those who fought against the powers that finally took charge (in this case, the pro-Russia forces). The persecution translated into risks of unjust punishment, forced disappearance, torture, and even death (see, e.g., Szczepanik, 2019). Also, relatives and friends of persons identified by the authorities as "separatists" or "terrorists", unwilling to cooperate with the new regime's law enforcement in prosecutions targeting these persons (i.e., not reporting information about wanted relatives or not confirming their guilt), live in constant fear of being persecuted by the authorities. The testimony of a Chechen asylum seeker can serve as an illustration of this:

> They [Chechen leader Ramzan Kadyrov's forces] killed my younger brother. They invented all accusations and sins blaming him for every crime of the Chechen war. It's now the everyday practice of contemporary Chechnya: if any member of your family was charged with war-related accusations, by default it means that all members of your family will suffer. We had such a situation when people openly told me: "you will not find peace on the territory of the Republic". That's it!
>
> *PLMICh10*

The culpability of relatives, in particular parents, stems from traditional laws that sometimes prevail in the daily practices of formal social control, even though Chechnya is technically a republic of the Russian Federation where federal legal acts excluding such assignment of responsibility, being a form of revenge, are binding (Kaliszewska, 2019; Szczepanik, 2019). Thus, parents are blamed for deeds committed by their children, regardless of their age and independent life choices. Families of such alleged "terrorists" may have their property taken or destroyed and be forced to leave Chechnya. In circumstances when the perspective for freedom from persecution and unjust treatment by the authorities and the security services are scant, those directly involved in the fighting and those associated with them look for possibilities to leave the country, as illustrated by a quote from another Chechen who came to Poland after 2015 and by 2019 had been granted subsidiary protection.

> [...] my two step-brothers were killed [...], 18 people were killed. [...] I was an accomplice. They sent me already twice to prison, and wanted to send me for the third time. On the third time, they took me, beat me up, they broke my arm and tortured me. I didn't want my family and my children to live the life I was living. I wanted for them a peaceful life, a normal life as humans could have. So, I decided to leave the country.
>
> *PLMICh14*

In contemporary Chechnya, the constant fear of persecution, unjust detention, violence, and torture characterises the lives of all Chechens opposing (even not openly) the Russia-backed Chechen government. One of the interviewees directly said how their lack of support for the Chechen or Russian president translates not only into a level of fear but also to living conditions:

> […] there is no war or bombing, people have villas. [However,] there is a guerrilla war. Now, the ones who support Putin will have a distinct life, and the ones who don't, are persecuted, killed, sent to prison (…) People are living in fear.
>
> *PLMICh14*

Not without reason, Chechnya earned the label of "the republic of fear". Despite the improvement of the economic condition of the republic and visible restoration after the war destruction, the social bonds remain in degradation, due to threats posed by the authorities and the common crisis of trust towards those in power, but also towards those well-known, and previously trusted, such as neighbours, acquaintances, or family (see also Kaliszewska, 2019; Szczepanik, 2019).

Importantly, Chechens cannot easily find asylum in other Russian republics, since, as explained by one of the interviewees:

> In another territory of Russia [one] should be registered. So to be registered authorities send a request for confirmation to Chechnya. In that way, it is not difficult for them to find […] out [where this person is].
>
> *PLMICh11*

Simultaneously, as claimed by some of the interviewees:

> The Russian government doesn't allow Chechens to live a normal life because if you are Chechen, you are already blamed.
>
> *PLMICh09*

And thus, the will of being out of reach of the Chechen and Russian authorities forces people to go not only outside Russian territory but also outside other territories strictly dependent on Russian politics. This is why Chechen nationals do not feel safe in Belarus, where they go first before they make an attempt to enter the EU through the Polish-Belarusian border. There is evidence (e.g., evoked in the case *M.K. and Others v. Poland* adjudicated by ECtHR, see also Szczepanik, 2019) that asylum procedures are not applied properly towards Russian citizens in Belarus. It is claimed that it is an element of a broader problem, namely an almost not-existent asylum system in Belarus. Regarding Chechen nationals, however, the Belarusian authorities consider Russia a safe country, which is to justify sending back persons with Russian citizenship (including Chechens) to Russia and Chechnya, where they may be subjected to violence (including forced disappearance) and persecution (see more, Szczepanik, 2019, pp. 35–36).

The loss of trust, triggered by armed conflicts, internal fights, and the unpredictable actions of security forces, was indicated as one of the crucial factors contributing to the decisions by asylum seekers from various regions to leave their home countries. An asylum applicant from Syria mentioned the fear of being assaulted by neighbours with whom in the pre-war period they had good contact (PLMISY24). Lack of trust often appeared in the accounts of Chechen nationals, who feared denunciation or persecution based on unfair associations with "terrorist" activity, that is, opposing the Chechen government (see also Kaliszewska, 2019; Szczepanik, 2019).

Persecution and Violence towards Certain Social Groups

Being a member of a religious minority in non-democratic regimes increases the risk of being persecuted and thus contributes to the pressure to leave the country. An Iraqi asylum seeker claimed that as a Christian:

> [I] found difficulty to live recently in Iraq because there was oppression from the side of organisations, terrorist groups, against Christians in Iraq [...] it made me scared for my family, household, and my children. We thought of leaving our country and getting out.
>
> *PLMIIr28*

In many countries, violence towards women, ignored or even provoked by a state's policies, remains a serious problem. The situation in Chechnya, where local laws and norms normalise such violence, was reflected by several female Chechen interviewees[4] applying for international protection in Poland. The problem is, however, that domestic violence as such and violence towards women are not a premise for granting international protection unless it is a systemic problem of the state, the authorities of which contribute to the phenomenon (Górny et al., 2017, p. 10). Chechen women escaping violent environments enter the asylum path, as was confirmed in our research. Single mothers with children approaching the Polish border and asking for asylum are not rare cases. One of the Chechen interviewees admitted that she left her husband "because it was impossible to live with him. He was a monster. He beat [me], he drank alcohol" (PLMICh03). Also, children may be victims of violent fathers, which usually constitutes a key factor pushing the women to search for protection in a place where customary laws, in particular Sharia law, are not executed.

In Chechnya, fleeing a brutal husband and establishing relationships with another man after divorce may be a life-threatening situation for women, as reflected on by one of the Chechen asylum applicants:

> According to the Muslim law, if a wife has cheated on her husband or has a different man, according to Sharia law, she must be killed. [...] it's a great shame.
>
> *PLMICh03*

As this interviewee explained, even the fact that she was divorced when she entered another relationship did not prevent the efforts of her male relatives to take revenge on her. She managed to leave Russia and arrive in the EU with her daughter and thus avoided not only the violence but also losing contact with her child. The latter situation is sometimes a part of the traumatic experience of Chechen women as their children are taken by the families of their fathers and kept away from their mothers for not obeying Sharia law (see also Kaliszewska, 2019; Lazarev, 2019).

Having a certain nationality or being a member of a certain social group may also be the reason for persecution, or at least discriminatory practices, in countries other than the country of origin, such as countries where forced migrants grow up or where they first try to find better living conditions. Such an experience was described by a Yemeni man who was unable to live either in Yemen, his country of origin, which is affected by internal conflicts and a humanitarian crisis, or in Saudi Arabia where he grew up. He compared the latter country to hell and stated that:

> [as Yemeni in Saudi Arabia] you are not able to find a job easily, they treat you very badly in governmental offices, very bad treatment by the police, traffic police [...] Once I received a ticket just for the fact that I am from Yemen, just a ticket like this ... [...] Human rights do not exist and have no value in Saudi Arabia, not for the people who are working with those foreign workers [...]. The Saudis come to work and relax, and we work [...] They imposed bigger taxes on people who are residing there. The cost of residency there is very high, that's one thing, and the other thing is that they started to deport people who are not Saudi.
>
> *PLMIYe29*

Notably, for people already staying away from territory where threats to life are the most serious, as in war-torn Yemen, the probability of being deported to the country of origin may constitute the main driver for an asylum seeker to look somewhere else. From the perspective of human rights protection, the European Union seems the right place to ask for protection, as confirmed by the story of the Yemeni quoted above, who has already been granted international protection by Polish authorities. The problem is, however, that the access to the very asylum procedure is limited, usually by the practice of pushbacks, observed at different parts of the external EU border (Strik, 2020). Poland with its control practices at its eastern border is not an exception in this respect (as confirmed in this chapter; see also, e.g., Białas et al., 2019; Chrzanowska et al., 2016; Szczepanik, 2018).

Consequences of Misinterpreting Motives of Mobility

Ascribing economic motives to asylum seekers particularly concerned the dominant group of asylum applicants in Poland between 2000 and 2020, namely persons with Chechen origin (Szulecka, 2019, 2016). However, economic motives were also often associated with other forced migrants who came from distant places and on the way to the EU passed through countries deemed by the Polish authorities as safe. Therefore, the efforts (and financial means) of forced migrants invested in long, partially or fully irregular and unsafe, travel to the EU were usually interpreted by the Polish authorities as proof of "asylum shopping", a form of mobility to be tackled in the same way as irregular migration (Szulecka, 2016). The statistics on the discontinuance of the asylum procedure due to the absence of asylum applicants on the territory of Poland and numerous motions from other EU states to Polish authorities under the Dublin Regulation served the authorities as justification for the mentioned perceptions. All these facts convince us that a more insightful look at the reasons and outcomes of seeking asylum in Poland is necessary.

The interviewed legal experts supporting forced migrants in various procedures (including the appeals against refusal of entry, negative first-instance decisions, or decisions on detention) frequently pointed to a lack of attention paid by the authorities to the reasons for leaving a country (push factors) and the reasons for the preference destinations other than Poland (pull factors). The allegedly unfair decisions issued by the state's authorities seemed to be used to the detriment of forced migrants in consecutive procedures, thus reproducing the perceptions of asylum seekers as bogus or as irregular migrants interested in social assistance provided by other EU states. The call for a more nuanced approach to the reasons for entry and reasons for onward mobility was expressed in the opinion of one public official acting for human rights protection:

> I really don't like [the situation] that every time I speak to the officers there is a belief that the asylum procedure is abused. Of course, it is, we all know that it is [...]. However, such a belief that every foreigner [abuses the procedure] when they enter and even say that something happened in their country, is so strong among the officers conducting the interview [during the border check] that it interrupts the fair performance of the duties. [...] these people who theoretically should be admitted, do not enter Poland. [...] This is a kind of a vicious circle. On the one hand, non-nationals come and are pushed back at the border. [...] [despite] their often quite dramatic stories about their countries of origin, about their faith there. [...] [On the other hand] the Border Guard officer speaking to the next family [at the border] has in the back of their head the families just let in and knows that they have already gone to Germany. [...] But this does not necessarily mean an instrumental approach to the asylum procedure.
>
> *representative of a public institution, PLMGN1*

In sharing this opinion, the expert emphasised the need for learning the wider context of forced migrants' decisions regarding, in particular, onward mobility. Such information should be provided to both the general public and public officials, including Border Guard officers who almost solely see persons lacking visas and asking for asylum at the border—arriving from more distant territories than the neighbouring countries—as abusers of the asylum system. And such a postulate, together with a call for insightful study of the reasons for leaving home countries, was supported by other human rights campaigners taking part in a group discussion or individual interviews. Indirectly, the need for applying a wider perspective when investigating the reasons for entering Poland with a will to apply for international protection was also stated in the domestic and international case law. The judicial assessment of the conduct towards forced migrants at the Polish eastern border assumed deliberate misinterpretation of reasons declared by potential asylum applicants at the border, supposedly proved by laconic official notes prepared by border guards, reducing the declared reasons to economic motives (Białas et al., 2019; Szulecka, 2022). Forced migrants' claims regarding experiences that could be considered as prerequisites for granting international protection (described above) seemed often ignored, just because of the common belief that those approaching Polish borders are not "genuine refugees".

Onward Mobility and Poland as a (Second Choice) Destination for Forced Migrants

The fact that the majority of the migrant interviewees experienced a transfer from other EU countries to Polish territory under the Dublin Regulation[5] indicates that Poland was not the preferred destination. Forced migrants first applying for asylum in Poland requested international protection also in other states or were apprehended in an irregular situation there. The common explanation given by the Polish authorities indicates the economic attractiveness of assistance provided to asylum applicants in other EU states or access to medical treatment seen as better than in Poland. However, based on the empirical data, it is necessary to highlight the crucial pull factor, which is the presence of family members or communities of co-ethnics in certain states. Chechen asylum seekers, predominant in Poland until 2020, used to go to Western Europe during the asylum procedure or even after obtaining any kind of protection in Poland. However, the established pattern of both reaching Polish territory to ask for asylum by Chechens and the presence of beneficiaries of international protection or other forms of protection originating from Chechnya in Poland led to the development of a Chechen community also in Poland. This may convince other Chechens to try their chances and adapt to Poland. One of the Chechen male interviewees admitted:

> I decided to come to Poland because I knew Poland welcomed Chechen asylum seekers. For a hundred percent, I believed that in Poland they would accept and help me. [...] among Chechens, up-to-date information about the situation in Europe or Poland is cycling around. I have chosen Poland because it is not far and not close. And there are also many Chechens, so I could eventually count on their help.
>
> *PLMICh09*

However, the presence of other Chechens in the destination country is not advantageous for everyone. Due to the previously mentioned lack of trust and constant fears of being "transferred" from Poland to their home country, some Chechen asylum seekers prefer to limit their contacts to the closest family members present in Poland. They are afraid that the knowledge about their place of stay may bring about threats to their safety, for example, if they are single mothers who ran away from Chechnya where they were at risk of violent treatment from ex-husbands or male relatives.

Apart from the Chechens who constitute an important group of forced migrants in Poland, in fact, until 2020,[6] there were no other distinct refugee groups that could be a strong pull factor for asylum seekers from other countries in crisis, such as Syria, Yemen, or Iraq. There were citizens of these countries among the beneficiaries of international protection granted by Poland or among holders of residence permits, but they did not constitute communities that forced migrants could see as a potential source of support. Therefore, as our interviews confirmed, Poland is chosen as a destination country by other asylum seekers than citizens of the neighbouring countries (Russia, Ukraine, and Belarus) usually only when the close family members are already present in Poland or another EU state relatively close to Poland. Poland becomes a second choice country if there are no chances for legalisation of stay (based on residence permits or international protection) in the preferred countries providing, allegedly, better assistance to their close families. The quote from a Syrian man confirms the crucial role of family connections in deciding where to go or where to stay, but also indicates how Poland eventually became the destination:

> [...] the reason that I wanted to leave Syria was to stay with my children. I was not thinking of Poland or Germany ... I wanted to stay with my children, in any country. We applied in Sweden for asylum. There, they received us normally just like any citizen, any person coming to apply for asylum there, we submitted our papers and we stayed. Ten months after applying for asylum they sent us a reply, that "here you go, we found out that you have a visa, that you have fingerprints in Poland". [...] We said: "Well, what's the solution now?" They said, "We will correspond with Poland, if Poland wants you, then we will send you to Poland, if they don't want you, then we will keep you here". [...] After one month they sent us a reply that "Poland agreed to receive you. So we will deport you to Poland". [...] They said that they don't want to give us visas, ah, residency in Sweden, so what could we do?
>
> *PLMISy24*

Interestingly, the presence of refugees from the same region or country is not always a factor increasing the attractiveness of a certain destination. The reasons are not only the already mentioned lack of trust, for example, in the Chechen context. As declared by one of the migrant interviewees, the possibility to live without the label of a refugee may be of great value, bigger than any material assistance offered. Such an approach can be exemplified by the experience of a Syrian man, who described his journey to Poland through Greece:

> When I was in Greece I already decided that I would go to Poland, but I couldn't do it so I came to Berlin by accident. [...] I bought a fake ID and booked a flight. [...] It was an Italian ID. I tried once [to go to Poland] but I was caught at the airport. In Greece. [moderator's question: "And then you decided to come to Poland, not to stay in Berlin?"] [...] Because Berlin, for a refugee, is not my favourite place. I mean I like it, it's more dynamic than Poland, but to stay there as a refugee I wouldn't go. Because I don't want to be labelled as a refugee. Like I don't want this label to follow me and the paperwork and everything in general. In Poland, there are fewer, fewer, fewer refugees. [...] I can avoid categorisation here, but in Berlin, I would always be categorised as "the refugee" or "the Syrian" or something like that.
>
> *PLMISy23*

In general, however, the issues determining the choices of asylum seekers, apart from border controls and accessibility of legal paths, are related to the presence of a potential source of support in adaptation, that is, families or friends already granted residence permits or international protection, or at least communities originating from the same regions and cultures, constituting the promise of easier adaptation (see also Koser, 1997).

In this context, the case of asylum seekers from Ukraine should be mentioned. Indeed, Ukrainian citizens were already the most numerous migrant group in Poland before the war, as they constituted at least a third of all foreign nationals granted any kind of residence permit in Poland (including those based on international or domestic protection). The crucial thing is, however, that the vast majority of Ukrainian citizens came to Poland for work, education, or family-related reasons.[7] Asylum seekers used to constitute a very small share of Ukrainian citizens coming to Poland. In their case, the presence of a Ukrainian migrant community in Poland was not necessarily the decisive factor in choosing Poland as a place to request asylum. Rather it was cultural and language proximity, and—even more important—geographic proximity and well-established transportation routes between the two countries, coupled with the relatively wide catalogue of legal paths accessible for Ukrainian citizens willing to enter Poland. Therefore, reaching Poland and requesting international protection was simply easier for Ukrainian citizens (and since 2020 also for Belarusian citizens, as mentioned in Chapter 4). Moreover, the pressure to leave Poland to seek options for legalisation in other EU countries was much lower than, for instance, persons from Chechnya, Iraq, or Syria. This does not exclude Ukrainians' aspirations to reach other countries that seem to be more attractive in economic terms, as in the case of a Ukrainian family with two small children from the Donetsk region that eventually decided to stay in Poland, where they were granted subsidiary protection:

> Well, languages are similar, Polish with Ukrainian [...] I was thinking about going to Germany [...] But what are we going to do there? We don't know English that much ... I understand that one can learn everything, but we've

> wanted to wait till the war would come to an end. So, we are going to wait there [in Poland]. Poland's close and Poland and Ukraine are like "brother countries".
>
> *PLMIUk16*

Nonetheless, for the majority of asylum seekers, Western or Scandinavian European countries still seemed more attractive. They tried to get there directly and ask for asylum in case they had other possibilities to reach EU territory, for example, based on a visa or in an irregular manner. The case of Syrians invited to the wedding of a relative can serve as an example here:

> Well, my brother had a wedding here and we actually came to Poland after having obtained a visa to attend his wedding. It was in 2012 [...] after one week or 10 days from that, we decided, me and my family, to go and try maybe in Germany, because, as we heard at the beginning from the people around, the refugee application in Poland is going to be hard and it's tough for the people to adjust here [in Poland]. So we decided; okay let's try to go to Germany. And we had some friends in Germany that could support us and tell us where to go ...
>
> *PLMISy21*

As mentioned above, the fact that Poland is treated as a transit country affects the practices of control at the border and the practices of receiving asylum applicants within the territory, especially after their returns to Poland under the Dublin Regulation. As legal experts among the interviewees emphasised, the common assumption shared by state bureaucrats that asking for asylum in Poland is only a short-term strategy of legalisation of entry onto the EU territory and stay in Poland means that both access to the asylum procedure and the course of it lack attention to the merits. Thus, people who seek protection may experience additional stigmatisation or even victimisation, for instance, when persons who survived state-based violence are placed in detention centres, which may only deepen their trauma (Helsińska Fundacja Praw Człowieka, n.d.; Ombudsman Office, 2018).

The way the authorities treat asylum applicants and even persons granted any form of protection may also have an impact on decisions to leave Poland and, if possible, to enjoy a more welcoming approach elsewhere. Thus, the government's perceptions may constitute a kind of "push out" factor contributing to the onward mobility (Klaus and Pachocka, 2019). However, if decisions on leaving Poland are taken before the asylum claim is processed by Polish authorities, there is high exposure to detection of unlawful stay in other countries, followed by transfer back to Poland under the Dublin Regulation. Upon their return to Poland, asylum seekers are usually subjected to detention, which is adjudicated by the courts at the request of the Border Guard. Importantly, such motions are justified by the argument that the forced migrant concerned tried to enter Poland unlawfully, which means in fact attempts to enter Poland without a visa but with the intent to ask for asylum (for more, see below).

One of the interviewed legal practitioners aptly reflected on the context in which forced migrants exercise their agency towards the common perceptions of them as "bogus" asylum seekers and administrative practices based on them:

> Would I stay [in Poland], if I came to Poland with the knowledge I have? Probably I would not stay because I could not count on any procedural guarantees. Six months without work? Surely, no. Lack of assistance in integration and 70 PLN[8] pocket money per month, taking into account the growth of prices of cigarettes … These are things that push [people] out. There is no sense in staying here. Here, the desperately poor people, single mothers bringing up their children, running away from their families, and unable to join their families elsewhere may stay. […] Other people must really experience this route[9] on their own to see that they will be returned [from other countries], that no one wants them in Germany, no one wants them in France. […] But [there are those] who could introduce changes, give the right to work at the very beginning of the asylum procedure, then they will have more opportunities to integrate. Maybe [they could] increase the amount of pocket money, which is at the moment a scandal.
>
> *legal practitioner from NGO, PLMGN1*

Even if the above quote points to economic aspects as determinants of onward mobility, it draws attention to two very important issues: procedural guarantees and opportunity structure to integrate into the host society (see more in Chapters 7 and 8). Even if in other countries forced migrants are not always welcome, the communities of co-ethnics may compensate for the lack of special integration programmes or social support. In case there is a lack of such support (no family or other close and trusted persons to whom forced migrants may turn), asylum seekers depend on the approach of both the host society and the authorities of the host states. One of the Chechen asylum applicants described his experiences and expressed understanding of other asylum seekers willing to leave Poland:

> When I came here I experienced some very unwelcoming moments with people here. They treated me not always well. So imagine, if refugees who come here will see that society is not welcoming them and don't want to have them here, they will be frustrated and not willing to integrate. There is no need to push people away just because they have different nationalities and religions. Nobody will just leave the country for their pleasure. People are forced to move out and have to find support and understanding from society. The homeland is the best place but when circumstances do not allow you to stay in your homeland you have to find another place.
>
> *PLMICh09*

This quote brings to the fore the main aspect often forgotten or misinterpreted by the authorities. The phenomenon of onward mobility is not only an answer to the low level of social assistance (see Chapter 7) or problems in accessing proper medical or psychological treatment (see Chapter 9). It is driven by a complex set of factors, some of which depend solely on political decisions, such as support for the practices deterring asylum seekers at the border ("push back" factors, Klaus and Pachocka, 2019). And even if onward mobility is eventually the decision of forced migrants, it seems, based on the accounts of migrant interviewees, that these decisions could be influenced in many ways. For some people, the supportive attitudes encountered in a different context—in the neighbourhood, at work, when contacting non-governmental organisations—could convince them to stay in Poland. In this light, the first contacts with Polish state representatives at the border cannot be ignored.

Access to the Asylum Procedure at the Eastern Border

Since 2016,[10] persons presenting at the eastern border of Poland (being at the same time the external border of the EU) and lacking documents authorising them to enter Poland have been more and more often refused entry and thus access to the asylum procedure. And with few exceptions,[11] asylum seekers had no documents (to be more specific, visas) allowing their entry onto Polish or EU territory, although they usually possessed identity documents facilitating Polish authorities the control procedures. Nevertheless, when persons lacking valid visas reached the border checkpoints at the eastern border, it happened that their declarations of the will to apply for asylum were either "not heard" or were misinterpreted and ignored. Whereas misinterpretation was confirmed by courts at the domestic and international levels (Białas et al., 2019; Szulecka, 2022),[12] from the migrants' perspective, the practice of refusing entry was simply an act of ignoring their request for asylum and sending them back to the country where they were neither safe nor could stay for a long time due to procedural or financial reasons.

Notably, the refusals of entry were issued to asylum seekers repeatedly, especially at the border checkpoint that for two decades served as the main entry point for asylum seekers to Poland,[13] namely the railway checkpoint at Brest/Terespol at the border with Belarus (Białas et al., 2019; Chrzanowska et al., 2016; Górczyńska and Szczepanik, 2016; Szczepanik, 2018). Forced migrants' accounts referring to "blocked" access to the asylum procedure often mention this checkpoint, which attracted the attention of human rights campaigners, especially in circumstances when people experienced not just a few but sometimes dozens of attempts to enter Poland and ask for asylum. With time, after 2015, incidents of refusing entry to potential asylum applicants were reported also at other checkpoints on the eastern border,[14] especially the one in Shegynie/Medyka at the border with Ukraine, which in 2014 (and subsequently in 2022) became an important entry point for persons leaving Ukraine to seek asylum in the EU. Thus, the eastern border as such[15] became associated with the deterrence practices deployed towards asylum seekers in the post-2015 context.

Such practices were usually not connected with asylum claims submitted in other places, in particular Warsaw. They concerned usually non-nationals transferred back to Poland under the Dublin Regulation and, in rare cases, applications received from persons detained in the guarded centres upon the detection of their unlawful stay in Poland and initiation of the return procedure. Asylum applications submitted at airports, especially in Warsaw, in rare cases also concerned persons who were travelling by plane to another destination but with a stop in Warsaw. In that case, the person left the airport transit zone and turned to the Border Guard to ask for asylum in Poland.

According to arguments given by the Border Guard and the Ministry of Interior, refusals of entry were justified by the need to prevent uncontrolled and irregular migration, as well as to prevent abuse of the asylum procedure (Szulecka, 2019, 2016). Although for many of the interviewed forced migrants, Poland was not the preferred destination, the geopolitical position of this country meant that approaching their final destination (especially Germany, Austria, France, or Scandinavian countries) required reaching Poland first. Regardless of whether Poland was treated by forced migrants as a primary or second choice, the greatest challenge faced by them was access to Polish territory, especially since mid-2015. The vast majority of migrant interviewees experienced several "pushbacks" at the railway checkpoint in Terespol on the border with Belarus. Being refused entry and the possibility to apply for asylum became common, but not always an understandable experience for many asylum seekers; to the extent that being let in on the first attempt of entering Poland and asking for asylum became more a surprise than fully expected, stemming from the law in force, the consequence of requesting protection upon the border check (Szulecka, 2022).

Thus, every case of an asylum applicant who was let into Polish territory and whose application for asylum was received by the Border Guard upon the first attempt to enter Poland in Terespol seemed confusing or surprising. Even these individuals who had the experience of being let in on the first attempt perceived it in terms of being lucky rather than of exercising their right to asylum. A single mother from Chechnya crossing the border with her children, having no visas for this purpose, admitted:

> I knew that sometimes it was necessary to make several attempts to cross the border. I was ready for this, but they didn't tell me to go back. They let me cross the border at once.
>
> *PLMCh01*

In this case, according to the interviewee, how the border guards viewed her condition and that of her children was decisive. Other asylum seekers were not sure of the factors determining the decision on both refusing and allowing entry. For some it was a matter of luck, others admitted that they did not understand the decisions of the border guards. As one Chechen woman who was crossing the border with her children and husband emphasised, on every attempt at entering

Poland they possessed the same documents and declared the same reasons for entering Poland:

> They [the border guards] asked us where we were going and why. I thought they would let us in, but they didn't. We had to go back. [...] My husband was very tired and nervous. The same situation happened four times, with the same questions and the same answers. For the fifth time, it was the same woman officer who met us for the first time. When she took our passports and told us to go upstairs[16] I couldn't believe it. I thought she was joking. She let us in. Some people are let in during their first attempt. Some people are not. There were people with us who had been trying to cross the border for one month. Some of them had six or seven children. [...] I thought they would let us in at once but it turned out that we had to make five attempts to cross the border.
>
> *PLMICh02*

From the perspective of legal experts, the very lack of transparency is not the only problem faced by forced migrants approaching the border checkpoint. The greatest challenge in exercising human rights at the border, including the right to asylum, was the fact that during the border check, the border guards made assessments about whose declarations of will to apply for asylum would be respected and those whose would not be (see also Białas et al., 2019; Górczyńska and Szczepanik, 2016). In legal terms, the Border Guard is responsible only for the reception of asylum applications and passing it on to the competent authority, the Office for Foreigners, which is responsible for deciding whether the request for asylum is justified or not. Nevertheless, everyday conduct towards people lacking visas at the main entry point for asylum seekers included discretionary decisions on who "deserved" the possibility to enter Poland and apply for protection and who did not.

Despite the developing domestic and international case law indicating abuse of the competences of the Border Guard or improper administrative conduct (lack of written reports reflecting the course of preliminary interviews during the border check), the practices towards potential asylum applicants did not change (Szulecka, 2022). This led not only non-governmental actors but also some representatives of public institutions to conclude that the repeated refusals of entry issued to potential asylum applicants are an element of official policy. One representative of the public institutions involved in monitoring respect for human rights aptly described the state of play, saying that refusals of entry issued to persons seeking asylum are "branded by the courts, by the doctrine, but it does not change the practice of the [Border] Guard, which act according to instructions from the very top" (MGN1). Such a stance was confirmed by the European Court of Human Rights in the case of M.K. and Others v. Poland issued on 23 July 2020, in which multiple refusals of entry issued to three Chechen families were seen as an expression of a wider policy aimed at deterring asylum seekers (European Court of Human Rights, 2020). Despite other complaints submitted to ECtHR and other judgements confirming human rights infringements, efforts by human rights campaigners to improve access to the asylum procedure at the eastern border were undermined by the Polish authorities. The latter kept defending or even encouraging the practices observed at the border as a necessary step to prevent uncontrolled migration and abuse of the asylum procedure (Klaus, 2017; Szulecka, 2019, 2016). One of the interviewed representatives of civil society organisations briefly characterised access to the asylum procedure at the Polish eastern border this way: "[It] is aimed at deterring people, not to allow them to ask for protection. It is highly determined by the politics" (PLMZSO02).

The (Interrupted) Asylum Procedure

Waiting for the Outcome of the Asylum Procedure

According to the law, the decision on asylum applications should be issued within six months, but if there is a need to continue investigation of the case, the procedure may be prolonged. And many asylum seekers experienced this, although, as the representative of the Office for Foreigners claimed (e.g., PLMZOF02), Office employees make a great effort to stick to the terms stated in the law. Especially in periods when the numbers of asylum applicants dropped significantly (2017–2020), it seemed that completing the asylum procedures (in the first instance) within half a year was feasible. As exemplified by the expert interviewees, there are instances in which asylum applications, the examination of which is very complex, require repeated interviews with asylum applicants or are prolonged due to the need to verify new facts or new circumstances either declared by the applicant or revealed when studying the situation in the country of origin.

Regardless of the difficulties linked to the investigation of asylum claims in some cases, it should be emphasised that the periods of waiting for the decisions usually constitute a difficult experience for forced migrants. This is the case in particular, for persons undergoing proceedings that are prolonged for an extreme time, as in the case of a Chechen man who was waiting more than three years for a decision on his first asylum application. He came to Poland, alone, in 2015, when he was threatened in the Caucasus with prison for criminal offences that he did not commit. Persecution by the state authorities also affected his parents, whose house was regularly searched to find the interviewee. It is possible that the period of waiting for the decision in his case was affected by the number of applications submitted in the year when he asked for asylum. It was in 2015, when the number of applicants amounted to 12,000, which is one of the highest numbers in Poland's contemporary history of forced migration governance. As this man claimed, he waited for the decision, hoping that it would be positive. He admitted, however, that it was not fully clear to him why the period of waiting was so long and suggested that:

> I think an asylum seeker would feel good if someone from the authorities informed him/her about the reasons [for issuing a certain decision] which

> would help them to know about the period of time to get a positive decision. If he or she could know about this, they would breathe a sigh of relief and have some hope. Now you don't know what could have an impact on their decision. This uncertainty gives you feeling of discomfort.
>
> *PLMICh15*

The harshness of the waiting period may be mitigated by the opportunities offered to asylum applicants in Poland. Although the scope of monetary social assistance is seen as much less attractive than in, for instance, Germany or France, forced migrants appreciate the possibility to work in Poland legally in the course of the asylum procedure, in case the decision is not issued within a half year after the asylum claim was submitted (for more, see Chapter 8). Waiting for the decision still gives some hope that it will be positive. And this waiting period is spent outside the country of origin, which in turn contributes to the sense of safety. This should be, however, accompanied by some forms of activity, depending on age, the phase of the asylum procedure, and accessible forms of involvement.

As regards waiting for the decision on the asylum procedure, the crucial issue is the already mentioned uncertainty about the outcome. Information passed within refugee communities regarding the chances of being granted (or denied) international protection can sometimes contribute to unjustified fears or hopes (as well as to decisions to move to other countries). Asylum applicants tend to focus more on what is said by other asylum seekers than on the information that is provided by the officials. The latter, however, may not be easy to understand. To address this problem, asylum seekers are offered the possibility to consult their cases either with the employees of the Office for Foreigners or with the employees of civil society organisations offering legal aid. To be able to take advantage of this offer, forced migrants need information about such a possibility, which is not always the case, especially among newly arrived asylum seekers who have no previous experience of seeking asylum in Poland. An additional problem to be mentioned in the post-2015 context is the reduction of funds accessible to civil society organisations dedicated to assisting migrants and asylum seekers (Klaus et al., 2017; see also Chapter 8).

Asylum Procedure Involving Additional Control Measures

As already discussed, the onward mobility of asylum applicants who applied for international protection first in Poland is a common phenomenon. It concerns both leaving Poland during the asylum procedure or after it ends in a negative decision. The authorities see this as confirmation that forced migrants are in fact not interested in obtaining protection in Poland and try their chances in other countries that they consider more attractive. These arguments are, however, insufficient to explain the treatment received by forced migrants during the asylum or return procedures. One of the interviewed Chechen women, who came to Poland with her child, described her contacts with the border guards in Poland and border police in Germany (where she went while the asylum procedure was conducted in Poland).

She described how she discovered that either the border guards interviewing her earlier or the interpreter did not include the most important information explaining the reasons for her escape from Chechnya, namely the threat to her life posed by her ex-husband and male relatives, stemming from Sharia law, binding in Chechen society. The fact that this information was not included in the interview protocols almost led to the decision on her deportation to Chechnya. The interview protocols instead included general information about her family problems, which resulted in a negative decision on her first asylum claims. The omission of such crucial facts among the declared reasons for seeking asylum in Europe was noticed by border guards other than the ones who interviewed the woman for the asylum purposes and interpreted it as a possible deliberate action. The asylum seeker shared this view:

> I think that they do it on purpose. If they did their best and tried to understand me, if they wrote down everything, what I said, it would be different. They omitted the main thing. They wrote down, when I came and for what reason, but they wrote "She was in danger in Chechnya, because of the situation with her husband and with her child", but it I was not [being] in danger. I would be dead, if I had stayed in Chechnya. That's the truth. When the two men [...] read my protocol, they started to swear, they said "[...] they did it on purpose. We should tell them to come back and to rewrite this protocol". They said to me "You never read your protocols and they know it, that's why they write whatever they want. If they wrote exactly, what you said you would have received the status of asylum long time ago.
>
> *PLMICh03*

Ascribing "bad will" to asylum seekers seems to be an immanent feature of dealing with asylum applicants who gave up their asylum procedures and were eventually apprehended by border services in other states. Upon being sent back to Poland under the Dublin Regulation, they have to deal not only with their uncertain legal status (and risk of being deported to the country of origin), but they also have to face being perceived as "bogus" asylum seekers, as they are almost automatically seen by the state as a potential threat to public order. This, in turn, entails applying additional control measures.

For persons denied access to the asylum procedure at the border, who have been rejected for international protection and willing to appeal against these decisions, and, last but not least, detained in guarded centres for foreigners due to the "risk of absconding", as identified by the authorities, access to legal advice is particularly important. According to representatives of NGOs interviewed for the purpose of our study, the situation of those detained may be the most difficult. It happens that they are not only within the asylum procedure (usually the consecutive one) but also within the return procedure, initiated upon detection of their unauthorised stay in Poland. As claimed by one of the legal professionals representing NGO, the procedures towards such people are conducted in a way disrespecting the special needs of migrants. The issues of unauthorised border crossing and an alleged abuse of the asylum procedure seem to influence administrative decisions more than the circumstances of leaving the country of origin or reasons for asking for international protection in Poland or in another country (PLMZSO03).

Based on the statements of interviewees as expressed in our empirical study, for the asylum applicants reapplying for international protection and transferred under Dublin Regulations to Poland, waiting for the decision may be equated with being detained or subjected to measures alternative to detention (such as reporting regularly to the Border Guard). Even if isolative or non-isolative measures are eventually not applied, asylum applicants are threatened with being subjected to them. Such threats either came from the border guards themselves, who took part in their apprehensions or control activities, or are part of information transferred among asylum seekers having experience or broader knowledge of how the asylum system in Poland operates. A Chechen asylum applicant apprehended in another EU country after leaving Poland during the asylum procedure conducted in Poland reflected on her experiences related to the Dublin transfer and its consequences:

> The deportation itself was not so awful, but we were not aware that we were breaking the law. We had no idea. We were afraid to be placed in a closed camp. This is depriving you of your freedom like a criminal. We were afraid of that most. [...] We told them [the border guards after being escorted to the Polish border] that we didn't want to leave Poland, we wanted to apply for asylum. We were not put in a prison to my great happiness. It was the happiest day of my life. [Q (moderator's question): "Who told you that you could have been put to prison?"] R: The border guards. It depends on the border guards. I don't know what it depends on. Some people are put to prison, others are not. We didn't have passports with us.
>
> *PLMICh05*

Referring to the statements given by both asylum seekers and representatives of social organisations, detention centres in Poland are rightly associated with prisons—there are guardians and various barriers limiting the possibility to move around. There is no free access to such centres and persons detained there cannot leave them freely. Persons experiencing arrest and imprisonment in their home countries may be particularly exposed to mental harm triggered by isolation and restricted liberty. An asylum seeker from Yemen transferred to Poland under the Dublin Regulation from Germany stated:

> [...][I] actually heard that there, there is prison, so I was in a very bad psychological state because I was imprisoned for a year and 6 months, I mean ... [...] I relied on God, it was inside of me, I was wishing that the ground would open up and swallow me but not to return to the situation which I was in in the beginning, I mean, it is a very big problem for me, I mean, I was suffering because I went into prison ... [moderator's question: "Who told you that

> there could be a prison?"] People, people there from Yemen [...] people in Germany who were with us at the camp.
>
> *PLMIJe29*

According to legal professionals, the courts that decide about the detention usually accept the motions of the Border Guard and very rarely make a thorough assessment, whether in each and every case detaining a person is a necessary measure (AIDA, 2020; Białas, 2014; Szulecka, 2019). Certainly, it is a measure aimed at deterring asylum seekers, and thus may be treated as another "push out" factor (Klaus and Pachocka, 2019), whereas it should be treated as a measure of last resort to secure the administrative procedure (not as discouragement to not participate in it). Even if the conditions in the detention centres are acceptable and the personnel put efforts to mitigate the harms posed by the isolation (as confirmed by the NGO representatives), for any person, being deprived of liberty is an undesirable experience. In the case of forced migrants, it equates to feelings of being "punished" despite the lack of involvement in any criminal activity. One NGO representative commented on how asylum seekers recall being sent to the detention centres in Poland:

> [...] in fact, every person feels bad behind bars. This is the main problem—the lack of liberty. It [administrative detention] will always mean that a person who committed no crime is deprived of liberty for a few months. And even if you offer the best treatment you can, this person cannot understand why she/he sits behind bars.
>
> *PLMZSO01*

Being behind bars is certainly not understandable for children, who are placed in the detention centres together with their parents identified by the authorities as proving the high risk of absconding. And even if in recent years, according to the interviewed lawyers, the courts or the border guards more often decide to apply non-isolative measures, still families with children are detained, which raises serious concerns among human rights campaigners. Children are placed on premises with proper facilities for their age and needs (e.g., playgrounds), guaranteeing access to educational activities. Still, however, they remain in a closed-off area (Centrum Pomocy Prawnej im. Haliny Nieć, n.d.; Majcher et al., 2020; Niedźwiedzki et al., 2021).

In the context of detention, the deficiencies of the identification procedures should be mentioned. According to the law in force (as stated in Chapter 4), certain categories of foreign nationals, such as victims of torture and violence, cannot be placed in guarded centres for foreigners. It happens, however, that people are identified as belonging to such a category when they are already isolated. According to the interviewed experts, it also happens that despite negative prerequisites to be detained (e.g., health condition), they are sent to the guarded centres. Placing forced migrants in detention centres also should be considered from an economic perspective. Even if detention is treated as a measure allowing for effective performance of return decisions and prevention of irregular onward mobility (Szulecka, 2019), it both incurs emotional costs (or harms) on the side of asylum applicants and a financial cost on the side of the Polish authorities. An employee of a public institution in Poland emphasised that:

> I don't know how the Border Guard assess the so-called risk of absconding. But if there is no "Dublin record" taking a hundred pages and they can decide to apply the alternative [measure], I suppose that from both the perspective of costs and the mental health of the foreigner, alternative [measures] are better. If there is really no need to detain [a person].
>
> *PLMZOF01*

Based on the experiences of forced migrants subjected to additional measures of control (apprehension, Dublin transfer, detention or non-isolative measures securing the course of the asylum procedure), it has to be stressed that such measures are usually deployed towards people who had already experienced some forms of oppression. It is not fully clear whether such control measures—if perceived as "push out" factors—allow the authorities to achieve the goal of deterring asylum seekers. For some forced migrants, these are the unavoidable costs of finding the safety and better conditions. The fact that they bear this cost questions the common perception of asylum seekers as bogus or as economic migrants and instead shows how much a person can bear to avoid being returned to the country of origin.

Conclusions

Despite relatively common beliefs among the public administration in Poland associating forced migrants with the idea of "bogus" asylum seekers and economic migrants (Adamczyk, 2021; Zespół do Spraw Migracji, Ministerstwo Spraw Wewnętrznych, 2021, 2012), the asylum seekers interviewed within this project stated that, even if economic motives were among the drivers of their mobility, it usually meant the motivation to leave a country where military, political, or economic crises devastated the economy, made public goods or services inaccessible, or there was no possibility to access even basic healthcare or clean water and food. The key factors forcing people to leave their countries of origin are rather linked to threats to one's safety and physical or mental condition, affected by political repression or the risk of it, persecution due to political views or religion, or unjust treatment (including unjustified detention or forced "disappearance") by the state in reaction to activity opposing the authorities in a given country (in the studied cases, this refers mostly to the Caucasus region of Russia, namely Chechnya). The reason behind the decisions to leave their homes and undertake sometimes difficult journeys to destination countries also includes gender-based violence and femicide. The interviewed single mothers pointed to various forms of violence experienced by them and their children, and the need to seek freedom from violence outside their homes, in the countries and environments where the binding law does not allow any form of violence towards women.

The accounts of the forced migrants' and experts' opinions presented in this chapter show deficiencies in guaranteeing access to asylum in Poland. As the interviewed experts emphasised, the mentioned reasons for mobility are important at the stage of assessing asylum claims submitted by forced migrants to Polish authorities, but not at the stage of receiving asylum applications. Indeed, if the experiences referred to as reasons for asking for asylum in Poland were linked to domestic violence and strictly economic motives, asylum applicants could hardly expect positive decisions. The positive scenario (meaning the possibility to stay outside the country of origin) in the cases of people coming from regions seen as free from ongoing military conflicts (such as Chechnya or Iraq at present) entailed repeated asylum applications, and in rare cases being granted a form of international protection (more often the subsidiary one) or national protection in Poland. Waiting for these decisions and uncertainty regarding the result, combined with assistance during the asylum procedure seen as relatively poor, are certainly a difficult experience. However, in the Polish context, much more difficult—sometimes even more than traumatic experiences—concerned the access to the asylum procedure at the checkpoints at the external eastern EU border between 2016 and 2019.[17] There is evidence coming from various sources (empirical studies, human rights-related interventions, court verdicts) that, lacking a legal basis to do so, the reasons why an asylum seeker is wanting international protection were assessed at border checkpoints, effectively deciding whether the person could submit an application or not.

The situation of potential asylum applicants before 2016 was also not advantageous, as they often experienced refusals of entry when trying to enter Poland and apply for asylum at the main entry point for asylum applicants at that time, that is, the border checkpoint at Brest/Terespol. Before 2016, however, the deterrence practices towards potential asylum applicants were quite effectively negotiated by social organisations acting for human rights and migrants in general. Since 2016, as expressed by human rights campaigners, the deterrence practices observed at the border became not only common but also accepted or even encouraged by the state authorities, despite the fact that according to the law in force they were not acceptable. It seems that also forced migrants became adjusted to the idea that to ask for asylum at the eastern border of Poland, one must be prepared for numerous attempts to enter Polish territory and numerous "pushbacks" to the territory of the neighbouring state (most often Belarus).

Another issue worth attention is the situation of people whose asylum procedure was discontinued and then renewed, usually after their return from another EU country under the Dublin Regulation. Although such people were allowed to re-apply for international protection in Poland, their experiences, including the "Dublin record", meant that they were treated by the authorities as potential irregular migrants, for whom the procedures (both for asylum and return) should be secured by placing them in detention centres or subjecting them to restrictive measures alternative to detention. Such practices are allowed by the law in force; however, it is of note that in practice, they are applied towards people who are in difficult situations by the very characteristics of their status as asylum seekers with limited or no possibilities to return to their home countries, and often with experience with various forms of violence. Especially in the latter situation, placing people in detention centres is in breach of the law. There is evidence, however, that insufficient attention to the motions on detention submitted to the courts by the Border Guard has led to the excessive use of detention. In theory, it is to be used as a preventive measure (prevention of absconding), but in practice (especially from forced migrants' perspective), it is as punishment for leaving Poland before the completion of the asylum procedure.

Based on both forced migrants' opinions and opinions shared by experts, the economic aspects of the scope of protection offered in certain countries matter and may determine the mobility paths of asylum seekers. However, these are not isolated drivers of onward mobility. The latter is determined by the presence of family or ethnic communities in the most preferred destinations that may offer support, even in case the host state will not be welcoming and supportive. Among the drivers, one may also indicate the transparency of administrative procedure, shaping both the grounds for trust and distrust towards public administration. If public administration is seen as responsible for reproducing harm or even symbolic violence, it is very probable that persons experiencing this will not be willing to subject themselves to the rules they should obey as asylum applicants. Of importance also are all expressions of support addressed to both asylum seekers and those already granted any form of protection. They may be linked with state policies and practices (which was, however, not the case of Poland in the border control context), but they may also refer to the activity of non-governmental sectors that help forced migrants navigate numerous administrative barriers they encounter.

Notes

1 Due to the scope of this chapter, three interviews with practitioners and two interviews with local governors were not included in the analysis of the expert opinions.
2 The one organised on 10 December 2018.
3 The analysis informing the chapter was finalised in December 2021, which is before the full scale Russian invasion of Ukraine started on 24 February 2022, which resulted in a massive inflow of refugees from Ukraine to Poland and other European states, and consequently in special policy responses and *ad hoc* practices aimed at facilitating the mobility and legalisation of persons fleeing the war in Ukraine.
4 Altogether, there were 8 women of Chechen origin in the group of 30 migrant interviews in the RESPOND project.
5 It concerned 17 migrant interviewees (out of 30), 13 of whom were Chechen nationals.
6 When Belarusian citizens started coming to Poland to seek asylum and became predominant among the asylum applicants in Poland. This concerns also 2021.
7 Before 24 February 2022 when the mass inflow of refugees from Ukraine almost reached the annual number of economic migrants in Poland within one week.

8 Approximately EUR 15.
9 Onward mobility after submitting an asylum application in Poland.
10 Until the Russian invasion of Ukraine on 24 February 2022 and subsequent mass refugee mobility.
11 Applying usually to citizens of neighbouring Ukraine and Belarus, as well as rare examples of asylum seekers from the Middle East who obtained visas allowing their entrance into the EU.
12 Detailed descriptions of such practices may be found in ECtHR judgements, such as M.K and Others vs Poland (ECtHR, 23.07.2020), D.A. and Others vs Poland (ECtHR, 8.07.2021).
13 Until mid-2021 when a considerable share of asylum applications were submitted by non-nationals who crossed the "green border" in an unauthorised manner. Still, however, the majority of applications were received from persons arriving through the border checkpoints or within the territory from persons staying in Poland legally, for example, based on visas.
14 See, e.g., application no. 54029/17 to ECtHR (Sherov v Poland), communicated on 16 December 2020.
15 Before mid-2021, i.e., before the intensified attempts of crossing the "green border", this concerned mostly the checkpoints, not the border itself as such.
16 Due to the organisation of the Border Guard premises, being referred "upstairs" is equal to being let into Poland and having the asylum application received at the border checkpoint.
17 Our empirical study did not cover the experiences of forced migrants stuck at the Polish-Belarusian border in the second half of 2021 ("Humanitarian crisis at the Polish-Belarusian border. Report by Grupa Granica", 2021).

References

Adamczyk, A., 2021. Procesy migracyjne w Polsce a aktywność państwa w sferze bezpieczeństwa. *Rocznik Instytutu Europy Środkowo-Wschodniej*, 19, 261–278.

AIDA, 2020. *Country Report: Poland – 2020 update*. Asylum Information Database (AIDA).

Białas, J., 2014. Automatyzm w stosowaniu detencji cudzoziemców, in: Poszukiwaniu Ochrony, W. (Ed.), *Wybrane Problemy Dotyczące Realizacji Praw Cudzoziemców Ubiegających o Nadanie Statusu Uchodźcy i Objętych Ochroną Międzynarodową w Latach 2012–2014. Obserwacje Programu Pomocy Prawnej Dla Uchodźców i Migrantów Helsińskiej Fundacji Praw Człowieka*. Helsińska Fundacja Praw Człowieka, Warszawa, pp. 61–63.

Białas, J., Górczyńska, M., Witko, D., 2019. *Access to asylum procedure at Poland's external borders. Current situation and challenges for the future*. Helsinki Foundation for Human Rights, Warsaw.

Centrum Pomocy Prawnej im. Haliny Nieć, n.d. *Detencja dzieci cudzoziemskich w Polsce* [WWW Document]. Centrum Pomocy Prawnej im. Haliny Nieć. www.pomocprawna.org/detencja-dzieci-cudzoziemskich-w-polsce (accessed 13 March 2019).

Chrzanowska, A., Mickiewicz, P., Słubik, K., Subko, J., Trylińska, A., 2016. *At the border. Report on monitoring of access to the procedure for granting international protection at border crossings in Terespol, Medyka, and Warszawa-Okęcie Airport*, Analyses, Reports, Evaluations No. 2/2016. Association for Legal Intervention.

European Court of Human Rights, 2020. M.K. and others v. POLAND [WWW Document]. https://hudoc.echr.coe.int/eng#{%22sort%22:[%22kpdate%20Descending%22],%22documentcollectionid2%22:[%22GRANDCHAMBER%22,%22CHAMBER%22],%22itemid%22:[%22001-203840%22]} (accessed 20 August 2020).

Górczyńska, M., Szczepanik, M., 2016. *A road to nowhere. The account of a monitoring visit at the Brześć-Terespol border crossing between Poland and Belarus*. Helsińska Fundacja Praw Człowieka, Warszawa.

Górny, A., Grzymała-Moszczyńska, H., Klaus, W., Łodziński, S., 2017. *Uchodźcy w Polsce. Sytuacja prawna, skala napływu i integracja w społeczeństwie polskim oraz rekomendacje,* EKSPERTYZY KOMITETU BADAŃ NAD MIGRACJAMI PAN. Komitet Badań nad Migracjami PAN, Kraków – Warszawa. https://webcache.googleusercontent.com/search?q=cache:s9tm-KIpLyIJ:https://instytucja.pan.pl/images/2018/wydzialy/w1/Uchod%25C5%25BAcy_wPolsce_ekspertyza_KBnM_PAN.pdf+&cd=1&hl=pl&ct=clnk&gl=pl&client=firefox-b-d (accessed 24 October 2019).

Helsińska Fundacja Praw Człowieka, n.d. *Ofiara tortur zwolniona z ośrodka strzeżonego dla cudzoziemców po 10 miesiącach pobytu* [WWW Document]. www.hfhr.pl/ofiara-tortur-zwolniona-z-osrodka-strzezonego-dla-cudzoziemcow-po-10-miesiacach-pobytu/ (accessed 31 March 2019).

IOM, 2021. *2021 Migration in Ukraine. Facts and Figures*. https://iom.org.ua/sites/default/files/migration_in_ukraine_facts_and_figures_2021-eng_web.pdf.

Kaliszewska, I., 2019. *Sytuacja kobiet na Kaukazie Północnym (Czeczenia, Dagestan, Inguszetia)*. Wydział Informacji o Krajach Pochodzenia UDSC, Warszawa.

Klaus, W., 2017. Security First: The New Right-Wing Government in Poland and its Policy towards Immigrants and Refugees. *Surveillance & Society*, 1(15), 523–528. DOI: https://doi.org/10.24908/ss.v15i3/4.6627.

Klaus, W. (ed.), 2021. *Humanitarian crisis at the Polish-Belarusian border*. Report by Grupa Granica. https://grupagranica.pl/files/Grupa-Granica-Report-Humanitarian-crisis-at-the-Polish-Belarusian-border.pdf.

Klaus, W., Pachocka, M., 2019. Examining the Global North Migration Policies: A "Push Out – Push Back" Approach to Forced Migration. *International Migration*, 57, 280–293. DOI: https://doi.org/10.1111/imig.12575.

Klaus, W., Ostaszewska-Żuk Ewa, Szczepanik Marta, 2017. *Fundusze europejskie i ich rola we wspieraniu integracji cudzoziemców w Polsce*. Stowarzyszenie Interwencji Prawnej, Warszawa.

Koser, K., 1997. Social Networks and the Asylum Cycle: The Case of Iranians in the Netherlands. *The International Migration Review*, 31, 591–611. DOI: https://doi.org/10.2307/2547287.

Lazarev, E., 2019. Laws in Conflict: Legacies of War, Gender, and Legal Pluralism in Chechnya. *World Politics* 71, 667–709. DOI: https://doi.org/10.1017/S0043887119000133.

Majcher, I., Flynn, M., Grange, M., 2020. Central Europe: Declining Arrivals, Surging Antagonism, in: Majcher, I., Flynn, M., Grange, M. (Eds.), *Immigration Detention in the European Union: In the Shadow of the "Crisis"*, European Studies of Population. Springer International Publishing, Cham, pp. 131–175. DOI: https://doi.org/10.1007/978-3-030-33869-5_4.

Niedźwiedzki, D., Schmidt, J., Stępka, M., Tacik, P., 2021. *Strzeżone ośrodki dla cudzoziemców w Polsce jako kultura organizacyjna: analiza prawna, politologiczna, socjologiczna i antropologiczna*. https://ruj.uj.edu.pl/xmlui/bitstream/handle/item/284042/niedzwiedzki_schmidt_stepka_tacik_strzezone_osrodki_dla_cudzoziemcow_w_polsce_2021.pdf

Ombudsman Office, 2018. *Raport Krajowego Mechanizmu Prewencji Tortur z wizytacji Strzeżonego Ośrodka dla Cudzoziemców oraz Aresztu dla Cudzoziemców w Przemyślu* [WWW Document]. www.rpo.gov.pl/sites/default/files/Wyci%C4%85g-Strze%C5%BCony%20O%C5%9Brodek%20i%20Areszt%20dla%20Cudzoziemc%C3%B3w%20Przemy%C5%9Bl%202017.pdf (accessed 23 January 2018).

Rafalik, N., 2012. *Cudzoziemcy ubiegający się o nadanie statusu uchodźcy w Polsce – teoria a rzeczywistość (praktyka) (stan prawny na dzień 31 grudnia 2011 r.) CMR Working Papers* No 55(113). Centre of Migration Research, University of Warsaw, Warszawa.

Strik, T., 2020. Mechanisms to prevent pushbacks, in: Carrera, S., Stefan, M. (Eds.), *Fundamental Rights Challenges in Border Controls and Expulsion of Irregular Immigrants in the European Union. Complaint Mechanisms and Access to Justice.* Routledge, London, pp. 234–258.

Stummer, K., 2016. Forgotten Refugees: Chechen asylum seekers in Poland. Political Critique. http://politicalcritique.org/cee/poland/2016/forgotten-refugees-chechen-asylum-seekers-in-poland/ (accessed 19 February 2020).

Szczepanik, M., 2019. *Republika strachu. Prawa człowieka we współczesnej Czeczenii.* Helsińska Fundacja Praw Człowieka, Warszawa.

Szczepanik, M., 2018. Border Politics and Practices of Resistance on the Eastern Side of "Fortress Europe": The Case of Chechen Asylum Seekers at the Belarusian–Polish Border. *Central and Eastern European Migration Review*, 7, pp. 69–89. DOI: https://doi.org/10.17467/ceemr.2018.08.

Szulecka, M., 2016. Przejawy nielegalnej migracji w Polsce. *Archiwum Kryminologii*, 191–268.

Szulecka, M., 2019. Border Management and Migration Controls in Poland (RESPOND Working Paper Series No. 2019/24).

Szulecka, M., 2022. *The undermined role of (domestic) case law in shaping the practice of admitting asylum seekers in Poland.* European Journal of Legal Studies,14, No. SI, 171–209. DOI: 10.2924/EJLS.2022.006.

Zespoł do Spraw Migracji, Ministerstwo Spraw Wewnętrznych, 2012. Polityka Migracyjna Polski – stan obecny i postulowane działania, https://ec.europa.eu/migrant-integration/sites/default/files/2019-07/PMP_przyjeta_przez_Rade_Ministrow_31lipca_2012_2_.pdf.

Zespoł do spraw Migracji MSWiA, 2021. Polityka migracyjna Polski – kierunki działań 2021–2022, www.gov.pl/web/mswia/projekt-uchwaly-rady-ministrow-w-sprawieprzyjecia-dokumentu-polityka-migracyjna-polski--kierunki-dzialan-2021-2022-id179.

6

ACCESS OF ASYLUM SEEKERS AND REFUGEES TO EDUCATION

The Case of Polish Language Learning

Introduction

Education is considered one of the core domains of integration (see Introduction) and as such is also both a marker and a means (Ager and Strang, 2008). In discussions about the multifaceted integration process, the education domain is often narrowed to the formal educational system consisting of primary, secondary, and tertiary education. As such, it predominantly refers to children or youth, leaving aside adult refugees who have finished their education. However, after arriving in the host country, forced migrants must intensively learn, either formally or informally, how to navigate the institutions and cultural conventions of the new society. Foremost, they must learn the host country's language, which in combination with the respective cultural knowledge is regarded as a facilitator of integration (Ager and Strang, 2008). Although in some countries such as Germany and Austria, the knowledge of language and culture is treated as inseparable and therefore integration courses for refugees contain both dimensions, in Poland language learning comes first, and the Polish courses are complemented with an "orientation course" only at the beginning of the asylum procedure.

Access to formal education depends on, among others, the age and legal status of the asylum seekers and refugees, since these two factors condition access to various forms of education. While the provision of education for children, regardless of their legal status, is constitutionally guaranteed and the practised approach in Poland, access to education for adult asylum seekers and refugees is hampered by many systemic and non-systemic obstacles. Even if the problem of access is overcome, there are other impediments to integration in the area of education. It needs to be underlined here that refugees are generally better educated than other migrants (Muus, 1997; Sobczak-Szelc et al., 2020), which we assume is similar among this group in Poland, even though there is no data showing the level of education

DOI: 10.4324/9781003196327-6

of refugees juxtaposed with other groups of migrants. RESPOND research has shown that 57% of the interviewed forced migrants declared having higher education, and this figure was higher than the percentage of people with higher education in Poland (29%) (Eurostat, 2021). However, refugees rarely perform jobs corresponding to their education and qualifications (see Chapter 8), which leads to the question of what are the reasons for such a situation? Apart from the difficulties in the confirmation of diplomas obtained in the countries of origin, there appear to be other impediments, with the lack of knowledge of the Polish language among the most significant ones.

The purpose of this chapter is to present the legal and institutional aspects of the integration of asylum seekers and refugees in the domain of education and examine the actual practises of integration in one chosen area, namely Polish language learning. We focus on adult asylum seekers' and refugees' access to Polish language courses, together with their effectiveness and participants' motivations for starting and continuing their learning, in order to see what facilitators and barriers there are in host country language acquisition by applicants and beneficiaries of international protection. We also ask whether the practises of language education at each step of the integration process (reception during the asylum procedure and actual integration after being granted protection status) are coherent. In addition, by presenting the actual practises of Polish language learning by refugees, we aim to identify shortcomings as well as good practises in this area. This chapter elaborates on the findings of the analysis of in-depth interviews carried out with micro-level (asylum seekers, refugees) and meso-level actors (NGO representatives, local government representatives, and school practitioners) involved in the process of integration.

Asylum Seekers' and Refugees' Access to Formal Education

According to the Polish constitution, everyone has a right to education, and education is compulsory until the age of 18 (see Chapter 4). Thus, the right to education is guaranteed not only to Polish citizens but to all children living in Poland, including asylum seekers, who have free and unlimited access to education in public schools until the age of 18 or the completion of high school. Full-time compulsory education lasts nine years and it applies to pupils aged 7–15 years. It comprises the last year of pre-school education and eight years of primary school education. Later on, there is part-time compulsory education (obligation to be in education) for pupils aged 15–18, and it may take place either in school settings (a pupil attends an upper secondary school) or in non-school settings (e.g., a pupil follows vocational training offered by an employer) (Sobczak-Szelc et al., 2020, pp. 63–64). In the matter of providing minor asylum seekers and refugees with access to education, Poland complies with European Union policies and regulations in this respect.

Although minor asylum seekers and refugees have access to Polish schools and can benefit from some integrational instruments, such as a cross-cultural assistant or preparatory classes; their actual integration is far from ideal. Since we did not conduct interviews with minors who attend schools, our empirical data on the education of refugee children is limited. However, previous research showed that refugee children face more obstacles than other children with an immigrant background (Block et al., 2014; European Commission, 2013; Młynarczuk-Sokołowska, 2020). Not only do they have to adapt to a new language and culture, but they also often deal with disrupted or minimal prior education (Bloch et al., 2015). The challenges might also include a lack of documentation of their education, credentials, and diplomas. This makes it difficult to place them in the right programme/grade without a systematic assessment of their skills (Hoehne and Michalowski, 2016; Cerna, 2019). In addition, refugee children often deal with Post Traumatic Stress Disorder caused by trauma, pain, and the protracted lack of stability (Essomba, 2017).

It is argued that the education systems of OECD countries, including Poland's, are not well prepared to receive asylum seekers and refugees. The school curricula often do not provide the basic language skills and social competences that refugees need. Additionally, the education system is responsible for schooling refugees in a social context that is not always supportive of welcoming these newcomers (Młynarczuk-Sokołowska, 2020; Essomba, 2017). Furthermore, refugees are often affected by trauma and mental anguish, which, in the case of children, can considerably impact the construction and development of their personal identities (Essomba, 2017). Therefore, it is really important to provide refugee children with a strong emotional and affective component of teaching, which is not often possible to implement. As a consequence of the aforementioned impediments, the educational expectations of refugee children and their families are not always met (Essomba, 2017). In the case of unaccompanied minors, additional challenges stem from separation from their families (OECD, 2019).

Unlike in the case of children, the access of adult forced migrants to various forms of education differs depending on their legal status. Both asylum applicants and beneficiaries of international protection have access to education in various types of public schools for adults, public post-secondary schools, and vocational qualification courses under conditions applicable to Polish citizens (see Chapter 4). With respect to higher education, beneficiaries of international protection have free access to it, under the same conditions as Polish citizens. If asylum seekers want to begin or continue their studies, they have to pay tuition. To study in Poland, a person is required to have completed their secondary level education and hold a maturity certificate confirming eligibility to apply to university. By virtue of law, the lack of such a document in the refugees' case does not constitute an obstacle to study since there is an administrative recognition procedure especially for them (see Chapter 4).

With regard to recognition of foreign higher education degrees in Poland, the general rule is that a foreign degree giving access to further studies or the right to start doctoral proceedings in the country where it was awarded gives its holder access to second cycle studies, postgraduate studies, third cycle/doctoral studies, or the right to start doctoral proceedings in Poland. A foreign degree may also be recognised for the purpose of further education on the basis of an international agreement. If the obtained degree does not give access to further studies in a country where it was obtained, in order to continue education in Poland there is a need for confirmation or recognition of the degree (see Chapter 4).

Polish Language Education Provided for Forced Migrants: The Legal Framework

Knowledge of the host country's language is commonly perceived as an indispensable factor for the successful inclusion of migrants (including refugees) into the host society. Not only does it facilitate daily communication, but it also determines the opportunities for newcomers in the new country (see Chapter 8). Different studies confirm that migrants who participate in a language course within four years from their arrival in the host country experience positive long-term benefits of such participation (Hoehne and Michalowski, 2016).

Furthermore, a communicative or working level of knowledge of the host country's language is often a precondition for the right to a long-term residency or citizenship. Many EU countries provide and fund language courses for adult migrants. The Council of Europe points out the importance of tailoring such courses to the particular needs and learning patterns of adult learners (Council of Europe, n.d.; Koehler, 2017, p. 24).

Under EU law, the Qualification Directive (Article 34) stipulates that integrational support provided for beneficiaries of international protection has to consider their specific needs. Knowledge of the language of the host country has been recognised as a need by the fourth Common Basic Principle for Immigrant Integration Policy in the EU. The document considers knowledge of the language, the history, and the institutions of the host country as essential to successful integration (Council of the European Union, 2004).

Despite the EU's recognition of the indispensable role of knowledge of the host country's language for integration, there is no universal model of language learning practised by all EU countries. The countries also differ in their approach to language education provided for beneficiaries of international protection, from a model of obligatory participation in language courses provided by the public institutions for free (Germany, Sweden, Austria, and Italy), to a model of semi-obligatory courses (or obligatory only on paper, but not provided for free) for participants of special integration programmes (Poland), to a model of no regulation when there is neither obligation nor availability of publicly funded courses for refugees (Greece) (Sobczak-Szelc et al., 2021, p. 53).

In Poland, in fact, there are three different approaches to Polish language education depending on age (different for those under 18 years old and for adults) and the legal status of a forced migrant. Children under an asylum procedure and subject to compulsory schooling, like all foreign children, who do not know Polish or whose level of Polish is not sufficient to benefit from education are entitled to additional, free Polish language learning in the form of additional lessons. These classes are conducted individually or in groups, for at least two hours up to a maximum of five hours a week (in a situation in which a child does not participate in the compensatory classes described below). Learning Polish continues until the student masters the language to a degree enabling learning and is neither time-limited (Ordinance of the Minister of National Education, 2017, Par. 17) nor determined by the legal status of the child.

Adult asylum applicants have Polish language classes and basic language learning materials guaranteed by the Law on Protection (Article 71(1)); however, they are not obliged to participate in the classes. Polish language courses in centres for asylum seekers are organised by the Office for Foreigners as a pre-integration action. The language classes are conducted by private entities selected through public procurement for the "provision of educational services for the needs of the Office for Foreigners". According to the conditions of the latest procurement announced in 2021, the entity responsible for the organisation of the courses has to provide Polish classes in every centre two times weekly (two hours each) for adults and five times weekly (one hour each) for children (Office for Foreigners, 2021). Although the number of hours of Polish classes increased between 2016 and 2019 from four to six a week after intervention by the Supreme Audit Office (in Polish: *Najwyższa Izba Kontroli,* NIK) in 2015, in the latest procurement in 2021 for unknown reason it was brought back to the previous quantity, namely four hours weekly. The NIK stated that four hours of Polish classes is not enough to learn the language to a level for functioning in the local community (Baczyński-Sielaczek, 2016). The situation gets complicated if an asylum applicant lives outside the centre, then he/she can either attend the course organised in the centre or use learning opportunities provided for free by NGOs. However, the Office for Foreigners does not provide any Polish language courses outside the centres.

On the other hand, beneficiaries of international protection are obliged to learn Polish if they participate in an individual integration programme (IIP) and if there is a need for their participation in a course (Law on Social Assistance, Article 93(1); see also Chapter 4). The vague "need" is assessed by a social worker who decides whether a beneficiary's knowledge of Polish is at a sufficient level. Since the IIP cannot last longer than 12 months, the obligation of learning Polish does not go beyond this period. In addition, the Law on Social Assistance stipulates that the beneficiary of an IIP should cover the expenses of a Polish language course using the cash benefits received through IIP (Article 92(1)(b)). Importantly, assistance for a foreigner (including the cash benefit) may be suspended in case of, among others, unjustified absence from Polish language courses of longer than 30 days (Law on Social Assistance, Article 95(1)). It needs to be underlined that participation in the IIP does not include automatic registering at a Polish language course, because it depends on the availability of the courses. Assessment of the need to learn Polish is made by a social worker from the family support centre responsible for mentoring the beneficiaries of the IIP. However, it is not specified what level of Polish language the beneficiary of an IIP should reach after accomplishing the programme (Pawlak, 2019).

Practise of Polish Language Learning by Asylum Seekers and Refugees

The success in acquiring Polish language skills by forced migrants is conditioned foremost by the possibilities of learning the language. There is no surprise that out of the three following groups—children, adult asylum seekers, and adult refugees—the first one is considered the least problematic or the fastest learners with regard to the acquisition of host country language skills (Isphording, 2015). Apart from the additional Polish classes provided for foreign children, the detrimental factor is their daily contact with the language from participation in classes where other subjects are taught in Polish and co-education with their Polish peers. Our respondents, parents, and teachers of asylum-seeking and refugee children confirmed that the children are able to learn Polish quite fast in such conditions. Nevertheless, right after placement in Polish schools, children usually do not speak Polish at all, and the first months are a challenge for both pupils and teachers. The language barrier, but also the educational gap stemming from the conflicts in their countries of origin or protracted journey, means asylum-seeking children are often placed in a lower grade than their age indicates (Pachocka et al., 2020, p. 77). Another challenge appears for children with speech articulation problems since a speech therapist who can recognise and work with speech impairments in non-popular foreign languages can be hardly found in Poland (PLMIKa30).

To overcome the linguistic barriers, the Office for Foreigners provides Polish language lessons for children in the centres for foreigners, which include help with homework and compensatory classes, as well as classes preparing newcomers to study in Polish schools. The teacher conducting the classes stays in touch with the schools attended by the children, which allows for the exchange of information on their progress and problems in learning and gives the opportunity to adapt the conducted classes to the needs of the children. In addition, the Office provides the pupils with textbooks and accessories (so-called school layettes) if they do not receive them in schools (European Commission/EACEA/Eurydice, 2019) (Hajduk, 2018).

As part of the project *Polish for a Good Beginning* (*Polski na dobry start*) carried out by the Office in cooperation with the foundation Linguae Mundi, a curriculum of Polish as a foreign language was developed for asylum-seeking children who have just enrolled in schools in Poland. As part of it, a teacher's handbook containing lesson plans and educational materials for pupils was prepared. As the Office for Foreigners explained, the programme takes into account the specific communication needs of children under an asylum procedure, including realistic and socio-cultural content. It also includes the acquisition of basic skills, as well as simulations of communication situations at school (Office for Foreigners, 2017).

Furthermore, asylum-seeking and then refugee children face different problems with linguistic education in Poland, namely the lack of access to education in their native tongue in schools. Although previous research shows many benefits of teaching migrant children in their native language, like strengthening their linguistic and academic development together with the development of their secure identity (European Commission/EACEA/Eurydice, 2019), such a policy is still not very common in the EU, and almost non-existent in Poland. A kind of support for asylum-seeking and refugee children stipulated by law (Law on School Education, 2016), which at the same time does not replace the native language education, is the presence of a cross-cultural assistant who, in principle, should speak a language understandable for the children. However, due to the variety of ethnic backgrounds of the children and the languages they speak, it is impossible for schools with high numbers of refugee children to hire as many cultural assistants as there are languages spoken by the children.

Like the children, adult asylum seekers and refugees are also treated by the state as people who need institutional support in learning the Polish language, but their access to courses and attendance obligations are different and depend on their legal status. As mentioned earlier, asylum seekers living in the centres for foreigners are provided with Polish language classes organised by the Office for Foreigners. Participation in the language classes in the accommodation centres is not obligatory. Despite the introduction of some incentives in 2015, such as prizes[1] for the highest attendance and/or the best results in the group, overall attendance has remained low. According to a survey by the Institute of Public Affairs, in 2016 only 45% of accommodation centre residents attended the Polish classes, and of them, only half were attending classes always or very often (Baczyński-Sielaczek, 2016).

Our in-depth interviews with asylum seekers point to a wide range of reasons for this situation. Among the individual reasons were traumatic experiences that precluded asylum seekers from focusing on learning, as in the case of one Chechen woman:

> Sometimes, I attend these classes. I don't have patience for that, that's why I started to see a psychologist to calm down a little bit. I can't concentrate on what the teacher is saying. I am thinking about my situation all the time.
>
> *PLMICh03*

Another impediment was the lack of early childcare provided in the centres for foreigners, at least for the class periods, so women could leave their youngest under care:

> I attended the course, when I was in the camp, but I had a little baby, which was very much connected with me and I couldn't attend the course all the time.
>
> *PLMICh08*

The Office for Foreigners is not obliged to run nurseries in the centres of foreigners and there is no such facility in any centre. It is worth adding that providing child-care is not included in the conditions of tenders for the organisation of language classes announced by the Office.

To some of our respondents, the Polish courses organised in the centres seemed to be focused too much on theory than on practise. One Ukrainian woman attended classes in the accommodation centre but practise was more important to her, therefore she used every opportunity to speak the language:

> I spoke using very short sentences. But for longer talks in Polish, there were opportunities in the centre with guards, with people in the office.
>
> *PLMIUk19*

It must be added that the communicative method of teaching refugees the Polish language has been introduced quite recently, in 2015, when a special textbook prepared by Foundation Lingua Mundi was published. Before, it was at the discretion of the language course provider which teaching method would be followed.

To increase attendance in the Polish courses, the Office for Foreigners enforced some incentives and adjustment measures, like increasing the number of course hours and dividing participants into groups according to their level, but these actions did not bring the expected results. Our respondents from the Office guessed that the motivation for not learning the language is directly related to the working plans of asylum seekers:

> It seems to me that maybe the Ukrainians are starting a job right now. After six months, if they do not have a decision issued, they can apply for a certificate that they can take up a job. Later, these language skills are needed.
>
> *PLMZOF3/4*

There is also an ongoing discussion about whether Polish language classes for asylum applicants should be mandatory. Some practitioners expressed that opinion and underlined the integration value of the courses:

> They are provided with Polish language classes, but almost nobody attends them. This is unattractive and they are not obliged to do so, but in my opinion, they should be. If someone applies for refugee status, wants to integrate and wants to stay in Poland, he/she should be forced, however, during the procedure—especially since it is very long—to learn the Polish language.
>
> *PLMZP1*

Opponents of obligatory Polish language courses argue that it is the responsibility of the central government to increase the motivation among asylum applicants to learn the language. Some representatives of social organisations claimed that in a situation when knowledge of Polish is not taken as a favourable factor in granting someone international protection (and it cannot be taken as such or it would be against the spirit of the 1951 Geneva Convention), asylum applicants have no incentive to learn it. Second, they are not aware that knowing Polish, together with their integration progress, can be considered an asset in the procedure of issuing a residence permit for humanitarian reasons, which is a form of national protection:

> Their future in Poland does not depend on whether they know the language or not unless this procedure lasts long enough that someone far-sighted would say that in four years when I would speak good Polish and someone would like to expel me, I will say that there are humanitarian reasons, that I have integrated myself and I know the language. But people don't think about it right now. If they are not asked to learn, the system of learning incentives was not created, then they lose a year, two years. The language is especially important.
>
> *PLMZSO3*

Previous research on the topic shed some light on another important aspect of the lack of motivation to learn the host country's language. Asylum seekers often do not choose the country they stay in and sometimes their migration path is not complete until they receive international protection status (Ortiz, Kralik, and Bianco, 2020, p. 69). Asylum applicants in Poland often leave the country and seek better life opportunities in Germany or other Western European countries (see more in Chapter 5), therefore they might not be keenly interested in learning Polish.

Our interviewees confirmed that one of the factors hindering participation in the language classes is the decision to reside in private accommodation, outside the centre for foreigners. Since language learning is not obligatory during the asylum procedure, asylum applicants do not have the motivation to look for opportunities to learn Polish on their own (PLMIUk18). Second, those with private accommodation, in order to make a living, usually work, either legally if they have the permission or not, and they do not have free time for attending the classes. One stated:

> After I arrived in Warsaw, I asked a friend about classes. She told me, there are language classes at the Foundation, and I signed up there. Then, I couldn't attend the classes because I was working.
>
> *PLMICh14*

If asylum seekers who live in rented flats or houses are determined to learn the language, they usually attend free Polish courses offered by NGOs, although the availability of such courses depends on location and funding.

Despite the criticism about the obsolete methods of teaching Polish in the centres for foreigners, a significant finding from the interviews with forced migrants was that those asylum seekers who regularly attend Polish language classes are satisfied with the results (PLMIUk19, PLMIJe29, PLMIKa30). The three mentioned respondents whose native languages (Ukrainian, Arabic, and Kazakh) belong to different language families (Slavic, Semitic, and Turkic) prove that language proximity is not the only motivation or de-motivation factor behind attending the Polish classes. Another challenge revealed during the fieldwork was the hesitance of male asylum applicants to participate in the courses. The possible reason for this is stereotypes rooted in culture, with men from the Caucasus or Eastern Europe perceiving participation in language classes as an activity for women and children, and not for them.

Together with the change of legal status after asylum applicants are granted international protection, the problem of a lack of motivation is replaced by other factors. Although the beneficiaries of international protection are obliged to attend a Polish language course, if they are participants in an IIP and they do not know the language well enough, the practice shows that the average attendance rate remains low, although this varies by location. As indicated by the NIK, the actual participation in Polish classes of beneficiaries of an IIP varied from 20% in Pruszków and Łuków, to 50% in Biała Podlaska, and 70% in Warsaw, and averaged 35.6%. The average number of Polish lesson hours during an IIP was four per week, however, situations in which the level, scope, and frequency of the participation in the course were not specified were common (Najwyższa Izba Kontroli, 2015, pp. 40–42).

Although recognised refugees officially enter the proper integration stage, their access to Polish language education becomes much more difficult than before, providing they were residing in the centre for foreigners. The first problem appears when refugees need to find the right course on their own. The ones organised for free by NGOs are usually overcrowded, and it is difficult to find the right group level there. The ones run by private language schools are expensive, and the price can be a deterrent factor, even if it is reimbursed by the family support centres. In addition, Polish language classes are often held when refugees work or are in locations far from their places of residence. The lack of organised childcare during language classes also makes it difficult for women who take care of children to attend the class, thus preventing them from taking part. Similar systemic oversights are not conducive to the successful integration of refugees if most of them encounter major obstacles at the language learning stage. Such state policy can even be an incentive to leave the country of residence (Korniychuk, 2016, pp. 16–17).

Among the objections presented by the refugees and beneficiaries of subsidiary protection we talked to was that there was a lack of effectiveness in the courses. A female beneficiary of subsidiary protection who attended a course provided by the family support centre said openly:

> I attended the course, but during this course I didn't learn to speak Polish.
>
> *PLMICh01*

Respondents repeatedly confessed that the courses did not meet their expectations in learning to communicate in the language:

> When I got a status, they told me that I have to go through some Polish language classes. I went to these classes and what was the most interesting thing

> you know? They told me to take a piece of paper and pen and write down. I told them I can't write in Polish. They told me, write what you hear. It wasn't efficient for me but living here and having conversations with people, the language knowledge came by itself.
>
> *PLMICh09*

The above quotation mirrors deficiencies of the Polish model of language education provided for refugees. In a situation with a faulty systemic approach to teaching adults the Polish language, the lack of methodology of teaching based on the needs of learners and the lack of different approaches depending on the group's native languages, it is impossible to expect refugees to master the language. If the courses cannot meet the most basic needs of refugees in the form of learning to communicate in the language, they certainly cannot answer the needs of vulnerable groups. It turned out that the non-availability of language courses tailored for refugees with specific needs was especially difficult for elderly people:

> In the beginning, one should learn the language. And for us, I am 65 years old, my wife is 62 years old, it is difficult, and there are no schools which would teach us the language. Our Polish language level is barely A1. Because I was not attending school, the only place where I studied is the foundation, and as I told you, if I learned [something] today, tomorrow I would forget half of it. Because there is no usage of the language, we don't have people that we would talk to in a continuous manner.
>
> *PLMISy24*

Apart from the poor quality of the language courses and their mismatch to the needs, our respondents complained about the lack of possibility to combine work with the Polish course. The latter obstacle was a reason for quitting the language course for three of our respondents (PLMICh07, PLMISy22, and PLMICh14).

Another issue revealed by our research was the complete non-availability of Polish language courses in some communities. A man from Chechnya had not attended any Polish classes for the last 10 years due to this situation:

> They didn't have here in [this city] any Polish classes like for example there are in other countries.
>
> *PLMICh11*

Another respondent compared the situation of host country language learning in Poland and Germany and pointed to big gaps in terms of integration through the language acquisition possibilities:

> In Germany, there are German courses everywhere: for learning the language, teaching language, so, for refugees in Germany it's very easy to join any

> course, but here the situation is very difficult. If we didn't have the chance to have these courses at NGOs, I wouldn't have the possibility to learn Polish.
>
> *PLMISy22*

It only proves that integration possibilities are also considered by refugees when they decide to leave Poland and move to its western neighbour. In fact, Germany provides much better host country language learning opportunities than Poland (Sobczak-Szelc et al., 2021, p. 27).

Interestingly, almost all interviewed refugees admitted that they are aware of the importance of learning the Polish language for their life in Poland and integration with the society. An example of such an observation is the following reflection made by a man from Chechnya:

> First of all, you need the knowledge of the language for yourself. For any kind of communication, a person has to know the language. Without language it would be hard because you would have to ask others all the time for translations. The knowledge of the language makes his/her life and the life of others easier. If you go to foreign country, you have to speak the language. [Q: Someone forced you to learn the language or you wanted to learn it by yourself?] R: I think my life here forced me to learn the language.
>
> *PLMICh15*

Although positive examples of Polish language learning were rare, some were reported. An example was provided by a woman from Chechnya who could not attend a regular course due to taking care of her children, including one with disabilities:

> The teacher comes to my flat to teach me Polish once a week. She comes for 4 hours. I started to study Polish last year.
>
> *PLMICh04*

With regard to our Ukrainian respondents, their Polish speaking skills sounded better than that of respondents of other nationalities. In addition, all of them chose Polish as the language for the interview, although they were given a choice between Polish and Russian. It is only further proof that language proximity—both Polish and Ukrainian are Slavic languages in the Indo-European language family—significantly facilitates second language acquisition. A woman from Ukraine told us a story of her husband who managed to learn Polish to a working level in a year during his IIP (PLMIUk19). Another respondent from Ukraine was able to learn Polish to a working level owing to work and private relations with Poles:

> I learned the language at work, by ear, maybe because I studied the violin at music school, because I need to do everything by ear. I learn the same way when someone tells me something. I hear, I try to remind myself, sometimes

> I don't understand something, for example, "jak się masz" and "siema". It is the same, only shorter, or not "na razie" only "nara". And such slang. And after that you can hear who is learning the language, because some friend, she studied Polish at school, and then at the university. And she doesn't speak like on the street, but like a professor. And everyone says, "your Polish is cool, we can't hear that you are a foreigner, but your Polish is like of a professor. You don't have this type of "siema, nara".
>
> *PLMIUk18*

Our interviews with forced migrants do not allow us to make any generalisation about Polish language learning attitudes of female and male refugees, since the attitudes of our respondents varied depending on many different factors, including gender but without significant influence. However, one of our expert interviewees brought up an issue concerning migrants with a Muslim background, which can hamper women's participation in language courses:

> There is no space for these cultural differences that can make some things difficult to accomplish. For example, learning Polish for a woman who comes from a Muslim environment that is very conservative. She can't attend Polish classes because her husband won't let her.
>
> *PLMZLG2*

With regard to refugees' motivation for learning the host country's language, our empirical research confirmed that fundamental to learning Polish is the integrative factor, namely the participants' willingness to integrate into the host country's society. Also significant are previous learning experiences (indicated by the level of education or existing knowledge of foreign languages) and self-confidence or anxiety. Surprisingly, external expectations, namely those made by the host country, by the course provider, and by the society, as revealed by previous research (Ortiz, Kralik and Bianco, 2020), were not mentioned by our speakers.

A refugee from Syria told us his ideas for improving the Polish language learning system. First, he pointed out the lack of Polish classes tailored specifically to refugees:

> We could make it better, as I told you in the beginning, let them make proper schools for teaching immigrants or the refugees who are coming to this country, that they teach them the language, this would facilitate integration very much.
>
> *PLMISy24*

Second, he suggested linking Polish courses with cultural orientation education:

> The person who is coming should learn the traditions and habits of the country where he/she is coming to, so if I am coming to Poland I should learn the habits and traditions of the Polish people. How do they live, [so] I live like them. This would make relations much easier, that the most important thing

> is the language and learning the habits and traditions of the country, and how they live, and take into consideration the economic and political situation that is present in the country. Once I know the law in the country I will integrate in the country and I will live according to law and live a good life.
>
> *PLMISy24*

Although such a combination of language and cultural orientation classes is practised in some European countries, such as Germany, Austria, and Sweden, in Poland there is no specific programme or cultural orientation courses offered for asylum applicants or even recognised refugees. Cultural orientation is carried out individually as social work by social workers in the centres for foreigners or as a part of the IIP. However, there is no standard for either the content of what actually is being taught or the quality of the information about Polish culture given by a social worker (Pawlak, 2019, p. 74).

A serious problem is the limitation of the obligatory period of participation in Polish language courses to 12 months. The NIK confirmed the earlier statements by the language learning methodology experts and NGO representatives that the one-year duration of such courses is insufficient to master the language. Furthermore, although the law has made attending Polish classes obligatory for participants of an IIP, no funds from the state budget were allocated to set up a system of Polish language education or even organise Polish language courses, with only small amounts coming from the budgets of local governments. Therefore, the obligation to learn Polish during the integration programme is almost exclusively carried out by NGOs (using EU funds). Judging by the latter, the NIK foresaw that the continuity of courses would be threatened due to the significant delay in the entry into force of the new financial mechanism of the Asylum, Migration and Integration Fund (AMIF) for 2014–2020 (Najwyższa Izba Kontroli, 2015, pp. 40–42). Although this NIK report was published six years ago, there have not been many improvements in the field of Polish language education for adult refugees since then.

An interesting finding of the RESPOND research is that social workers often put refugees' need to work ahead of their need to learn the Polish language, arguing:

> If someone takes up a job and works from 8 a.m. till 4 p.m. and it is not possible for him/her to attend a Polish language course, then we recognise that work is more important. They will also have some contact with Polish at work, so they will naturally learn, and yet become independent.
>
> *PLMZP1*

According to another practitioner, sometimes social workers faced difficulties with enforcement of the Polish language learning obligation:

> If a person [...] does not want to do something, still does not attend Polish lessons, then no one is able to take him/her to Polish language lessons. The decision is always up to the client.
>
> *PLMZP2*

Later in the interview, this practitioner pointed to self-motivation as a crucial factor behind one woman learning the language:

> There is also such a thing in language acquisition as self-study. [...] When she decided to learn Polish, she turned on the television and lived with the television non-stop, entered into social relations. She is a phenomenon to me ... she wanted to learn.
>
> *PLMZP2*

As mentioned before, access to Polish language education for refugees would not be possible without the activity of NGOs working in the field of migration. In general, NGOs offer foreigners free language courses, but asylum seekers and refugees have priority in registration. The courses are organised by the Ocalenie Foundation (in Warsaw, Łomża, and Łódź), the Multicultural Centre in Warsaw, Foundation for Somalia (Warsaw), Homo Faber Foundation, Centre for Voluntarism Association, Foundation for the Rule of Law (in Lublin), Centre of Support for Immigrants (in Gdańsk), Caritas (in Szczecin and Białystok), Nasz Wybor Foundation (in Warsaw and Cracow), and others. However, due to the huge interest in the courses, the mentioned foundations usually cannot provide enough places for all those willing to participate. In addition, there is no certainty of continuation of the courses due to the lack of stability of funding for the NGOs. As foreseen by the Supreme Audit Office, there was a period of either discontinuity of language courses or a decrease in the offer provided by NGOs after the suspension of AMIF funding in 2015 (Sobczak-Szelc et al., 2020, p. 78).

In conclusion, our research confirmed that Polish language acquisition is considered by both forced migrants and institutional respondents (governmental and non-governmental) as an essential factor of integration. In addition, our respondents, in general, shared the opinion that the Polish language courses, available for adult asylum seekers and refugees (if available), are insufficient and not effective.

Conclusions

Access to education for forced migrants is perceived and organised differently depending on the age (if under 18-year-olds are considered) and their legal status (whether it concerns asylum applicants or beneficiaries of international protection). Regarding the first group, it is fully recognised by the state that education is an indispensable factor in integration, so asylum-seeking and refugee children have full access to school education and are provided with instruments supporting their learning. Two of the mentioned instruments are especially worth highlighting: cross-cultural assistants and preparatory classes, which were introduced as a tool for supporting migrant children in their first year of education. In the area of Polish language education, children are first provided with additional Polish classes, right after their placement in the centres for foreigners, and then again after their registration in school. Nevertheless, the language barrier, along with the cultural barrier, is still the most significant one considering the need for children's integration in education.

With regard to adult asylum seekers and refugees, based on the education opportunities available to them, the primary focus is on their Polish language education. Therefore, building on the Ager and Strang theoretical framework (2008), the marker and means of integration (education) heighten the aim of acquisition of the most important facilitator of integration, namely the language. However, access to Polish language classes is organised differently depending on the legal status of the forced migrants. While asylum seekers have relatively easy access to Polish language classes, provided they live in the centres for foreigners where the classes are held, the situation is more complicated for beneficiaries of international protection. Although the latter group is obliged to attend a Polish language course during their 12-month participation in the IIP, the practice shows that the majority of refugees do not do this for various reasons, including a lack of courses in some localities, inability to reconcile employment with participation in a course due to work hours, and the low attractiveness of the courses (i.e., their failure to meet the needs of refugees). It turns out that the model of semi-obligatory courses in Poland (Sobczak-Szelc et al., 2021, p. 77) is not efficient, and without introducing a state-financed system of teaching refugees the Polish language, Poland cannot expect they will easily acquire the language skills enabling their full integration in all domains, such as finding work according to their professional qualifications.

The period of the COVID-19 pandemic has appeared to be enormously challenging for education in general, and forced migrants were even more prone to exclusion in this domain. Owing to the high mobilisation of NGOs and schools, asylum-seeking and refugee children have been provided with laptops enabling their participation in online classes. The situation has been much more difficult for adult asylum seekers. Polish language courses in the centres of foreigners were suspended for a couple of months and no online alternative was provided by the course organisers. With regard to those attending courses organised by NGOs, there was also an interruption in the continuity of the education, although it was overcome when appropriate online meeting applications were introduced.

Note

1 These were material prizes of a didactic value of 100 PLN for an adult with the highest attendance and at the same time the best learning results in a given semester in each centre or for two people with the same results with prizes worth 50 PLN each.

References

Ager, A., Strang, A., 2008. Understanding integration: A conceptual framework. *Journal of Refugee Studies*, 21, 166–191. DOI: https://doi.org/10.1093/jrs/fen016.

Baczyński-Sielaczek, R., 2016. *Język polski w ośrodkach.* Wyniki badania ewaluacyjnego, Warszawa: Instytut Spraw Publicznych.

Bloch, A., Chimienti, M., Counilh, A.-L., Hirsch, S., Tattolo, G., Ossipow, L., de Wenden, C.W., 2015. *The children of refugees in Europe: aspirations, social and economic lives, identity and transnational linkages*. Country reports-Working paper. Geneva: SNIS.

Block, K., Cross, S., Riggs, E., Gibbs, L., 2014. Supporting schools to create an inclusive environment for refugee students. *International Journal of Inclusive Education,* 18, 1337–1355. DOI: https://doi.org/10.1080/13603116.2014.899636.

Cerna, L., 2019. *"Refugee education: Integration models and practices in OECD countries"*, OECD Education Working Papers, No. 203, OECD Publishing, Paris, DOI: https://doi.org/10.1787/a3251a00-en.

Council of Europe, n.d. *Courses and assessment* [WWW Document]. Linguistic Integration of Adult Migrants (LIAM). www.coe.int/en/web/lang-migrants/courses-and-assessment (accessed 19 October 2021).

Council of the European Union, 2004. COMMON BASIC PRINCIPLES FOR IMMIGRANT INTEGRATION POLICY IN THE EUROPEAN UNION.

Essomba, M.À., 2017. The right to education of children and youngsters from refugee families in Europe. *Intercultural Education,* 28, 206–218. DOI: https://doi.org/10.1080/14675986.2017.1308659 (accessed 15 November 2021).

European Commission, 2013. *Study on educational support for newly arrived migrant children (Website)*. Publication Office of the European Union, Luxemburg.

European Commission/EACEA/Eurydice, 2019. *Integrating Asylum Seekers and Refugees into Higher Education in Europe: National Policies and Measures*. Publications Office of the European Union, Luxembourg.

Eurostat, 2021. Population by educational attainment level, sex and age (%) – main indicators, Eurostat Database, available at: https://ec.europa.eu/eurostat/databrowser/view/edat_lfse_03/default/table?lang=en (accessed 20 November 2021).

Eurydice, 2019. *European Commission/EACEA/Eurydice, 2019. Integrating Students from Migrants Background into Schools in Europe: National Policies and Measures. Eurydice Report.* Luxembourg: Publication Office of the European Union.

Hajduk, S., 2018. Edukacja dzieci w procedurze uchodźczej. *Urząd do Spraw Cudzoziemców: Biuletyn informacyjny kwiecień,* (3), 6.

Hoehne, J., Michalowski, I., 2016. Long-term effects of language course timing on language acquisition and social contacts: Turkish and Moroccan immigrants in Western Europe. *International Migration Review,* 50, 133–162. DOI: https://doi.org/10.1111/imre.12130.

Isphording, I., 2015. *What drives the language proficiency of immigrants?* IZA World of Labor, 177, doi: 10.15185/izawol.177

Koehler, Cl., 2017. *Continuity of learning for newly arrived refugee children in Europe (No. 1), NESET II ad hoc question*. NESET.

Korniychuk, A., 2016. *Nauka języka w integracji uchodźców – doświadczenia innych państw*. Instytut Spraw Publicznych, Warszawa.

Law on School Education, 2016. In Polish: Ustawa z dnia 14 grudnia 2016 r. – Prawo oświatowe (t.j. Dz.U. z 2020 r. poz. 910).

Law on Social Assistance, 2004. In Polish: Ustawa o pomocy społecznej z dnia 12 marca 2004 r. (t.j. Dz.U. z 2019 r. poz. 1507 z późn. zm.).

Młynarczuk-Sokołowska, A., 2020. *Na uchodźczej ścieżce. Doświadczenie przymusowej migracji w procesie edukacji formalnej*. Forum Pedagogiczne, 10, pp. 147–162.

Muus, P.J., 1997. *Shifting Borders: the Inclusion and Exclusion of Refugees and Asylum-seekers in the Netherlands, in: Exclusion and Inclusion of Refugees in Contemporary Europe*. ERCOMER, Utrecht.

Najwyższa Izba Kontroli, 2015. *Pomoc społeczna dla uchodźców. Informacja o wynikach kontroli*. Departament Pracy, Spraw Społecznych i Rodziny, Warszawa.

OECD, 2019. *Ready to Help?: Improving Resilience of Integration Systems for Refugees and other Vulnerable Migrants*. OECD Publishing.

Office for Foreigners, 2017. Polski na dobry start – projekt dlacudzoziemców. [Online] Available at: https://udsc.gov.pl/polski-na-dobry-start-w-osrodkach-dla-cudzoziemcow/, (accessed 25 November 2021).

Office for Foreigners, 2021. Przetarg nieograniczony. Świadczenie usług edukacyjnych na potrzeby Urzędu do Spraw Cudzoziemców, available at: https://zamowienia-udsc.ezamawiajacy.pl/pn/zamowienia-udsc/demand/notice/public/37263/details (accessed 18 November 2021).

Ordinance of the Minister of National Education, 2017. In Polish: Rozporządzenie Ministra Edukacji Narodowej z dnia 23 sierpnia 2017 r. w sprawie kształcenia osób niebędących obywatelami polskimi oraz osób będących obywatelami polskimi, które pobierały naukę w szkołach funkcjonujących w systemach oświaty innych państw (Dz.U. 2017 poz. 1655).

Ortiz C., Mónica, Kralik, R., Bianco, R., 2020. Refugees' L2 learning: new perspectives on language motivation research. *XLinguae,* 13, 64–80. DOI: 10.18355/XL.2020.13.04.05.

Pachocka, M., Pędziwiatr, K., Sobczak-Szelc, K., Szałańska, J., 2020. Reception Policies, Practices and Responses. Poland – Country Report, Multilevel Governance of Mass Migration in Europe and Beyond Project (#770564, Horizon2020) Report Series.

Pawlak, M., 2019. Nauka języka polskiego i orientacja kulturowa, in: Górska, A., Koss-Goryszeska, M., Kucharczyk, J. (Eds.), *W stronę krajowego mechanizmu ewaluacji integracji. Diagnoza sytuacji beneficjentów ochrony międzynarodowej w Polsce.* Warszawa: Instytut Spraw Publicznych, pp. 53–57.

Sobczak-Szelc, K., Pachocka, M., Pędziwiatr, K., Szałańska, J., 2020. Integration Policies, Practices and Experiences – Poland Country Report. Zenodo. DOI:https://doi.org/10.5281/zenodo.4008666.

Sobczak-Szelc, K., Szałańska, J., Pachocka, M., 2021. *The integration of asylum seekers and refugees in the field of education and the labour market – Comparative Thematic Report, Global Migration: Consequences and Responses.* Zenodo.

7

ACCESS TO HOUSING BY ASYLUM SEEKERS AND BENEFICIARIES OF INTERNATIONAL PROTECTION

Introduction

Housing is one of the most important basic needs that anyone claiming asylum and refugee status must be provided with or take care of themselves. The quality of housing, including its spatial location, has crucial influence on the pace of foreigners' integration into the new socio-cultural conditions of the host country, as well as on the psychophysical condition of those escaping war or various types of persecution in their home countries. The high concentration of immigrants in a given locality (usually certain districts of big cities) may, on the one hand, facilitate initial familiarisation with the new place and country but on the other hand can delay the process of integration (Alba and Nee, 1997).

As shown in other studies (e.g., Pachocka et al., 2020; Szulecka et al., 2018) and in Chapter 2, although Poland is a new net-immigration country (Pędziwiatr et al., 2021; Strzelecki and Pachocka, 2020), persons seeking asylum have been arriving to the country since the early 1990s (Grzymała-Kozłowska, 2017). One key issue with housing provision for them is not their concentration in certain parts of cities but rather their location far from urban centres where they have fewer opportunities to interact with members of the host society and limited access to the labour market.

This chapter sheds light on the housing conditions of people seeking asylum in Poland and those with different forms of international protection. It analyses statistical information on the provision of accommodation for asylum seekers in the existing centres for foreigners in Poland as well as outside them and evaluates key problems linked with the provision of housing allowances. Beneficiaries of international protection, namely those who have received a positive decision on their asylum application, should leave these so-called refugee centres[1] within two months from the moment of receiving the decision. In analysing the experiences of

DOI: 10.4324/9781003196327-7

persons with international protection with access to housing, we also assessed their transition from being provided with some form of shelter or very modest housing allowances during the asylum procedure to a situation in which they might be deprived of any assistance in this regard.

The chapter begins with a description of the institutional framework of housing provision to asylum applicants and beneficiaries of international protection in Poland and then, in the following sections, it assesses the experience of asylum seekers with housing in Poland. It takes into account the experiences of those who choose to be accommodated during the asylum procedure in the centres for foreigners, as well as those who opt for housing allowances and accommodation outside of them. It separately examines the experiences with housing of beneficiaries of international protection.

The Institutional Framework of Housing Provision for Asylum Seekers

Before we shed light on the experiences of forced migrants with housing in Poland, it is necessary to briefly sketch the institutional framework of this provision in Poland and some background information about it.

Among the legal acts binding in Poland and providing detailed rules regarding reception conditions, the Law on Protection is particularly important since it includes articles (70–86) that lay out the elements of assistance that foreigners applying for international protection in Poland are entitled to, including the provision of housing. Apart from accommodation, foreigners staying in the centres for foreigners are entitled to, among others: (a) all-day group meals in accordance with their cultural standards, (b) financial assistance in the form of "pocket money", (c) financial aid for the purchase of personal hygiene products, and (d) one-time cash assistance for the purchase of clothing and footwear (Office for Foreigners, 2019a, pp. 4–5).

Importantly, the Law on Protection specifies in Article 71 that a foreigner shall be granted a financial benefit to cover his/her cost of stay in Poland outside the centre for foreigners (excluding the cost of medical care) when it is required by organisational aspects or it is necessary to: (1) ensure the foreigner's safety (including the special situation of single women), (2) protect the public order, (3) protect and maintain family ties, and (4) prepare the foreigner to live independently outside the centres for foreigners after receiving refugee status or subsidiary protection. As one of our respondents from an NGO pointed out, the requirements to justify staying outside the centre are nowadays not strictly followed. She pointed out that:

> Today, no longer do these conditions need to be fulfilled. Fifteen years ago, it was obligatory to provide medical or security arguments, but not now. (…) In practice, it works in such a way that everyone who submits an application to obtain the housing benefit gets it.
>
> *PLMZSO1*

One of the reasons to allow people seeking asylum to live outside the centres for foreigners, and hence the growing popularity of this type of accommodation in the last decade, was revealed by another NGO expert. This respondent mentioned a discussion with one of the employees of the Office for Foreigners, who argued that paying housing allowances to asylum seekers is less costly for the state than accommodating them in the centres and maintaining the centres. Our interviewee even suggested that this is a win-win situation as long as people seeking asylum are also provided with some additional integration instruments (PLMZSO3).

As we show below, the most recent statistical data as of the end of 2021 show the option of living outside a centre for foreigners was the most popular form of housing among those seeking international protection in Poland. As described in Chapter 4, the Law on Protection stipulates that accommodation (along with material assistance and medical care) is provided to all asylum seekers during the entire period of the procedure and up to two months after the final decision on their case. If an application is discontinued, assistance is offered for up to 14 days after that decision becomes final. If applicants receive a final negative decision, they must leave the territory of Poland within 30 days, so they should not need to take advantage of social assistance beyond this time limit.

As already mentioned in Chapter 4, to benefit from this assistance, asylum applicants have to register at one of the reception centres within two days of submitting the application for international protection. If they do not reach the centres within 48 hours, their asylum proceedings are discontinued. As Szulecka, Pachocka, and Sobczak-Szelc (2018b, p. 42) aptly point out, nonappearance at a reception centre usually stems from the fact that asylum seekers, who are often assisted by members of their families already living in Western European countries or by paid intermediaries, decide to travel across Poland to get to other countries where they also apply for international protection (see also Chapter 5).

The Law on Protection and some other more detailed legal acts[2] describe elements of material assistance to be provided to those seeking international protection, including the provision of housing. The reception system for asylum applicants is coordinated by the Office for Foreigners, with its head office in Warsaw and branch office in Biała Podlaska, 30 km from the border with Belarus and the border-crossing point at Brest-Terespol. The Office is responsible for providing social assistance, including housing, to people seeking international protection.

Foreigners eligible for the cash payments receive assistance in the amount specified in the Ordinance on the amount of assistance for foreigners applying for international protection. The amount of assistance depends on the number of family members, from PLN 25 daily per person for singles to PLN 12.50 per person for the fourth and next member of the given family (Table 7.1) (Ordinance of the Minister of Interior and Administration of 19 February 2016, Par. 6(1) and (2)).

Despite the growing cost of living and inflation, this level of financial support to asylum seekers living outside the centres has remained unchanged for more than 15 years. These payments are supposed to be sufficient to cover all living expenses of a foreigner in Poland, including housing and food. It is worth remembering that

TABLE 7.1 Allowances for asylum seekers living outside the centres for foreigners

Number of people in a family	*Daily amount per person*	*Monthly amount per person*
1 person	PLN 25 (around EUR 6)	PLN 750 (around EUR 187)
2 people	PLN 20 (around EUR 5)	PLN 600 (around EUR 150)
3 people	PLN 15 (around EUR 4)	PLN 450 (around EUR 112)
4 people and more	PLN 12.50 (around EUR 3)	PLN 375 (around EUR 94)

Source: Office for Foreigners, 2019a.

asylum applicants are not allowed to work in Poland in the first six months of the examination of their applications for international protection so they cannot legally improve their financial situation (see also Chapters 4 and 5). The only additional allowance that those living outside the centres can receive is the one for school utensils and didactic materials for children (Chrzanowska and Czerniejewska, 2015, p. 7), as well as help in learning the Polish language and basic educational materials, financial assistance to cover the costs of extra-curricular activities, and recreational and sports activities for children; funds to cover the cost of public transport in order to participate in the procedure for granting international protection, to undergo medical treatment or protective vaccinations, or in other particularly justified cases (Law on Protection, Article 71(4)).

The asylum seekers during the procedure are not eligible for any social benefits available for citizens or foreigners having a residence permit, including the "500+" child benefit introduced by the Polish government in 2015. It means that, in light of the law, all the needs of the asylum seeker are to be met by the Office for Foreigners. However, as we show below, everyday practice significantly differs from these legal provisions, and foreigners need to search for diverse ways (e.g., illegal employment or help from the NGO sector) to satisfy their needs.

According to the latest statistical data published by the Office for Foreigners, at the end of June 2021 there were 3,796 foreigners whose applications for international protection were being processed. The vast majority of them lived outside of the centres for foreigners and only 19% (713 persons) were accommodated in the 10 operating centres. Two years earlier (as of 30 June 2019), there were 2,963 foreigners whose proceedings for international protection had been initiated and 44% lived in one of 11 centres for foreigners, while the remaining 56% were being paid cash benefits to cover the cost of living outside the centres supervised by the Office. At that time (in 2019), 62% of the foreigners entitled to receive social assistance from the Office for Foreigners were Russian citizens, 18% came from Ukraine, and 5% from Tajikistan (to mention only the largest groups) (Office for Foreigners, 2019a).

As one may see in Figure 7.1, for many years only slightly more people were choosing to live outside of the centres for foreigners than in them. This situation changed radically in 2020, since one may see a significant rise in the number of

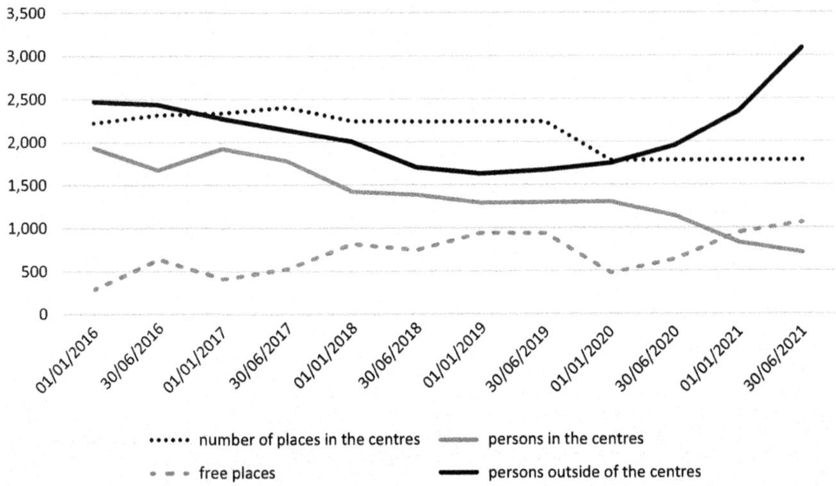

FIGURE 7.1 Number of asylum seekers accommodated in the centres for foreigners and outside of them, and the total number of places and free places between 2016 and 2021

Source: own elaboration of the data provided by the Office for Foreigners (2021).

people who choose to live outside of the centres. Despite the decline in the total number of available places in the centres (two were closed in the last five years), the number of free places rose to more than one thousand. In 2019, there were on average 118 people accommodated in each centre, but by mid-2021, the number had dropped to 71 (Office for Foreigners, 2021, 2019b).

For most of 2021, the Office ran 10 centres for foreigners, including 4 centres that belonged to the Office and 6 in rented premises[3]. Apart from these centres, the Office runs Foreigner Service Centres (mostly for persons using services outside the centres for foreigners) in Warsaw and Lublin (Office for Foreigners, 2019b).

Almost all the centres for foreigners are located in the eastern part of Poland (Figure 7.2). Six centres are located very close to Poland's eastern border, either in Lublin Voivodeship or in Podlaskie Voivodship, and the rest in Masovian Voivodeship or in Kuyavian-Pomeranian Voivodeship. Out of the 10 centres run by the Office throughout most of 2021, only 2 were located in big cities with more than 250,000 inhabitants (Warszawa-Targówek and Białystok), with the majority located in small cities (e.g., Biała Podlaska) or rural areas.

The centres in Biała Podlaska, 30 km from the border-crossing point in Brest-Terespol, and in Podkowa Leśna-Dębak, in the suburbs of the Capital City of Warsaw, perform the functions of reception centres. In other words, they serve as the first contact places where asylum seekers are accommodated and registered before they are moved to other centres for foreigners in different parts of Poland. The reception centre in Biała Podlaska is for first-time asylum applicants, while the centre in Podkowa Leśna-Dębak serves mostly as a reception centre for asylum

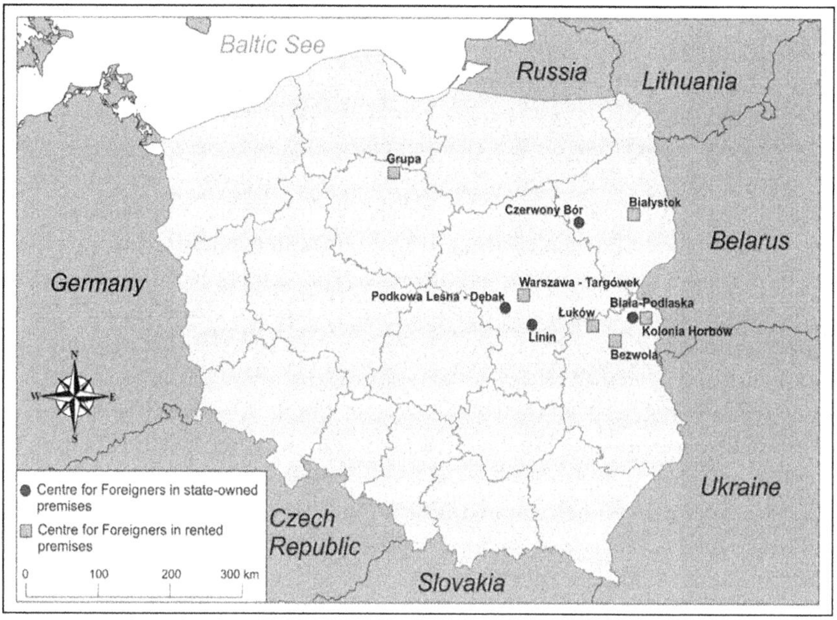

FIGURE 7.2 Location of the centres for foreigners in Poland (July 2021)

Source: Prepared by P. Jaczewski.

seekers transferred to Poland within the framework of the Dublin Regulation (see Chapter 4).

As one of the employees of the Office for Foreigners (PLMZOF3/4) informed us during the interview, the location of these reception centres is closely linked to how the migrants applying for international protection in Poland arrive in the country. Most frequently, they arrive in Poland from Belarus or Ukraine. Other migrants are transferred back to Poland (in line with the Dublin Regulation), usually from Western European countries, often by planes arriving at Warsaw airport or received by the Polish Border Guard from German or Czech border police at the checkpoints along the internal EU border. Asylum seekers can request to be placed in a particular centre, for example, to reunite with some family members or to join friends, and such requests are usually accepted. Also, centres located in either bigger or smaller cities tend to be more popular than those in rural areas.

As far as accommodation in the centres is concerned, all of them are open-type facilities, so foreigners are free to leave them at any time. However, while staying in the centres, foreigners must follow some rules specified in the Ordinance on the rules of stay, which some may perceive as restricting some of their freedoms. They are obliged to, among others, show particular care for the safety of minor children remaining under their custody, respect quiet hours from 10.00 p.m. to 6.00 a.m., and return to the centre before 11.00 p.m.

The residents are accommodated in double, four-person, and multi-person rooms depending on the situation of a particular individual or family. With the exception of the centre in Czerwony Bór where foreigners receive a per diem instead of prepared meals, in the other centres, a full-board canteen is offered to asylum seekers. Apart from meals, in all the centres, the residents are provided with so-called "pocket money" (PLN 50 per month), financial aid for the purchase of personal hygiene products (PLN 20 per month), one-time cash assistance for the purchase of clothing and footwear (PLN 140), and financial aid to cover the cost of transportation for strictly specified purposes (taking part in proceedings for international protection; presenting oneself for medical examinations or protective vaccinations; other justified cases). The centres also offer the possibility to learn Polish and basic materials necessary for learning, access of foreign minors to public schools and covering the costs of tuition and a cash equivalent for meals, the possibility for preschool children to participate in educational and adaptive activities, and the chance of having the costs of extra-curricular, recreational or sports activities for children covered (Office for Foreigners, 2019a, pp. 4–5, and Ordinance of the Minister of Interior and Administration of 19 February 2016 on the amount of assistance for foreigners seeking international protection, Par. 2.1–6.1).

At the same time, the Office for Foreigners claims to pay a lot of attention to the issue of respect for the religious and cultural identity of people applying for international protection, and—in cooperation with other bodies—to try to ensure security and compliance with public order at the centres and in their immediate vicinity (Office for Foreigners, 2019a, p. 5).

As far as the special provision of housing for vulnerable persons and groups is concerned, the legal basis for it can be found in the Law on Protection in Article 68 (see Chapter 4). If there is a need for accommodation in the centre for foreigners in a single room or in a room adapted to the needs of a disabled person or in the centre for women and children only, then such applicants are considered as requiring special treatment in the field of social assistance (Article 68(2.1)). Also, the applicant is treated as vulnerable when there is a need to place them in a treatment institution, a nursing care institution, or hospice, or when it is necessary to place them in foster care corresponding to their psychophysical condition (Article 68(2.2–3)). Another prerequisite to consider an applicant as a person requiring special treatment as regards social assistance applies to cases when it is necessary to adapt the applicants' diet to their health (Article 68(2.4)).

The vulnerable groups that the Office seems primarily to take into account are single women and women with children. In order to improve their safety, the Office for Foreigners designated one centre solely for this group in 2010, the centre for foreigners in Targówek in Warsaw. According to the Office, from the very beginning, the centre was fully occupied (Office for Foreigners, 2019b, p. 9). At the end of 2021, the centre was closed due to a change of ownership, but special wards of the reception centre in Podkowa-Leśna Dębak were dedicated to single women and single women with children (Chlabicz and Nowosielska, 2021).

Representatives of NGOs during interviews pointed to numerous issues linked with this particular centre for vulnerable persons. The most significant criticism was that there was only one such centre in Poland, and it could be easy to track down a given woman with children. This is crucial from the point of view of the safety of vulnerable persons:

> This is the only centre in Poland for women bringing up children on their own. What protection are we talking about?
>
> *PLMZSO5/6*

Apart from that, the same interviewee mentioned several other problems concerning this centre for foreigners:

> Living conditions there are terrible. There are bed bugs and sick children. Children sleep on the floor because it is not possible to sleep in beds because of the danger of being bitten by bed bugs. You can't get rid of them.
>
> *PLMZSO5/6*

Apart from setting up the centre for single women and mothers with children, in recent years the Office for Foreigners adopted and implemented the action "Policy of protection of children against abuse in centres for foreigners" in cooperation with the "We give children the strength" Foundation. This policy was a result of the project "We protect children in refugee centres—a comprehensive system to protect children from violence and abuse", co-financed from the national programme under the Asylum, Migration, and Integration Fund and from the state budget (Office for Foreigners, 2019a, p. 9).

The Institutional Framework of Housing for Beneficiaries of International Protection

The Constitution of the Republic of Poland of 2 April 1997 stipulates in Article 52(1) that: "Everyone shall be guaranteed freedom of movement in the territory of the Republic of Poland and the choice of place of residence and stay". This means that the beneficiary of international protection decides independently where he/she will live. Polish law does not offer separate legislation regarding housing for foreigners, including refugees. Beneficiaries of international protection are generally subject to the same rules as Polish citizens. Two key laws can be identified regarding housing policy in general: the Law on Tenancy and Housing and the Law on Housing Allowances[4]. However, foreigners' rights on access to housing are limited in terms of property rights. They can purchase flats, but if they purchase land or a house, they must obtain permission from the Ministry of the Interior and Administration (Koss-Goryszewska, 2019, p. 28).

Despite the freedom to choose one's place of residence, for procedural reasons, in particular to benefit from the Individual Integration Programme (see Chapter 4) or when applying for a flat from commune housing resources, the voivodeship and poviat the beneficiary of international protection declares their residence is important.

Although the state does not offer preferential access to housing for refugees, a kind of housing support (rather housing counselling) is offered as part of the integration activities under the Law on Social Assistance. The family support centre is obliged within individual integration programmes (IIP) to provide assistance in obtaining housing to refugees, including in a protected flat, if possible (Law on Social Assistance, Art. 93(1)(1)). In addition, the beneficiaries of IIPs are entitled to receive monthly cash benefits to cover, among others, housing costs (Art. 92). Sometimes, housing assistance is implemented as part of the poviat's own tasks (e.g., special projects). In practice, this means that the only gateway to special or dedicated housing solutions for refugees are those offered by local authorities.

This is well reflected in the activities implemented by the Warsaw Family Support Centre on the basis of the relevant provisions[5]. According to them, that centre is entitled to apply for the conclusion of a rental (lease) agreement to an apartment from the housing resources of the Capital City of Warsaw, for persons with refugee status or subsidiary protection. However, the Warsaw Family Support Centre (WFSC) cannot submit more than five applications annually. A rental agreement may be concluded with a person who resides in the flat in which the density does not exceed 6 square meters of living space per person and this person/family is in poverty (which is defined by the income criterion based on the average monthly income per member household). The 2019 edition of the housing contest for flats set aside by the municipality for persons with international protection was open to people who, among others, completed an IIP in Warsaw and did not have legal title in the form of ownership or joint ownership of a dwelling, were not a party to any flat rental agreement, did not have the right to reside in a communal/social apartment, were not on the list of people waiting to sign a contract to rent an apartment from the housing resources of Warsaw, or had received from the competent office of a Warsaw district a refusal to qualify for the list of people awaiting to rent a flat from the housing resources of Warsaw (WCPR, 2019).

The Warsaw Family Support Centre's housing support also includes providing assistance to refugees in the form of organising their temporary stay in a protected (sheltered) flat, which results from the provisions of the Law on Social Assistance (Articles 93 and 53). A stay in a sheltered flat can be granted to a person who, due to a difficult life situation, age, disability, or illness, needs support in everyday life, as well as a foreigner who has obtained one of the international protection forms in Poland. The flat is a form of social assistance that prepares people staying there, under the care of specialists, to lead an independent life or to replace a stay in an institution providing full-time care[6]. Stay in protected housing can be granted to foreigners who:

- are beneficiaries of international protection or members of their families,
- are staying in Warsaw and intend to settle there,

- expressed their will to implement an IIP or are already under an IIP coordinated by the Warsaw Family Support Centre,
- have difficulties in integration,
- are affected by a difficult life situation, especially in housing, as confirmed by the WFSC social worker,
- demonstrate a commitment to solving life problems.

The period of stay cannot exceed 12 months, and in particularly justified cases may be extended by three months. Foreigners bear the full cost of living there.

The report by the Supreme Audit Office published in 2015 indicated that the beneficiaries of IIPs most often lived in premises rented on the free market. Only a few families used a protected flat or a flat from the commune's housing stock. Housing assistance in the audited family support centres most often consisted of providing foreigners only with information on possible forms of access to flats (NIK, 2015).

It is rare in Poland that local authorities provide refugees with free access to an apartment. This possibility was created by the project WITEK–"Warsaw test project of integration of foreigners with regard to the needs of the labour market", initiated and coordinated by the Capital City of Warsaw in 2017–2019. Most participants took advantage of this opportunity, considering this even more important than professional support in accessing the labour market. Material security in the form of a flat for more than two years gave them a sense of stability and security (Gać and Pachocka, 2019).

Some of the key challenges related to housing for beneficiaries of international protection that will be analysed in greater detail below include the limited supply of affordable housing, high rental costs (especially in big cities), discrimination in the housing market, the lack of specialised housing counselling for beneficiaries of international protection, and the risk of homelessness after the end of institutional support under the IIPs (Koss-Goryszewska, 2019).

Asylum Seekers and Housing in the Centres for Foreigners

From the institutional framework of housing provision, we now turn to the practices, experiences, and perceptions regarding this dimension of the reception and integration systems in Poland. We start with analyses of the experiences of asylum seekers and then turn to those of the beneficiaries of international protection. As the experience with housing provision of the asylum applicants starts with the centres for foreigners, we begin with this type of provision and only later assess the situation of applicants outside of the centres. While doing so, we strive to juxtapose the opinions of the asylum seekers with those of the state administration, practitioners, and NGO actors.

There was rare agreement among our interviewees from the non-governmental and governmental sectors that the housing conditions in these centres have in recent years significantly improved. These improved conditions, according to some of the interviewed employees of the Office for Foreigners, can be matched with conditions provided to asylum seekers in Western European countries. One of these interviewees argued that:

> I have not been on many study visits, but from the stories, reports, and what I saw myself, we really have nothing to be ashamed of. Our conditions may be modest, but they are really very good. Especially in comparison to the situation in some countries where foreigners live in some barracks, in large halls, where it is not possible to keep the intimacy of the family. (...) We have at least comparable conditions, if not better. I know this also based on the opinions of foreign delegations that visit our centres. I have not heard any criticism yet. On the contrary, everyone is surprised that foreigners are in such good conditions.
>
> *PLMZOF3/4*

Migrants seeking international protection in Poland had generally a less rosy perception of the conditions in the centres. Before describing some of the main criticisms they raised, it is worth mentioning a couple of positive points that were made, too. Several interviewees pointed out that the centres have provided them with something very important—security. One of them, when asked if she liked the centre in which she was staying, answered:

> The main thing for me is that I am safe here, that nobody will come and kill me. I am alive, my child is with me. We are not starving. We have a room. Of course, it could be better, but for the moment, that will do for me. The main thing is that I feel protected. Nobody knows where I am.
>
> *PLMICh03*

Another element of the housing provision in the Office-run centres appreciated by their inhabitants was the possibility of interaction with other people and social life. An asylum seeker at one of the centres said:

> It looks like a hotel to me. Yes, we share the kitchen and the bathroom with other families. It is not convenient, but on the other hand, we have a social life. Women talk in the kitchen. (...) I can go out to the garden, rake leaves, like at home. I can't say I feel completely at home. We have been living here for some time, so we made our room cosy.
>
> *PLMICh05*

As is evident, this person is fully aware that the centre is not her home and yet she tries to make it a little bit like home. Similarly, a few other interviewees talked about the importance of socialising and spending time together with other inhabitants of the centres in their kitchen (e.g., PLMICh06 and PLMIIr26). One of the major reasons that prevented them from enjoying it more was the lack of money to buy items to cook. Another feature of the centres that was considered positive and mentioned by a few current or past inhabitants was the quite easy access to medical care in the centres.

One of the major critical remarks concerning the provision of housing in the centres for foreigners was linked with their location. Both our interviewees involved in providing assistance to foreigners and asylum applicants saw the location of the centres in both the countryside and sometimes (when applicable) within cities, as very problematic. The first issue was well captured by one of the practitioners, who pointed out that:

> When it comes to the centres for people in the procedure, I have the impression that they select them only on the basis of price. Whoever offers the lowest then wins. Nobody thinks whether there are refugees or not. Łódź Grotniki, for example, or Czerwony Bór near Łomża. I apologise for the expression, but you can't find bigger shitholes. The conditions for integration are zero. They have empty buildings so let the foreigners live there. Nobody takes into account how close these places are to cities, about the possibility of interaction with people and entering the labour market. This is completely out of the picture. Only the price criterion—98% and 2%—I do not know what, whether there is a nice forest around. Dębak, for example, is a former missile defence unit in Warsaw. What [integration] are we talking about?
>
> *PLMZP*

This is how one of the people in the asylum procedure talked about her life in Podkowa Leśna-Dębak:

> I lived there for four months and it was very difficult. I had to be in the office in Taborowa street in Warsaw every Wednesday and I had to go to the bus stop through 3 km of forest together with the children. Sometimes, my friends who had cars gave me a lift. I also had a job. I cleaned in the kindergarten. It was difficult to get there from Dębak.
>
> *PLMICh02*

Later, this person talked about the relief she felt when she managed to secure a transfer to a centre in a big city where she lives close to people, shops, school, and her temporary job.

The location of the centres far from big cities is particularly problematic to vulnerable persons such as those with a disability. One such person interviewed in the course of the research pointed out:

> The location of the centre is very problematic—it's a big problem for me. How can I go anywhere? You can't go anywhere except by car. I've been here in the camp for two months and 10 days and I did not go out at all. If I need anything, my friends will bring it to me here. Anything I eat or drink

> or smoke, it comes to me here. I do not go out because once it was cold and another time there was no track for the wheelchair.
>
> *PLMIIr26*

The fact that many centres are far from cities not only limits the scope of interaction and integration of foreigners with the host society but also the actions of the NGO sector. As one of its representatives aptly pointed out:

> Because the centres are far away from some large urban agglomerations and often off the beaten track, it makes it difficult for NGOs to reach them. If we want, for example, to do some activities for people in Linin, we will find volunteers, but we would need to arrange transportation for them to take them there and back.
>
> *PLMZSO1*

An interesting problem linked with the location of the centres away from big cities was noticed by one of the interviewed representatives of the local authorities. He claimed that one of the centres:

> (…) was located in the wrong place. It became a very visible, dominant element there. If it functioned within a larger environment, it wouldn't be so noticeable, it would be lost in the crowd of people. This is a sparsely populated area because we know that these are small villages and a school with 150 pupils. Every element of behaviour that we cannot agree with is quickly noticed. Maybe it has good sides because there is a signal and there is a faster response. In the city, it could be more camouflaged, classified, because in urban society not all such things are noticed.
>
> *PLMZLG1*

In his own way, the quoted respondent referred to the issue of the visibility of minorities that in villages or small towns becomes clearer. However, moving the centres for foreigners to big cities will not resolve all the problems linked with this phenomenon and the frequent discriminatory perceptions and treatment of visible minorities especially seen during the significant recent securitisation of the idea of asylum seeker and refugee (Legut and Pędziwiatr, 2018; Łodziński, 2019; Pędziwiatr, 2019).

Another issue indicated was the location of some of the centres in cities, but on their outskirts or in some poor or "problematic areas". One NGO expert pointed out, for example, the centre for foreigners located in Targówek in Warsaw (closed in August 2021) was located "in the unfriendly part of the city, with the factories and where the concrete mixers drive every now and then" (PLMZSO1). Another expert complained also about the "dust in the area during the summer" in the area where the centre was located and that it was in on the outskirts of the city (PLMZSO2).

Yet, a different problem with the housing provision in the centres mentioned by a few of our interviewees was overcrowding. One asylum seeker with whom we talked recounted the following about the conditions in the centre:

> (…) in the past, it was not good. (…) Before, there were 14 people in a room. All the countries, Iraq, Yemen … Now in the new room, it is me and three other guys, two Kurds, and one Yemeni.
>
> *PLMIIr27*

On the other hand, another asylum seeker described his and his family's living conditions in the centre for foreigners like this:

> Maybe we were lucky, or maybe the management decided like that, but they gave us a very spacious room. There were four big rooms in the centre, and one of them was ours. We fit in. On the one side, there were children, on the other, us. We separated the sides with wardrobes.
>
> *PLMIUk19*

People seeking international protection who lived in the centres for foreigners also complained about conflicts with other inhabitants of the centres. One of our Ukrainian interviewees claimed that ethno-religious tensions were one of the major reasons why she decided to move out of the centre. She argued that:

> It was hard to stay together with Chechens and their different attitudes to women and to people relations. (…) It was one of the reasons I wanted to live in my own flat, not to depend on anyone. I wanted to be a host in my own house.
>
> *PLMIUk20*

Instances of conflict and even violence in the centres were also mentioned by some of the interviewees from the civil society organisations and local governments. One NGO expert (PLMZSO2) claimed that the scale of violence was particularly high in the centre in Targówek in Warsaw where there were only women and children. These conflicts were "between residents, between children, between residents and children" and even the police were unable to control them. Our interviewee put most of the blame for this situation on the authorities who had created such a large centre for women with children. The number of people staying in the centre at the time of the interview was around 150. According to the respondent, this crowding was the main reason for the high level of tension and violence in the centre.

Conflicts rooted in cultural and religious differences in other centres for foreigners were also pointed out by one of the interviewed representatives of the local authorities (PLMZLG1). According to this interviewee, these differences were the main reason why asylum seekers, in spite of the very modest housing benefits, preferred to live outside the centres. One of the employees of the Office for Foreigners informed us that in order to prevent conflicts:

> There is a bit of a tendency not to mix nationalities too much, and some know-how about how to locate the people in the centres so as to avoid tensions [related to] different backgrounds.
>
> *PLMZOF2*

At the same time, another person we interviewed from the Office said that in one of the centres they needed to intervene to prevent strong ethnic homogenisation. This interviewee pointed out that:

> We try to avoid situations in which the centre was typically Chechen, that persons of no other nationality stay there, only Chechens. We had such a situation in one of the centres. The case was quite mediatised. In one of the schools attended by the children from our centre, there was some nasty incident. One of its consequences was the decision to try to change slightly the nationality structure in this centre and reduce the number of Chechens in favour of persons with other nationalities. (...) We succeeded in achieving this.
>
> *PLMZOF3/4*

Another recurring point of criticism among the migrant interviewees and NGO representatives is the amount of "pocket money" given to asylum seekers while living in the Office-run centres. One Chechen asylum applicant (PLMICh06) pointed out that she would like to cook for her children more often instead of receiving food from the canteen, but for PLN 70 in pocket money per month, it was not possible. The very low amount of pocket money given to those who stay in the centres for foreigners also has an impact on their daily functioning outside the centres. An interesting observation about this was made by a social organisation respondent, who stressed that:

> The pocket money they get is terribly low, it is not enough for anything, for example, to travel by public transport. It forces people to travel without a ticket and exposes them to fines, penalties, etc.
>
> *PLMZSO1*

One important criticism from the NGO experts working with asylum seekers was that apart from food and shelter, the centres for foreigners offer very limited activities for their inhabitants. According to some of our interviewees, this is linked not only with the legal and financial aspects of the functioning of these centres but also with the qualifications of their personnel. Some actors from the NGO sector complained that many employees of the centres do not have adequate qualifications to work at such premises. One of them argued, for instance:

> People who are said to be social workers in the centres are not social workers. (…) They do not need to have a degree in social work. There is no career path at all for a social worker working with people seeking international protection.
>
> *PLMZSO5/6*

As far as vulnerable people are concerned, as mentioned above, there is a fairly good legal basis for providing services for them (including housing) in the Law on Protection. The interviewed employees of the Office for Foreigners claimed that also in practice special needs of vulnerable persons are addressed adequately. The Helsinki Foundation, which monitors the asylum system in Poland, however, highlights in its reports the malfunctioning mechanism of identification of vulnerable persons, as well as the issue of placing vulnerable groups in detention centres (AIDA, 2020).

It is important to mention also the crucial role played by various NGOs in the assistance of asylum seekers and beneficiaries of international protection with housing. From a wide range of NGOs involved in the help of asylum seekers in the centres or outside them, some of the most frequently mentioned by our interviewees were the Ocalenie Foundation and the initiative Chlebem i Solą (With Bread and Salt). One of the interviewed asylum seekers said, for instance:

> After arriving in Poland, I stayed in Dębak for seven months and meanwhile, I got a work permit. I was working officially, but to live in one room in the camp among those different nationalities it was very hard. (…) Thank God that there exists such an organisation like the Ocalenie Foundation. (…) Those open and kind people, trying to help us as much as possible. Thanks to this organisation (…) my children take additional exercises and I'm getting moral, psychological, legal support. Everything that is going on positively in my life now is thanks to the Ocalenie Foundation. I am saying it honestly because they gave me a house, household appliances, cleaning supplies. They help how they can, me and my family. I'm thankful to them.
>
> *PLMICh13*

Another interviewee acknowledged the aid of the initiative Chlebem i Solą:

> We live in one of the districts of Warsaw. Why there? Because we didn't have any alternative. The foundation Chlebem i Solą posted an advertisement on the internet and then some people answered these ads. (…) There were two rooms with a kitchen, an old house, after renovation. So, we went there.
>
> *PLMIUk20*

Asylum Seekers and Housing Outside the Centres for Foreigners

As shown earlier, the majority of asylum applicants in Poland live outside the centres for foreigners operated by the Office for Foreigners (a particularly visible trend since 2020). One of the major problems with this housing provision, mentioned equally frequently by the civil society actors as well as persons seeking international protection in Poland, is the insufficient level of financial support provided by the state to cover the cost of living outside of the centres for foreigners. As mentioned above, a single person receives a monthly benefit of PLN 750 to cover all the costs of life outside the centres while a four-person family receives PLN 1500.

One of the interviewed practitioners argued that the extent to which housing needs are satisfied for people seeking international protection

> (…) depends on their personal expectations because everyone is different. For some people, one room with a kitchen will be enough, and for someone else who used to live in a large house, it will degrade his/her dignity and comfort. (…) I can't say it is tragic because these are just the conditions in this country. One cannot turn a blind eye to the fact that in this country sometimes families of two generations live in a 37 square metre flat. It is just a fact. If someone thinks that he/she will live in 65 square metres, it is not always [the case] in our region.
>
> *PLMZP2*

This interviewee also claimed that in one medium-size Polish city, PLN 1200 was sufficient in 2018 to pay for all the costs of the rental of a fully-furnished two-room or three-room flat.

> If someone rents a room in a single-family house, it is PLN 400–450. It is true that people may prefer to be more independent, but these prices can still be found.
>
> *PLMZP2*

The respondent also suggested that the cash benefits to self-cover the costs of one's stay in Poland were adequate.

However, the vast majority of actors from the NGO sector as well as some asylum seekers interviewed in the course of the research complained about the level of the financial support provided by the Office to cover the cost of living outside the centres for foreigners. For instance, one asylum seekers who would like to live outside the centre if she could afford it argued that to rent a flat:

> I would need to have a permanent job. I receive PLN 1500 when I work, and I would need to pay for everything for the flat. But I also need the money for food and for the children's clothes. I certainly would like to rent a flat. We go to bed at 8 p.m. and sometimes it is noisy here.
>
> *PLMICh02*

She was unable to leave the Office-run facility despite its numerous drawbacks because she did not earn enough money and would not receive sufficient financial support from the Office.

Some representatives of social organisations were even more vocal in their criticism of the level of support provided by the state to the asylum seekers who decided to live outside the centres. One of them pointed out that, for example:

> The level of financial support can be sufficient to rent at maximum a room because one cannot even dream about renting an apartment for this money and yet [still have] some resources to buy food. A couple with a child gets PLN 1350 for three persons. This amount is not sufficient to survive even in small towns in Poland.
>
> *PLMZSO2*

A similar opinion was expressed by another respondent from the NGO sector, who argued that PLN 750:

> (...) certainly does not allow one to rent an apartment. Sometimes a room. In Warsaw, room prices are even higher. So, to find a room for PLN 400 borders on a miracle. This has a direct impact on the housing conditions (...) They are sometimes literally substandard—people live in basements or in attics without heating, or a lot of people live in a very small space and this is done without the consent of the owner. So, they rent a flat as a family of five [persons], and then they also take in a cousin with his/her children.
>
> *PLMZS01*

These opinions are supported by numerous research reports. In one of them, from 2017, one may read that the amount of so-called benefits outside the centre has not been raised since they were introduced in 2003 (see also Chapter 4). In the same period, the costs of living have significantly risen. In 2016, for example, the subsistence level—that is, the minimal amount of financial resources below which there is a biological threat to human life—according to calculations by the Institute of Labour and Social Affairs amounted to PLN 555 for a one-person household and PLN 472 per person in a four-person household. Hence, if a four-person family in 2019 was paid a PLN 1500 cash benefit to live outside the centre, then it was already almost PLN 100 per person less than the subsistence level in 2016.

A report by the Association of Legal Intervention based on monitoring the housing conditions of refugees describes the situation of persons seeking international protection in Poland. It points out that asylum applicants "in order to support themselves have to earn some extra money, most commonly by working illegally. And even then, they usually rent apartments of substandard quality or rent them together with two or three families". At the same time, the authors of the report argue that foreigners who are in the asylum procedure are never threatened with extreme homelessness. If they are unable to make a living by renting an apartment on the free market, they can at any time opt-out of the "out-of-centre" benefits and return to one of the Office-run centres for foreigners (Chrzanowska and Czerniejewska, 2015, p. 8).

Here, it is worth mentioning that this opinion is not shared among all of the researchers analysing the situation of people seeking asylum in Poland. Kinga Wysieńska, for example, in her report on various dimensions of homelessness among refugees and people seeking international protection in Poland, argues that not only foreigners living in the centres run by the Office for Foreigners but also those who are recipients of the benefits living outside the centres experience homelessness, or they are *exposed* to it. The first group of foreigners (those living in the centres) are exposed to it because they are staying in collective accommodation, whereas those receiving the benefit, due to its minimal amount, cannot adequately cover the cost of rented premises on the free market (Wysieńska, 2014a, pp. 5–6).

Poor housing conditions due to insufficient financial support were also mentioned in the project interviews by employees of the Office for Foreigners. One interviewee said openly that "the out-of-centre benefit is too low and it is difficult to survive with it" and that the agency's control visits regularly show that "migrants are renting flats or houses that are lived in by a higher number of people than they should be" (PLMZOF3/4). These situations are also confirmed by numerous accounts of people seeking international protection in Poland. For instance, one of our migrant respondents said:

> The thing I would like to change in the first place is an apartment. Here, the accommodation issue is very hard, unlike in other countries. I lived for almost one year in my sister's apartment because it was hard to rent a flat. In the one apartment, we lived with almost 15 people.
>
> *PLMICh11*

The process of monitoring the housing conditions of asylum seekers living outside of the centres by employees of the Office for Foreigners is also not very consistent and there are no serious consequences of a negative assessment.

The research data also show that other practitioners and members of social organisations try to provide assistance to foreigners in search of housing. A practitioner from one medium-size Polish city pointed out, for example:

> If someone is looking for a flat somewhere, we talk about it and we are also looking for such a flat. We call people who rent flats or provide these addresses where we know people have been renting flats for many years. It is hard to call them hotels—let's call them workers' hotels. We provide asylum seekers information about where someone is renting an apartment at a decent price and in good conditions.
>
> *PLMZP2*

This help is very important since foreigners seeking protection have to tackle not only the issue of very limited funding for accommodation but also problems related to discrimination in the housing market. This problem and some interesting ideas for addressing it were mentioned by an interviewee in the NGO sector, who said:

> There is high resistance on the part of flat owners, apart from the financial barrier. (…) However, an interesting grassroots initiative has been launched by With Bread and Salt over a year ago. They search for flats for both asylum seekers or refugees without separating the two groups and they have achieved huge success in this field. They work through Facebook, through various social media and such networks. They found several dozen nice apartments in the last year or so.
>
> *PLMZSO1*

It is also important to mention the key barrier for vulnerable people to move out of the centres, namely a financial one. Its key elements were aptly noted in this observation by a civil society actor:

> Certainly, for everyone, in the long run, the best is accommodation outside of the centres for foreigners (…) a lot of people who would want to move out of the centres cannot afford it because they know that they have no "extra money", because they are single mothers or people with disabilities. It is certainly the case that the financial support is not diversified in any way depending on the specific needs of a given person or family.
>
> *PLMZSO1*

As will be shown below, some vulnerable asylum seekers prefer to live in the centres for foreigners to have easier access to the medical services provided there or that can be arranged easier with the help of the centre's staff.

The Experiences of Beneficiaries of International Protection with Housing

Some of the key issues that emerge yet at the stage of pre-integration, or while claiming asylum, frequently continue to the period after one has received international protection. Some of the most important ones are the lack of adequate and affordable accommodation, discrimination in the housing market, and limited support from the state institutions. As one of the interviewed practitioners very pertinently argued:

> (…) if someone has a problem with paying for his/her apartment, or has no financial means to sustain himself/herself, then they will not think about learning Polish or somehow cultivate themselves culturally. This is Maslow's Pyramid above, and we didn't provide the basic ones.
>
> *PLMZP1*

The lack of adequate and affordable rooms, flats, and houses also has been one of the issues most frequently pointed out by actors from the non-government sector. Refugees tend to settle in big cities where the labour markets are bigger; hence, there are more offers for suitable jobs (PLMZSO2). On the other hand, the access to cheap and adequate housing might be limited in such cities.

Some of our interviewees from social organisations rightly pointed out that the difficulty of finding adequate housing for persons with refugee status or other types of international protection is part of a general shortage of affordable housing. According to experts, there is a shortage of about 2.1 million houses in Poland. This situation most frequently affects people with medium and low income. They neither have access to cheap mortgages nor finances to buy the apartments. The social housing in the country estimated at 150–200 thousand premises is absolutely insufficient for the needs of the population (Chabasiński, 2018).

One of our interviewees pointed out that:

> Housing is one of those things that do not work in Poland at all. Our experience often shows that when we talk about a problem that affects refugees, we de facto talk about a problem that affects everyone. The refugees just have a harder time than the rest of society with the same problem (...) There are too few cheap flats, too few social housing options, and these flats are poorly managed. There is also a lack of relevant legislation that could put more flats on the market. There are flats that are empty and people do not want to rent them and keep for themselves as a form of capital investment. There are countries where there are legal solutions that prohibit such a situation.
>
> *PLMZSO2*

Another interviewee from the social organisations argued that the lack of access to cheap housing is what she considered "the biggest barrier in the integration process". She said:

> This is the first human need, to ensure a sense of security when you have a roof over your head (...) Only then can you think about work, qualifications, retraining, etc.
>
> *PLMZSO1*

She persuasively argued that if this basic need is not provided, then it is difficult for migrants to advance in other dimensions of integration.

As already mentioned, persons whose applications for asylum were assessed positively have the right to apply for social housing through the same channels as citizens of Poland. If they meet the conditions, which in each locality might be different, then they can get municipal or social housing. They also face the same barriers as Poles—the small housing stock, competition for such housing, long queues, and waiting times. Sometimes, as one of our interviewees from the social sector noted, they also face discrimination on the basis of being foreigners. One of our interviewees said that it is not uncommon to hear a narrative that if there are not enough houses for "us", "we" should not provide them to "aliens"

(PLMZSO1). Discriminatory practices towards refugees in the housing market make access to decent housing increasingly difficult. The negative portrayal of refugees further aggravates their situation in the housing market. It makes the offer of the prospective houses and flats, which they could rent, increasingly scarce. One NGO representative argued that:

> The problem with flats also forces refugees to leave Poland, because in the West, it is easier to find a flat and there are fewer prejudices.
>
> *PLMZSO2*

This interviewee also claimed that they have people on their team who speak Polish with and without a foreign accent. If persons with the accent enquire about a given flat, they much more often hear that the offer is not valid. This interviewee also recalled a situation when a young Chechen couple was looking for an apartment. A few times they had a situation where the landlords agreed to rent the apartment to them, but later refused to do so, when they learned that they were from Chechnya. More recently, this couple was going to sign a contract and when the owners saw that the girl was in hijab, although she spoke perfect Polish, they refused to sign it (PLMZSO2).

Several beneficiaries of international protection pointed out that sometimes even though they had the necessary financial resources for a given flat, their owners refused to rent these flats to them. One person pointed out that:

> It was very difficult to find a flat because their owners refused to rent them to refugees, or to foreigners. (…). After the tenth refusal, I thought, "how come one receives protection, but cannot find a flat". It was difficult, difficult.
>
> *PLMIUk19*

Our findings confirm earlier research on the experiences of discrimination in the housing market by refugees. One such study of both a quantitative and qualitative nature was carried out by Kinga Wysieńska in 2014. It showed, among other things, that Chechen men (also part of our research) were the group most frequently discriminated against (Wysieńska, 2014b).

The research into anti-refugee and anti-Muslim prejudices partially confirms the aforementioned interviewee's point on the levels of discrimination towards persons perceived as "aliens" in contemporary Poland (e.g., CBOS, 2016, 2015; Zick et al., 2011). As argued in the chapter on narratives (see Chapter 3), these prejudices were very effectively mobilised and used in the parliamentary elections in 2015 that overlapped with the peak of the migration-management crisis (Legut and Pędziwiatr, 2018; Pędziwiatr, 2017, 2016). According to some representatives of social organisations, the lack of affordable housing is the key reason why many people who claim asylum in Poland treat the country only as transitory (PLMZSO1). One may find this observation also in some other studies on the situation of refugees in Poland. The latest annual report of the Association of Legal Intervention points out that one of the major reasons persons with international protection leave Poland has to do with the lack of "housing security" (Chrzanowska et al., 2020).

Adequate housing as the most important need was also frequently stressed by the interviewed beneficiaries of international protection. One argued, for example, that when he had been granted international protection his first need was an apartment, because:

> without a flat you can't move any further. You can't think about finding a job, etc. Currently an apartment issue is the main problem.
>
> *PLMICh10*

Our research data shows that those persons who seem to have particularly big problems with finding the right accommodation are those who have been living in one of the refugee centres financed by the Office for Foreigners during the whole asylum procedure. The majority of asylum applicants decide to live outside of such centres and seem to learn about the difficulties of finding adequate housing at an earlier stage of their stay in Poland. One of our interviewees who was in a difficult situation during the transition with a family from the refugee centre to living outside it pointed out that:

> We had only 3–4 days more in the centre and then we were about to be on the street.
>
> *PLMIUk20*

She was also surprised that the small allowance paid to her and members of her family would stop being paid after a positive decision on their asylum application had been issued. She said:

> I was in shock. I could not understand how they cannot give us money.
>
> *PLMIUk20*

Our research data show the difficulty some families experience when transferring from the refugee centres to independent accommodation and in financially managing to find a new house before receiving access to the financial support within the IIP. Signing a rental contract usually means that one needs not only adequate funds to pay for the monthly rental fees but also a deposit for the rented property. Many persons moving out of the refugee centres do not have savings that would allow them to pay for such costs.

This transition period and the search for adequate housing have been facilitated by different actors. Some of the most frequently mentioned are the different social organisations, members of social networks, and representatives of the local authorities. For instance, the interviewee mentioned above was helped by activists from With Bread and Salt (Chlebem i Solą). She described this assistance in the following way:

> I called Chlebem i Solą. They took photos of us. And in the centre, I met a woman from Kyrgyzstan, and she also was moving out from the centre. We agreed to look for a flat together, since we could share the bills, and together we had 1500 zł. (…) Chlebem i Solą found a house for us and invited us to see it. We saw it. It is the same house where we live now, we have lived there till now. Why there? Because we didn't have any alternative. Chlebem i Solą posted an advertisement on the Internet and then some people answered it. (…) When we arrived, the landlord on the same day went for shopping and bought a fridge and a washing machine. We also had help from Chlebem i Solą, they collected things for us. I was very grateful. It was like a fairy tale to us that we moved out from the centre, that we received a status.
>
> *PLMIUk20*

We may learn from this excerpt also that it is not uncommon for refugees, in order to be able to afford to rent a certain flat or house, must do so with other persons or families to share the cost of rental. Subletting parts of the flats or houses is another practice of dealing with scarce financial resources when renting an adequate room, flat, or house. As one of our interviewees pointed out, sharing a room or flat with another family is frequent since "it is cheaper this way" (PLMICh08). The phenomenon of subletting parts of flats and houses is closely linked with overcrowding.

Among other frequently mentioned organisations helping refugees in the context of housing has been the Ocalenie Foundation. Numerous persons with international protection approached by us in the course of the research expressed their appreciation of the Foundation's efforts in helping them to rent flats and houses. One interviewee said:

> It is a great house, which is rented for me by the Ocalenie Foundation. Partially I pay house rent, partially it is paid by the Foundation. (…) I have been living here for more than 4 months. We have all the necessary furniture and supplies.
>
> *PLMICh13*

In the case of the above-mentioned interviewee, the Foundation not only found him a place to live but also partially covers the costs of the place in which he lives.

Among other facilitators who have helped our interviewees to find their flats and houses when they moved out of the refugee centres were members of their ethnic community and friends, but sometimes also strangers whom they had met coincidentally online or offline and who decided to help them. One interviewee pointed out that:

> Our Chechen friends were living here before and they had planned to move out. They asked if we wanted to take it. We did because before we were living in a one-room apartment. Everybody wants more comfortable living conditions, so we decided to move here.
>
> *PLMICh10*

Another female interviewee recalled that:

> The woman from my daughter's school helped me. Her neighbour works in administration. He helped me to find this flat. The owner is a very good person. He wanted to get PLN 1600 a month for this flat, but when I told him I couldn't pay him PLN 1600, he agreed to charge me PLN 1200 a month.
>
> *PLMICh04*

This account also shows the flexibility on the part of some apartment owners who are willing to rent their properties for a lower price than originally requested.

One of the strategies employed by the beneficiaries of international protection in finding adequate housing is to apply for social housing. Generally, access to this pool of flats, as mentioned earlier, is on an equal basis with other residents of a given part of Poland. In practice, it means that if they qualify for such housing they must wait for many months, if not years, to be allocated a flat from this source. One of our interviewees recalled her experience with applying for social housing:

> We applied for a social flat, but we received a negative answer (...) They wrote that we had collected 22 out of 28 points. And I knew it from the beginning, because we had a normal income, we both work, we have a neat apartment. I didn't expect that we would get a social flat. But the municipal employee told us that one could apply for a social flat every year. So ok, maybe after 10 years we will get it.
>
> *PLMIUk19*

Our data also shows that sometimes the application process for social housing is an important factor in why some people do not change their current inadequate housing arrangements. One interviewee argued that:

> I cannot rent a bigger room than 6 square metres for 1 person, as I have applied for a social flat. (...) If I rent a bigger room, they will not give me the flat, they will tell me that I have enough space.
>
> *PLMICh08*

Another interviewee also mentioned that her efforts to obtain social housing is one of the reasons that keeps her with the family in the house where the roof is leaking when it rains and where "the landlord does not do anything about it" (PLMIUk20). She claimed that she did not search for any new place because she had applied for a communal flat and "I should not change my place of living, I should stay in the house where I live now" (PLMIUk20). She also said that it is the first reason for her housing immobility, but not the main one. She pointed out that the main reason is the proximity of her daughter's school:

> I really don't want to change it. We have already changed five schools for her. It is my dream that she can live close to the school. Now it takes her only five minutes to be in the school. I would like her to get used to the school where she has friends. She really likes having friends, and now she has some.
>
> *PLMIUk20*

As far as spatial integration is concerned, the research data show a high preference among the interviewed persons with international protection to live in cities. They mentioned numerous advantages of life in a big city such as good schooling, work, sport, and transportation. One interviewee stated: "Here is a civilization, everything is very accurate, good and nice" (PLMICh13).

Meanwhile, others, like the following interviewee, said they were aware that finding an adequate place to live in a city for a reasonable price is not easy:

> I'd like to live in a bigger city where you have more opportunities, chances to do more or find people who have the same point of view or interest as I do. (…) At the same time, it is also more problematic, because accommodation is more expensive in bigger cities.
>
> *PLMICh10*

Our interviewees were fully aware of the difficulties linked with finding adequate and affordable housing in big cities where the majority of them wished to live. As we have shown above, apart from the housing problems similar to those faced by Polish citizens, persons with international protection face additional challenges. Discrimination in the housing market and insufficient social, cultural, and financial capital are some important ones. As shown above, the beneficiaries of international protection were assisted in addressing some of these problems by actors from the governmental and non-governmental sectors. This assistance is always very much appreciated by the refugees and has also played a key role in the facilitation of their integration with the host society.

Conclusions

In this chapter, we have looked at the housing conditions of persons seeking asylum in Poland and those with different forms of international protection through the perspective of legal regulations, their implementation, and how refugees perceive this system and integrate into it.

Our results show that the inadequate quality of housing results in slowing the adaptation of the foreigners to the new socio-cultural conditions of the host country and may have a negative impact on their physical and mental condition. As shown above, housing is a primary issue not only for the asylum applicants in Poland who live in the centres run by the Office for Foreigners and outside of them but also for persons who have already obtained some form of international protection. The situation of the beneficiaries of international protection in Poland might be even more difficult since they cannot rely on the support provided by the Office for Foreigners in this regard in the form of accommodation in one of the refugee centres or a modest housing allowance.

As shown earlier the majority of asylum seekers decide to move out of the refugee centres while their applications are being processed. Thus, the shock of being forced to find suitable accommodation is frequently avoided before a given person is granted international protection.

According to our fieldwork data, those foreigners who lived outside of the facilities run by the Office for Foreigners during the asylum procedure seemed better prepared for the numerous challenges of finding adequate housing for a reasonable price after their applications for protection were positively assessed. The chapter confirmed also a very important role played by actors from the non-governmental sector that facilitate access to housing for refugees and persons with subsidiary protection.

We also have shown that sometimes the difficulty of finding adequate and affordable housing is one of the important reasons why some beneficiaries of international protection decide to leave Poland in search of better living conditions in Western Europe where there might be a denser diaspora and other support networks.

Notes

1 These are in fact centres for foreigners applying for international protection, but in the Polish language they are simply called "refugee centres".

2 In particular, the Ordinance of the Minister of Interior and Administration of 19 February 2016 on the amount of assistance for foreigners seeking international protection (Journal of Laws 2016, item 311) and Ordinance of the Ministry of Interior of 23 October 2015 on the rules of stay in the centre for foreigners (Journal of Laws 2015, item 1828), both unchanged as of January 2022.

3 The state-owned centres were located in Podkowa Leśna-Dębak, Biała Podlaska, Czerwony Bór near Łomża, and Linin. The remaining six facilities were leased from external entities through agreements concluded as part of public procurement procedures. They were located in Białystok, Kolonia Horbów, Bezwola, Łuków, Grupa near Grudziądz, and Warszawa-Targówek. The centre in Warszawa-Targówek was closed in August 2021.

4 The Law on Tenancy and Housing regulates the principles and forms of protection of tenants' rights and the principles of managing the housing resources of the commune. It indicates, among others, the rights and obligations of owners and locators of flats, defines housing stock (resources) of the communes and the rules of rent of social housing (subsidised housing). The Law on Housing Allowances, in turn, regulates the principles and procedure for granting, determining the amount and payment of housing allowances, as well as the competences of authorities in these matters.

5 Resolution No. LVIII/1751/2009 of the Council of the Capital City of Warsaw of 9 July 2009 on the principles of renting flats that are part of the housing stock of the Capital City of Warsaw in conjunction with Regulation No. 43/2013 of the Director of the Warsaw Family Support Centre of 10 September 2013.

6 Details of this form of social support are contained in Regulation No. 11/2015 of the Director of the Warsaw Family Support Centre of 24 February 2015 regarding the principles of functioning of protected apartments for foreigners run by the Warsaw Family Support Centre.

References

AIDA, 2020. *Country Report: Poland – 2020 update.* Asylum Information Database (AIDA).

Alba, R., Nee, V., 1997. Rethinking assimilation theory for a new era of immigration. *The International Migration Review,* 31, 826–874. DOI: https://doi.org/10.2307/2547416.

CBOS, 2015. *Postawy wobec islamu i muzułmanów (Attitudes towards Islam and Muslims).* Centrum Badania Opinii Społecznej, Warsaw.

CBOS, 2016. *Stosunek Polaków do przyjmowania uchodźców (No. 24/2016), Komunikat z* Badań. Warsaw.

Chabasiński, R., 2018. W Polsce brakuje mieszkań – aż 2,1 miliona. A będzie tylko gorzej. Bezprawnik. https://bezprawnik.pl/w-polsce-brakuje-mieszkan/ (25 June 2020).

Chlabicz, B., Nowosielska, P., 2021. *Granice wytrzymałości. Jak wygląda sytuacja w ośrodkach dla cudzoziemców?* Dziennik-Gazeta Prawna.

Chrzanowska, A., Czerniejewska, I., 2015. *Raport z monitoringu warunków mieszkaniowych uchodźców w Polsce.* Stowarzyszenie Interwencji Prawnej, Warsaw.

Chrzanowska, A., Dobrowolska, O., Jaźwińska, M., Mickiewicz, P., Pulchny, A., Sadowska, M., 2020. *SIP w działaniu. Prawa cudzoziemców w Polsce w 2019.* Stowarzyszenie Interwencji Prawnej, Warsaw.

Gać, J., Pachocka, M., 2019. Warszawski testowy projekt InTEgracji cudzoziemców z uwzględnieniem potrzeb rynKu pracy (WITEK) – Opracowanie końcowe z realizacji Umowy nr PS/B/VI/3/10/203/2017. Warsaw.

Grzymała-Kozłowska, H., 2017. *Strategie adaptacji kulturowej w społeczeństwie polskim cudzoziemców starających się o ochronę i nią objętych, in: Uchodźcy w Polsce Sytuacja Prawna, Skala Napływu i Integracja w Społeczeństwie Polskim Oraz Rekomendacje, Ekspertyzy Komitetu Badań Nad Migracjami.* Komitet Badań nad Migracjami PAN, Cracow-Warsaw.

Koss-Goryszewska, M., 2019. Mieszkalnictwo, in: Górska, A., Koss-Goryszeska, M., Kucharczyk, J. (Eds.), *W stronę krajowego mechanizmu ewaluacji integracji. Diagnoza sytuacji beneficjentów ochrony międzynarodowej w Polsce.* Instytut Spraw Publicznych, Warsaw, pp. 27–30.

Legut, A., Pędziwiatr, K., 2018. Sekurytyzacja migracji w polityce polskiej a zmiana postaw Polaków wobec uchodźców, in: Jończy, R. (Ed.), *Sami Swoi? Wielokulturowość We Współczesnej Europie.* Dom Współpracy Polsko-Niemieckiej, Gliwice-Opole, pp. 41–51.

Łodziński, S., 2019. Uchodźcy jako "podejrzana społeczność" (suspect community). Polska opinia publiczna wobec udzielania pomocy uchodźcom w okresie maj 2015 – grudzień 2018. *Studia Socjologiczn-Polityczne* 1, pp. 31–60.

NIK, 2015. *Pomoc społeczna dla uchodźców.* Najwyższa Izba Kontroli, Warsaw.

Office for Foreigners, 2019a. *Guidebook: Department for Social Services.* UDSC, Warsaw.

Office for Foreigners, 2019b. *Miesięczny raport z działalności urzędu – czerwiec 2019.*

Office for Foreigners, 2021. *Miesięczny raport z działalności urzędu – czerwiec 2021.* UDSC, Warsaw.

Pachocka, M., Pędziwiatr, K., Sobczak-Szelc, K., Szałańska, K., 2020. Reception Policies, Practices & Responses: POLAND Country Report, Multilevel Governance of Mass Migration in Europe and Beyond Project (#770564, Horizon2020) Report Series.

Pędziwiatr, K., 2016. *Islamophobia in Poland: National Report 2015 (European Islamophobia Report 2015).* SETA, Istanbul.

Pędziwiatr, K., 2017. Islamophobia in Poland: National Report, in: Bayralki, E., Hafez, F. (Eds.), *European Islamophobia Report 2016*. SETA, Istanbul, pp. 411–443.

Pędziwiatr, K., 2019. The new Polish migration policy – false start. openDemocracy. www.opendemocracy.net/en/can-europe-make-it/the-new-polish-migration-policy-false-start/ (accessed 25 June 2020).

Pędziwiatr, K., Brzozowski, J., Mucha, J., Stonawski, M., 2021. *Imigranci w Krakowie: od studentów do przedsiębiorców*. Nomos, Cracow.

Strzelecki, P., Pachocka, M., 2020. Migration processes in the countries of Central and Eastern Europe – transformation from net emigration to net immigration countries, *Report of SGH Warsaw School of Economics and the Economic Forum 2020*. SGH Publishing House, Warsaw, pp. 235–267.

Szulecka, M., Pachocka, M., Sobczak-Szelc, K., 2018. *Poland – Legal and Policy Framework of Migration Governance, Multilevel Governance of Mass Migration in Europe and Beyond Project (#770564, Horizon2020) Report Series*. Zenodo. DOI: https://doi.org/10.5281/zenodo.1418583.

WCPR, 2019. *Konkurs mieszkaniowy 2019* [WWW Document]. Warszawskie Centrum Pomocy Rodzinie. http://wcpr.pl/nasze-uslugi/cudzoziemcy/-konkurs-mieszkaniowy-2019 (accessed 3 July 2020).

Wysieńska, K., 2014a. *Czyj jest ten kawałek podłogi? Wyniki badań dyskryminacji uchodźców w dostępie do mieszkań*. Instytut Spraw Publicznych, Warsaw.

Wysieńska, K., 2014b. *Niewidzialni i niepoliczalni – rodzaje i skala bezdomności uchodźców i osób w "procedurze"*. Instytut Spraw Publicznych, Warsaw.

Zick, A., Küpper, B., Hövermann, A., 2011. *Intolerance, prejudice and discrimination: a European report, FES-Projekt gegen Rechtsextremismus*. Friedrich-Ebert-Stiftung, Forum Berlin, Berlin.

8

INTEGRATION OF ASYLUM SEEKERS AND REFUGEES ON THE LABOUR MARKET

Introduction

Asylum seekers and beneficiaries of international protection integrate into the labour market with much more difficulty than other migrants, even if their skills and education are comparable. This difference occurs regardless of age and knowledge of the host country's language (Peromingo, 2014, pp. 76–77). According to an analysis carried out in OECD countries, it takes up to six years for refugees to achieve a level of employment and income similar to the level achieved by persons migrating within the family reunification scheme. Moreover, according to the results of the 2014 EU Labour Force Survey, refugees need even 20 years to reach the level of the native population in the mentioned area (OECD, 2016). This appears because, in addition to challenges faced by economic migrants such as a lack of language proficiency or social and professional networks, they often suffer from psychological distress and disabilities, which lower their ability to integrate into the labour market. This is further strengthened by the period of suspension and uncertainty about their future during the asylum procedure. Also, their qualifications and work experience often have been gained in challenging conditions. Finally, many of them cannot provide proper documentation to prove their level of education and skills, and they arrive with weak, if any, attachment to the host country (OECD, 2016). Nonetheless, the possibility to perform any work already during the procedure is indicated as an essential factor of physical recovery after all the traumatic events that asylum seekers face in the region of origin and on their way to the safe country. Early access to the labour market also allows for better integration if the decision on their asylum application is favourable.

Poland's economy is the sixth-largest economy in the EU (as of 2020). For a long time, however, Poland had been a net-emigration country and not very attractive for economic migrants or beneficiaries of international protection (Górny and

DOI: 10.4324/9781003196327-8

Kaczmarczyk, 2019; Kaczmarczyk et al., 2020). Only since EU accession in 2004 has Poland experienced steady economic growth resulting in a gradual rise in the number of employed persons and, simultaneously, a decline in the unemployment rate in the country[1] and transitioned from a net emigration into an immigration country at the same time (see Chapter 2).

This chapter examines the access and adaptation to the labour market of both asylum seekers and beneficiaries of international protection in Poland. We show how the change of legal status from an applicant for international protection to a person granted refugee status or subsidiary protection affects the situation of these people in the labour market. The chapter refers to the challenges and facilitators that influence the labour market integration process and how asylum seekers and refugees respond to these factors.

Data related to the employment of asylum seekers and beneficiaries of international protection in the formal and informal labour market in Poland are very limited. Neither the data nor official reports describe the process and its scale. The goal to study this process in a more in-depth manner requires empirical research involving both forced migrants and professionals dealing with the issue of their adaptation to the labour market. This chapter is based on qualitative interviews with meso-level actors and interviews conducted with asylum seekers and beneficiaries of international protection. However, as just 6 out of 30 interviewees applying for asylum in Poland confirmed working experience during the asylum procedure in Poland, and only 4 of them worked legally during this time (3 Chechens and 1 Ukrainian), the information about the working conditions during the procedure are mostly based on the interviews with representatives of the Office for Foreigners, NGOs, and practitioners dealing with immigration, asylum, and integration issues in Poland (for more information about the structure of the sample, see Chapter 1).

This chapter is structured as follows. The first section is dedicated to the implementation of provisions on access to the labour market by asylum seekers and beneficiaries of international protection. The second section presents the types of jobs performed by asylum seekers and beneficiaries of international protection. The following, consecutive sections are dedicated to the two most significant challenges that asylum seekers and beneficiaries of international protection need to overcome to access the labour market—language and recognition of education and qualifications. The last part focuses on the role of gender in the labour market.

Legal and Institutional Aspects of Forced Migrants' Adaptation to the Labour Market

Asylum seekers often want to perform work as soon as possible. The majority of the interviewed forced migrants, regardless of their region/country of origin, declared a willingness to find a job in Poland, as underlined by one of the officials from the Office for Foreigners: "We have a lot of telephone calls (...) when foreigners ask about the possibility of taking up a job in Poland" (PLMZOF2). However, after submitting an application, they are not allowed to work for six months. This period by some officials from the Office for Foreigners is perceived as too long, even if it is in line with EU law. The experts suggest that a three-month-long period preceding the possibility to enter the labour market could be a better solution (MGN2).

After six months, asylum applicants need a certificate that allows access to the labour market. Certificates are issued upon request of asylum applicants whose procedure lasts longer than six months (see Chapters 4). Even this step means many challenges for asylum seekers. The first is a lack of information about whether and how they can receive documents giving them access to the labour market. What is significant is that this concerns both asylum seekers and potential employers. All interviewees, whether forced migrants or experts involved in forced migration governance, confirmed that many asylum seekers had no knowledge of the legal conditions regarding their access to the labour market and job opportunities and that "not all asylum seekers are aware that they can apply for this certificate" (PLMZOF2). Even more significant is that potential employers do not know that the certificate with a temporary ID document gives asylum applicants the right to work and they demand a "work permit", even if a work permit per se does not apply to this group according to Polish law. Regrettably, there is no special information campaign for employers regarding the possibilities of hiring asylum seekers. This misunderstanding is then repeated by asylum applicants, as during the interview with one Kazakhstan female interviewee:

> I could work in a beauty salon. I found a place where they would give me a job, but I need to have a work permit and a residence permit.
>
> *PLMIKa30*

One of the officials from the Office for Foreigners (PLMZOF1) pointed out that asylum applicants even try to receive a work permit from voivodes,[2] although they are not entitled to obtain them, as work permits are issued only to migrants (upon the request of the employers) having or applying for other legal titles to stay in Poland (Pachocka et al., 2020).

In practice, the number of requests lodged for certificates is not high. If we compare this number to the total number of asylum applications, we observe that it amounts to 13–17% of the latter (Table 8.1). Despite the lack of knowledge about the certificate issued to asylum applicants, according to the employees of the Office for Foreigners, another factor contributing to the low number of certificates issued is that asylum seekers receive a first-instance decision on their application for international protection within five months, which means that they are not entitled to apply for a certificate to work earlier. Not without significance is the high number of asylum seekers leaving Poland after submitting their application for international protection. This is evidenced by the large number of discontinued proceedings (Pachocka et al., 2020) and directly affects the issuance of certificates allowing asylum applicants to work in Poland. Importantly, the data of the Office for Foreigners also shows quite a significant number of refusals concerning requests for issuing a certificate submitted by asylum seekers (e.g., 49% in 2018) (Table 8.1).

TABLE 8.1 Number of requested certificates and decisions issued to applicants between 2017 and 2021 (September)

	2017	*2018*	*2019*	*2020*	*2021*
Number of asylum applications	5,104	4,165	4,093	2,803	1,683
Number of requests for the certificate	689	588	686	619	368
Percentage of requests for certificates from asylum applications	13%	14%	17%	22%	22%
Number of issued certificates	459	301	486	481	221[a]
Number of refusals	230	287	200	138	117[b]
Percentage of refusals	33%	49%	29%	22%	32%

Notes:
a Data for the end of June 2021.
b Data for the end of August 2021.

Source: Own elaboration based on data received from the Office for Foreigners.

According to the interviewed experts, there are two explanations. First, asylum seekers apply for permission to work legally earlier than the mentioned six-month wait. Second, the decision on granting international protection may become final before the request is examined (Pachocka et al., 2020).

For a long time, the certificate was valid only until the end of the procedure before the Office for Foreigners. If asylum seekers appealed to the court or reapplied for protection, they were not allowed to work at that time. Therefore, in a situation when someone received a final decision within the first six months and then appealed against this decision in the court and submitted a new application (or more applications), they were not allowed to work legally for even a few years, provided that each new procedure did not last more than six months (MGN2, AIDA, 2020; Pachocka et al., 2020). The practice in this area has changed. The entitlement to a certificate applies not only to those asylum seekers whose procedure has been prolonged in the first instance but also to those whose whole asylum procedure before both bodies (Office for Foreigners and Refugee Board) has exceeded six months. Also, juridical practice regarding the validation has changed. Courts started suspending the implementation of the negative decisions of the Refugee Board more often, which means that people who appeal to the courts may legally perform work and use the certificate in the appeal procedure (Pachocka et al., 2020).

The situation of forced migrants changes significantly after receiving one of the protection statuses. Beneficiaries of international protection as well as members of their families receive access to the Polish labour market and different vocational activation instruments equal (with some exceptions) to those enjoyed by Polish citizens. However, despite the lack of legal restrictions, beneficiaries of international protection face a lot of informal barriers. For instance, officially, there are no obstacles for beneficiaries of international protection to perform liberal professions.

In practice, however, they may face difficulties related to access conditions of some liberal professions, such as lawyer, where one must have three-and-a-half years of apprenticeship. Therefore, access to this job directly after receiving protection is not possible (Pawlak, 2019). Although these types of restrictions apply to all migrants, for beneficiaries of international protection, this is perceived as an additional barrier.

The labour market policy implemented by the local (county) labour offices (see Chapter 4) envisages job search assistance. The type of support, such as individual professional advice, advisory interview, preliminary interview, and individual professional information, is differentiated from individual advice and includes different types of internships and training up to paid internship programmes (Table 8.2). Programmes offered by the local labour offices are addressed to all clients and there are no tailored programmes for migrants, including refugees unless one of several privileged groups. Those who fulfil the conditions and find themselves in a special situation in the labour market (such as young refugees, people with disabilities, or their caregivers) may apply for inclusion in a special programme within labour market institutions (PLMZP2). As the interviewed experts emphasised, beneficiaries of international protection need to be aware of those options, which is rarely the case.

Between 2011 and 2020, most of the support delivered by local labour offices to refugees in Poland were focused on individual activities such as individual professional advice, advisory interview, preliminary interview, and individual professional information (see Table 8.2). As mentioned by one of the investigated NGO experts, some of these activities are limited to enrolment in the database and invitation to an appointment in a few months' time when the applicant's language skills improve. Importantly, vocational training was attended only by those who were able to find information about it on the office's website and applied for it (PLMZSO1). For those who do not know the language, such support was not available (Sobczak-Szelc et al., 2021).

In general, local labour offices are rated quite negatively by NGO representatives working with refugees:

> I do not remember that there were ever actions targeted specifically at refugees at the labour office. I know a few refugees who took advantage of the opportunity to attend a Polish language course or any vocational courses organised by the labour office. (…) As I was looking through it some time ago, I was struck by the fact that there are no refugees or migrants there [among privileged groups]. This is a specific group that requires another type of interaction due to these linguistic or cultural differences. And I don't think anything has changed in this area. According to my experience, refugees treat the labour office only as a health insurer (…) and as an annoying institution that looks for any job for them. If they do not take the first, second, third job offer, they bear the consequences. But these are often job offers where they have no chance to support themselves.
>
> *PLMZSO1*

TABLE 8.2 Type of support delivered to beneficiaries of international and national protection between 2011 and 2020 by local labour offices

Type of support	*2011*	*2012*	*2013*	*2014*	*2015*	*2016*	*2017*	*2018*	*2019*	*2020*	*Total*
Individual professional advice	43	105	141	118	82	69	104	64	74	18	818
Advisory interview	37	54	69	86	81	68	101	68	74	21	659
Preliminary interview	14	84	114	65	4	6	4	2	3	0	296
Individual professional information	20	31	35	25	21	26	40	34	41	16	289
Group professional information	22	37	46	45	7	28	12	16	11	5	229
Referral to work	16	16	16	26	20	31	43	30	25	5	228
Vocational training	14	18	17	24	24	31	25	16	9	3	181
Referral for an internship	7	15	22	27	16	20	18	7	12	8	152
Referral to socially useful work	4	7	7	14	16	21	14	8	12	7	110
Other[a]	29	32	55	29	13	13	13	32	14	15	245
Total	206	399	522	459	284	313	374	277	275	98	3207

Note: [a]Thirty requests for the certificate have not yet been considered or their results have not yet been registered.

Source: Own elaboration based on data received from Ministry of Economic Development and Technology.

Based on the provisions, another important actor involved in assisting the adaptation of refugees to the labour market in Poland are the family support centres. Although they are not directly involved in job search or training, they are responsible for the implementation of the individual integration program (IIP), with a crucial role in implementing it played by social workers. Within the IIP, beneficiaries of international protection are supported in persisting in their chosen way of gaining adequate work and language skills. Sometimes, they are assisted in finding suitable employment opportunities in the labour market (Grzymała-Kozłowska, 2017; Sobczak-Szelc et al., 2020).

A significant role in funding activities towards third-country nationals, including refugees, in the EU Member States is played by EU funds. During the previous EU Multiannual Financial Framework (MFF 2007–2013), there was an opportunity to choose among a wide selection of professional courses and internships offered not only by the labour offices but also by NGOs. Those activities delivered productive results according to one of the interviewees' claims; of those who took part in training between 2011 and 2013, the vast majority are still working for the same employer. After 2014, however, due to cuts in the Asylum, Migration and Integration Fund (AMIF), the number of trainings was significantly limited. For instance in 2014, 198 people participated in the IIP programme in Mazovieckie Voivodeship. However, merely 13 out of the 198 participated in any training co-financed with EU funds either through NGOs or local government units. The most popular trainings were on welding or to obtain driving licenses. These courses did not correspond to jobs taken subsequently by foreigners. Only 37 participants of those involved in the IIP found a job, usually in gastronomy, as interpreters, or as labourers (MUW, 2014). It is worth mentioning, however, that data regarding training and the effectiveness of the IIP in relation to labour market inclusion are not collected in a systematic way (Pachocka and Sobczak-Szelc, 2020; Sobczak-Szelc et al., 2020; Szałańska, 2019).

Finally, those willing to start their own company face different kinds of barriers. Beneficiaries of international protection, despite no formal barriers to run their own business, face challenges on the bureaucratic level. They can benefit from the same subsidies and facilitations as Poles, but most documents and information systems are in Polish. Furthermore, refugees are supposed to deliver different kinds of documents, which they may not have or have no knowledge of how to get them. Some NGOs such as the Polish Migration Forum or the Foundation for Somalia make an effort to help migrants facing these difficulties. Nevertheless, there are opinions that the access of beneficiaries of international protection to run their own business is advantageous, but also troublesome if not accompanied by migrants' awareness of what it means to be an entrepreneur in Poland. As one of the NGO representatives commented:

> [Refugees] don't know what it means to run a business, how many pitfalls there are, they set up companies, various other forms of business and later they have problems.
>
> *PLMZSO2*

Types of Jobs Performed and Their Determinants

Finding a job is crucial for many applicants for international protection as the allowance provided by the Office for Foreigners for asylum seekers is rather low. Issues such as phone calls, internet access, or other non-basic needs are not delivered by the centres for foreigners or are limited in scope, and "70 PLN per month is not enough" (PLMICh06), as is the case of those accommodated in the centres for foreigners. The centre covers expenditures related to travel by public transport in procedure-related issues. If the asylum applicants have other needs, they often travel without a ticket, which exposes them to fines and penalties. In addition, the amount of the allowance "has not been changed for X years, since I can remember, I do not know if it has been at least a dozen years or so", as indicated by one NGO expert (PLMZOS1) (Pachocka et al., 2020). Those who are accommodated outside the centre receive a financial allowance for all costs of their stay in Poland. The amount received depends on the family composition (see more AIDA, 2020).

The situation of asylum applicants in the labour market is difficult. After receiving the work certificate, their access to employment is not limited. However, the availability of jobs is determined by the place where they live (in the centres for foreigners or outside them). Therefore, they look for any paid activities in the neighbourhood of the centres or the place of residence. Due to the relatively high demand on the Polish market for seasonal employment in agriculture and horticulture, as well as the fact that some centres for foreigners are located outside large cities and in rural areas, this is conducive to employing asylum seekers. The opinion of one of the interviewees that "[t]he whole Linin centre near Góra Kalwaria collects apples and strawberries depending on the season" (PLMZSO1) indicates the trend that was already observed in previous research in Poland (Abdoulvakchabova, 2012; Klaus, 2007, 2017a; Pawlak, 2019; Ząbek and Łodziński, 2008). The most common sectors of work taken during the procedure include agriculture (mostly undocumented work), security services, construction, small gastronomy, services at the reception centre for the centre inhabitants (manicurists or hairdressers, mostly working undocumented), "handyman" activity, and car repair. Some of the inhabitants of the centre may gain additional pocket money from occasional work inside the centre, such as help with cleaning the centre or with translations. However, the offer of such jobs is limited, and they are not well paid. The additional payments may be as high as only 50 PLN (about 12 EUR) per month. Probably because the payment is low, only 5–10 people in a given centre engage in this type of work and receive this financial supplement (Pachocka et al., 2020).

According to the interviewed experts, the sectors and forms of employment characterising the work of asylum applicants often do not differ much even after a positive decision on their status is granted. While for the first year after receiving one of the protection statuses the beneficiaries of international protection receive financial support within a special integration programme, the amount of money granted to them is rarely enough to meet some basic needs. Therefore, they start to look for job opportunities as soon as possible. They are aware that they may face many difficulties, which was apparent in the statement of one of the interviewees, who responded with sarcasm when asked about plans for employment:

> I will have to take up a job. (…) [Q: What kind of job?] R: Cleaning. They won't employ me as a minister, will they?
>
> *PLMICh08*

Indeed, the most popular jobs performed by the beneficiaries of international protection are unskilled worker or craftsperson. Chechens and Ukrainians usually work in construction, transport, and vehicle mechanics. Chechen men also work in security services. This occupation is so common among this group that working in security services is sometimes called "a professional Chechen job" (PlMiCh13). Cleaning as well as jobs in gastronomy are usually performed by women.

Both asylum applicants and people already granted protection often are pushed into the informal labour market. There are two main reasons for this. The first one is connected to some employers exploiting the difficult economic position of their foreign employees, as they believe that foreigners can only be employed informally and will work for less money because they are desperate (PLMZSO1). The second is that the vast majority of asylum applicants and beneficiaries of international protection from the Caucasus and Chechnya are less educated and perform simple, low-paid jobs. Even if they work a lot, they may not earn enough to pay all their bills, particularly those who rent a flat. Consequently, they often prefer to work, even if they have another option, in the "grey market", because they can get a higher "net" salary, which makes it easier for them to support themselves compared to legal employment (PLMZSO1).

Furthermore, working in the informal labour market is related to the specificity of the sector in which migrants perform their work. Sectors such as construction, gastronomy (simple jobs), domestic work, and auto repair are some of the most commonly undertaken jobs in the informal sphere (without job contracts). Importantly, undeclared work in such sectors applies to all workers, not only foreign nationals. Domestic work is a striking example (Kindler et al., 2016). One of the NGO representatives commented about female forced migrants working in this sector as follows:

> Women clean up and care for children. It is almost never formalised. A king's ransom to whoever signs contracts with ladies who clean, care for children, or the elderly. Although I know of minor exceptions.
>
> *PLMZSO1*

The National Labour Inspectorate (NLI) has increased the number of inspections among employers to minimise employment irregularities, including the employment of foreigners, and at the end of 2019 launched a helpline for migrants through which they can obtain information on conditions of stay and work in Poland. Both of those actions positively affected the number of legally employed foreigners, including beneficiaries of international protection (PIP, 2019). It is notable, however, that the inspections carried out by the NLI pertain to employers, that is, entities that formally commission work to other persons on a work contract basis (or on conditions that should be based on a work contract). Therefore, undeclared employment and work performed in private houses or on farms remain, in general, beyond this institution's purview.

Despite the common unofficial character of the work performed by asylum seekers, there are cases of forced migrants who enjoy the opportunity to work lawfully in Poland, which was not accessible in their country of origin. For instance, one Chechen woman was working unofficially as a babysitter in her home country, and in Poland she found a job as a cleaning lady in a hotel (contract-based). In general, during the asylum procedure, foreigners often perform undocumented work. However, even if the beneficiaries of international protection have documented jobs, it rarely corresponds to the type of work performed in the region of origin. For instance, one of the micro-level respondents (PLMIUk20) admitted that despite the fact that he has higher education and experience in mechanical engineering, he cannot find a job. During the period the interviews were conducted, he was willing to find a job in a supermarket and gave up work in his professional field since, as he explained: "one needs to pass the exam, to study for the exam, in Polish language. And I don't want to. I don't want to go back to this".

The majority of the interviewed asylum seekers and beneficiaries of international protection in Poland were specialists in the country of origin: doctors,

TABLE 8.3 Change of job types

Interviewee	*Type of work last performed in country of origin*	*Current type of work*	*Situation in Poland*
PLMIUk19	Self-employed	Unskilled worker	Lower
PLMICh08	Unskilled worker	Unemployed	Lower
PLMIUk20	Specialist	Unemployed	Lower
PLMICh04	Self-employed	Unemployed	Lower
PLMIJe29	Manager/supervisors/director	Unemployed	Lower
PLMiIr28	Office worker	Unemployed	Lower
PLMICh07	Unskilled worker	Unskilled worker	Same
PLMICh09	Unskilled worker	Unskilled worker	Same
PLMICh11	Skilled worker or craftsman	Skilled worker or craftsman	Same
PlMICh14	Skilled worker or craftsman	Skilled worker or craftsman	Same
PLMIUk16	Skilled worker or craftsman	Skilled worker or craftsman	Same
PLMICh10	Specialist	Specialist	Same
PLMISy23	Specialist	Specialist	Same
PLMICh01	Unemployed	Unemployed	Same
PLMISy25	Specialist/student	Unemployed/Student	Same
PLMiSy21	Service employee or salesperson	Specialist	Improved
PLMISy22	Unemployed (student)	Specialist	Improved

Source: Own elaboration (Sobczak-Szelc et al., 2020).

bookkeepers, lecturers, IT specialists, teachers, or translators. Such jobs were usually performed by men (only two interviewed women had such occupations). Some interviewees performed work as unskilled (five persons) or skilled workers (four persons). The rest of interviewees used to work as service providers, were self-employed, worked in offices, or were technicians and managers. Their situation significantly changed after arriving in Poland. Only 4 of the 30 interviewees were employed during the asylum procedure. On the other hand, as many as seven within the investigated group were unemployed at the moment of the interview (Table 8.3). Five of them were women, who indicated family responsibilities as the main challenge (Pachocka et al., 2020). Among the interviewed forced migrants, many declared a deterioration of their professional situation in comparison to their region of origin. Most of them were unemployed. Only one of the self-employed persons in the country of origin had work, as an unskilled worker in Poland. Four interviewees managed to maintain their positions as specialists or were promoted to jobs at this level. This, however, was possible only because of their particular skills, self-confidence, strong motivation, and relatively young age. A good example is a Syrian interviewee who described his job trajectory from a kebab restaurant to finance:

> I was looking, and I found something like kebab, but it was not what I was looking for. It's not about ego. It's about what kind of job I would like to have, because I studied economics in Syria, though I wasn't able to finish it because of the war. So, I wanted a job related to financial stuff. And this is what I found. And it's cool.
>
> *PLMISy21*

This interviewee, a student in his country of origin, was working as a part-time musician. In Poland, he managed to find a job in line with his education. His testimony underlines the role of the trainings he received in the host country, and his work ethic and readiness for new challenges:

> (...) I worked in customer service, and then I got experience and after six months I got promoted, and again after six months I got another promotion. I moved to the compliance department / sanctions. I was working there for one year, and later I was promoted again. You know, they don't promote everyone, they promote the ones that are really working hard. And again, it's not about ego, I was really working hard, because I like the job. Me and my friends were always enthusiastic that we want to do something to get this position to get promoted. After you do a lot of work, in a good way. So, we built that up, and it was great, and I started to learn as I was doing a good job. And right now, I'm working with the sanctions (department) for two months. This was my last promotion.
>
> *PLMISy21*

Not less important is the issue of cultural sensitivities. For instance, Chechens, who frequently are practising Muslims, are not willing to work with pork or alcohol, and Chechen women are not always willing to work with men.

Age and career position in connection with flexibility and mobility in the labour market also play an important role in economic integration. Comparing the trajectory of a job search by two men from the Middle East reflects this statement. The first man is the husband of an Iraqi interviewee who used to work as a manager in an IT company in the region of origin. Despite his competence in the English language, he faced many difficulties in finding a job. He applied for jobs in companies, however without success. His wife justified his difficulties with his poor knowledge of Polish. This argument, however, was not so significant in the case of the younger Syrian refugee. Although his level of knowledge of the Polish language was low, since he had participated in language training organised by the family support centre for only three months, he managed to find a job according to his education and skills. As he explained, looking for a job is:

> (…) not difficult but it takes a lot of time. Because, interviews you need to wait for, and there are some other candidates, so it needs time…
>
> *PLMISy22*

Additionally, those forced migrants who also studied in the host country are in a better situation. Even if they need to repeat some years of studies, they are motivated enough to gain higher education with the help of their relatives and look for a job matching their education.

Among our migrant interviewees, there were both those who found jobs in a relatively short time and those who experienced a long and unsuccessful process of looking for a job. A few could rely on the networks they had created before arrival in Poland, for instance, a Syrian refugee explained:

> [I had been] working in translation already for a long time, and [I] had a network and acquaintances all around the world, so practically [I am] working with the same team that [I] used to work before. Before coming to Poland.
>
> *PLMISy23*

An important role also is played by various social networks, friends, co-ethnics, and other refugees. This is significant especially among the larger groups of asylum seekers and beneficiaries of international protection, such as Chechens, as explained by one of the interviewees:

> I just had some Chechen friends who were working in security service and they told me I can work with them. We, Chechens, help each other here.
>
> *PLMICh09*

Others, including those who have not found a job for a long time, rely on social aid and help from NGOs, especially those who are shortly after arrival and often without external support, do not know where to start the search or who to turn to, as one Yemeni interviewee, who admitted:

> (…) I am trying [to find a job], but till now, I don't know how… (…) I am trying with NGOs. Apart from help from the foundation (…) there is someone who is trying to, I mean, I tried to talk to him, so he could help me in so… Something like this… (…)
>
> *PLMIJe29*

Asylum seekers and refugees face many challenges in entering the labour market. It starts with the long period of exclusion during the first six months after submitting the application when they are not allowed to work. Then they face other obstacles, such as discrimination by potential employers and performance of simple and low-paid jobs, which pushes them into undocumented work. They often work below their qualifications and skills or do not work at all due to family responsibilities. Also influencing their situation are psychological problems such as trauma and depression. This all shows how, in order to achieve a good level of integration in the labour market, it is important to have appropriate information, social networks, adequate language training, and a welcoming atmosphere.

"This Is the First and Main Problem—the Language"

Language is the most crucial barrier faced by asylum seekers and beneficiaries of international protection in economic integration. This was the biggest challenge mentioned by all interviewed groups of respondents, who indicated that they experience the problem already at the stage of work training and the job search as it affects communication on all sides—institutional, employees, and employers.

With regard to public institutions, this barrier appears quickly, for instance, on the district labour office web pages and during work training, which are mostly available only in Polish. Just a few institutions offer some facilitations such as web pages in a language other than Polish or the "Zielona Linia" web page (*eng.* "Green Line"[3]), where information is available in three languages: Polish, English, and Russian. Moreover, the offer of work training in languages other than Polish is poor, which reduces the offer available for foreigners to individual assistance. For example, between 2011 and 2020, different forms of support in search of a job were offered 3,207 times (Table 8.2). Most often, the support concerned individual professional advice, advisory interview, preliminary interview, and individual professional information. While the practical activities are the most effective, they were also the least available. Different forms of referral to work or training between 2011 and 2020 were offered 671 times (Table 8.2).

This shows how important knowledge of the Polish language is for participation in any vocational training. The Iraqi interviewee noted in his testimony that the only available courses for him were language courses. When he wanted to participate in any vocational training, it came out that:

> (…) in order to learn anything, to help me find a job, they said it's not possible unless you know Polish. I mean, it was not available in English language. I wanted to attend courses in English language, so I could learn a vocation, which I could start working with even without using the Polish language… (…) it was not possible. (…) It was through the real labour office, I asked the labour office, and they said that I can't unless I know Polish language.
>
> *PLMIIr28*

However, even if the training had been offered in other languages the situation would not have improved significantly: "(…) It is not enough for them to finish the course. (…) It is not so bad when we do a tiler course in Russian, but in Arabic? Even if someone finishes such a course, anyway, they will not get a job because they do not speak Polish" (PLMZP1), as explained by one of the interviewed experts.

Even those who look for a job online may face linguistic issues. Advertisements for work in Poland are usually posted only in Polish and in the end, one needs to contact the employer in Polish as well. This was described in the testimony of one Ukrainian woman who mentioned how she found a job on OLX, a popular online marketplace:

> (…) I sent an SMS. It was difficult for me to speak through the phone at that time, since my language level was not good.
>
> *PLMIUk19*

Respondents of all nationalities mentioned the lack of knowledge of the Polish language as the main barrier when entering the labour market and regarding chances for promotion. In 2014, 18 people among the 198 participants of the IIP in Mazovian Voivodeship admitted that their poor knowledge of Polish was the reason for not taking up a job (MUW, 2014). On the one hand, a lack of self-confidence was mentioned by one Ukrainian woman, who did not feel comfortable with her knowledge of Polish, and as a result, it brought additional stress for her while working at the checkout in a grocery store:

> Maybe it was not very hard work, but I know that I speak with mistakes, and it is stressful for me. I am afraid of everything.
>
> *PLMIUk19*

However, mostly it is the issue of reluctance of employers who are not willing to hire someone without sufficient knowledge of Polish. Some interviewees mentioned situations such as, "Poles for example say, 'No Polish language, no job'" (PLMICh14) and another one reflected on his personal situation:

> Yes. I came to the first workshop and they asked me for my number; it was a hard time for me, because I could name car parts in Russian and Georgian, I didn't know Polish names! So, it happened two times that they asked me for my number [and they did not call back].
>
> *PLMIUk16*

The employers are also not willing to spend time explaining tasks or procedures that, in their opinion, should be obvious, so they are not interested in hiring people without fluency in Polish. Even if someone speaks communicatively, "basic Polish [is] immediately rejected. (...) The employer, for example, does not have time to explain that chickens must be put on higher shelves and turkey on lower shelves. Someone (a foreigner) may not understand this or require more time" (PLMZP1), as explained by one of the practitioners.

Refugees are aware that without learning the language they have almost no chances to work, as suggested by one Chechen interviewee: "You have to speak Polish to find a normal job apart from cleaning. (...) I have no choice. I am in a foreign country. First, I have to study the language" (PLMICh02). Our interviewees mentioned strategies for learning the language besides language courses to improve their opportunities in the labour market. The sister of one of the Syrian refugees had problems finding office work without knowing another language, either English or Polish. As she had a very basic knowledge of Polish, she was looking for work in a coffee shop. As her relative explained:

> It is simple work. It is just to get some practice with Polish and contact with Polish people and when she improves her Polish, she will try to look for an office job.
>
> *PLMISy25*

Recognition of Qualifications

The recognition of diplomas and qualifications constitutes a significant challenge both for refugees and the Polish integration system. A diploma certifying the completion of studies abroad may be recognised as equivalent to the relevant Polish diploma and professional title on the basis of an international agreement or through a recognition procedure (see Chapter 4). In case a given country is not on the list of those with which an agreement recognising diplomas has been signed, the refugee has to certify the diploma, that is, apply for recognition as equivalent to the Polish one. Even more difficult is the situation of those who had no opportunity to take their diplomas before fleeing their home and cannot ask for a copy due to the fear of persecution by authorities in the home country. This situation is frequent among refugees and their qualifications and competences remain unrecognised. Nonetheless, asylum seekers and refugees are conscious that they need to make an effort to increase their qualifications and raise their chances in the labour market; however, the procedure for recognition of qualification does not facilitate this process (Wysieńska and Karpiński, 2012). The lack of procedures for skills validation and recognition of qualifications results in a significant loss of valuable workers who are willing to integrate into the labour market, even if not entirely within their competences, then at least within the sector in which they had received their education and qualifications (Grzymała-Kozłowska, 2017).

The issue of recognition of qualifications emerges during the asylum procedure. Even if asylum applicants possess the certificate entitling them to work, no recognition of their competences or professional training is offered to them. Data on this subject also is not collected systematically by the public authorities. A positive decision on refugee status does not impact the access to and willingness to participate in the recognition of qualifications and diplomas of beneficiaries of international protection in Poland, which remains very low. This procedure is perceived as complicated, as each case is evaluated individually and is conditioned by the administrative procedures of a given university's faculty. It is difficult to receive any help from either the Polish state or non-governmental institutions, and it is very expensive. The fee can be as high as 50% of a professor's salary. The university determines the conditions and procedure for exemption from the fee (IOM, 2021). Refugees without recognised education are treated as those without diplomas from a college or high school. One of the investigated practitioners directly indicated the problem:

> It is complicated, and most refugees do not have these documents or only have a diploma, and there are no documents confirming the transcript of records. It is really a very complicated procedure and few people do it.
>
> *PLMZP1*

A family support centre may help their clients within the IIP program to go through the recognition procedure; however, it cannot pay for it. The labour offices deal with vocational training only and not with certifying the documents possessed by forced migrants (PLMZP1). In 2014, there were 198 participants in the IIP in Warsaw, out of which 98 were finished in the same year. Of the 106 adult participants of the IIP, 53 (50%) had secondary education and 32 (30%) declared higher education, while 14 (13%) had an elementary education. Only 45 of them (43%) possessed documents confirming professional skills. Further, 31 (29%) did not have documents confirming their education or professional qualifications and 30 declared no profession learned in the country of origin (MUW, 2014). All of these factors influence not only the amount of money they receive for their work but also the possibility for work matching their education or to obtain further qualifications (Sobczak-Szelc et al., 2020). In 2014, the reason most often given for not taking up a job among the participants of the IIP was the lack of an adequate offer matching their skills and qualifications (17% of all adult participants). Other reasons were related to the lack of childcare (12 people), bad health conditions (12), lack of motivation for taking up work (8), or insufficient knowledge of the Polish language (18) (MUW, 2015, p. 22).

Those beneficiaries who possess skills sought on the market that do not necessarily require recognition of their qualifications are able to find a job that matches their education and experiences more easily. This mainly applies to people with skills in particular crafts, IT, or linguistic qualifications. They are often young and able to adapt to the demands of the labour market. Such specialists look for advertisements for specific jobs that they can perform. For instance, one Georgian man was looking for adverts for mechanic jobs online:

> I came to Warsaw and started looking for a job. I grabbed a phone and started to make calls... (...) When I came to the third workshop, I met with the owner and I said to him that I have all the skills that he listed in his ad. He asked me, "When are you ready to start?" That was so nice! "Now!"
>
> *PLMIUk16*

Both asylum seekers and refugees who are willing to get the education and gain new skills may participate in training to improve their job qualifications, which is possible, however, only if organised either by local labour offices or NGOs. Vocational training for asylum seekers staying in the centres for foreigners were stopped when the funding from the AMIF was limited.

After the final decision on the asylum claim, the family support centres may refer people to some courses or practice during the IIP. This type of assistance requires, however, some flexibility and engagement from the centre's office workers, because each case is different. For instance, one Ukrainian interviewee already had work and did not want to participate in classes that were a couple of months long. Even if the classes were free, he would not be able to attend due to his current employment. Instead, the social worker from the local family support centre recommended he consider asking for an apprenticeship in his current workplace, which would lead to obtaining a certificate confirming his qualifications. He received permission, and therefore his work meant he gained both practical and theoretical knowledge. As he explained: "That was faster. I worked, I earned money and I got a certificate". Thanks to adequate advice and guidance, his situation became stable and he had the chance to develop his skills. He also mentioned his perspective for the future:

> We do everything when it comes to cars; mechanics, roofers... Today I don't need to attend any course... Although, maybe I would like to attend a course about hybrid cars, but I don't have time for it now. My boss said to me that when I am ready, he'll send me there.
>
> *PLMUk16*

The qualifications of beneficiaries of international protection are their assets and a starting point for their integration in Poland; therefore an analysis of each foreigner's capabilities and skills should be a starting point for planning any support in the field of their integration in the labour market, as noted by Kosowicz and Maciejko (2007).

Role of Gender in Access to the Labour Market

Another issue is the differentiation between men and women in performed jobs, which is mostly related to the region of origin of beneficiaries of international protection. One of the interviewees from the NGO sector described the differences between men and women among Chechens and other nationalities as:

> [about Chechens] Gastronomy—it is mainly women. (...) Chechens [men] will not go to work in gastronomy because it is not a male type of job. Women will. I think that when it comes to other cultures, it is not necessarily the same. For instance, a Georgian, especially if he is a chef (...) If men are present in gastronomy, then it is more likely that he is a chef and [has] higher [position], and [is] not kitchen help or [does not work] in a pub. Gastronomy is mostly a matter of washing the dishes, chopping vegetables, less often some [are] waiters, when it comes to refugees, because of the language barrier. (...) Women clean up and [also] babysit.
>
> *PLMZSO1*

Among the beneficiaries of international protection from other regions, these differences are not as significant. They mostly depend on the skills of a particular person. One NGO interviewee gave the example of single and childless men and women from African countries based on the 15–20 cases known to him. According to his claims, those who can speak French or English can easily find a job in an international corporation, even for simple jobs such as a helpline for clients, in gastronomy, or in hotels. The facilitation, according to the interviewee's statement, was their Christian confession, which is less burdened with rules regarding impure or inappropriate activities (PLMZSO3) than in the case of Muslims. However, their family status should also be taken into account as a factor influencing access to the labour market.

Women's access to the labour market is more challenging due to their cultural role as wives and mothers and as the ones who, according to cultural norms and values, "are traditionally responsible for taking care of children and family life" (PLMZLG1). This is particularly important among Chechens, one of the most significant groups of beneficiaries of international protection in Poland, with single mothers the most vulnerable. The majority of them, even if they had received any education, have never worked or have never had the experience of a stable job. Additionally, in a foreign country, they are usually deprived of support from their relatives and friends who gave them a sense of belonging and security in the country of origin (Chrzanowska, 2007; Sobczak-Szelc et al., 2020). Expectations regarding the traditional role of men as the breadwinner and the one who takes care of the household budget do not change in a new country (Chrzanowska, 2007). Women who are willing to access the labour market in Poland need to overcome not only a traditional passive position in the labour market but acquire new skills and habits related to everyday job duties (Sobczak-Szelc et al., 2020), even if their main goal is still to take care of children, as explained by one Chechen woman:

> My main goal is to raise the children, to support them. When they are 18, I will stop receiving the money for them. Now I am thinking about it. I can't work. I have a disabled daughter and I don't have any education. So, I am worried about that. My children will grow up. They will want to get married and I can't help them. I don't have a husband.
>
> *PLMICh01*

During the protection procedure and stay in the centre for foreigners, the only facilitation linked with prospective activity in the labour market is access to a kindergarten, which operates during precise hours. For single mothers, this gives only limited time for potential work or other activities (Pachocka et al., 2020). After receiving a positive decision on international protection, it is not easier, as the challenges increase. Refugees must then find accommodation, a job, and take care of the children at the same time. Without stable jobs, refugee women face difficulties to maintain a rented flat for a longer period (Sobczak-Szelc et al., 2020).

Conclusions

Asylum seekers receive access to the labour market six months after submitting an asylum application if the procedure exceeds this period. Both the interviewed asylum seekers and experts perceive this time as too long as the migrants within the procedure are both willing to work earlier, even after three months, and need additional money to satisfy their needs. If asylum applicants are entitled to work, they officially gain access to the training offered by local labour offices. Beneficiaries of international protection enjoy unrestricted access to the labour market and support offered by the state within special integration programs and offers generally available for job seekers in Poland.

Despite the legal framework, they face many obstacles while accessing the labour market. From the very beginning, they experience a lack of or poor awareness of the legal conditions. For asylum applicants, this influences both job opportunities and the relationship between them and potential employers who may not be aware of the conditions of employment of a person in an asylum procedure. This combined with a lack of sufficient knowledge about their rights in the labour market often pushes asylum seekers to the informal sector where they frequently remain even after the final positive decision. With regard to beneficiaries of international protection, we observed that employers are often unaware of the conditions of employment of such persons, which results in a reluctance towards hiring them or even outright discrimination.

One of the key problems in the economic integration of asylum seekers and beneficiaries of international protection on the labour market is their insufficient knowledge of the Polish language. This has a multidimensional impact on the possibility of integration, starting from the possibility of finding a job offer, through contact with the prospective employer, to the possibility of participating in training. Although beneficiaries of international protection have access to vocational training and employment-related education similar to Polish citizens, in reality this access is limited by the lack of language skills. The support of local labour offices is often limited to individual consultations, which are perceived as ineffective, especially in comparison with vocational training. Even if a given training is available in a foreign language, it may become worthless when knowledge of Polish is necessary to pursue work in a given sector. Finally, the type and duration of the training and employment-related education often do not correspond with the market needs.

Difficulties in the acquisition of work skills and lack of recognition of qualifications, as well as the expensive and complicated procedures for such recognition, are additional barriers to access the labour market, as discussed above. Those who cannot validate their qualifications work far below their competences and have unstable or low-paid employment. Even if they were performing jobs that demanded high skills in their countries of origin, in Poland most often they are unskilled workers or craftspeople. Although this phenomenon is clearly noticeable among migrants, it is particularly common among beneficiaries of international protection. In Poland, this challenge not only affects the overall process of integration but also the willingness to stay in the country. Beneficiaries of international protection, discouraged by a lack of the possibility to take a better job, leave the country and try their chances abroad, for instance, in Germany or Sweden. There, even if they work below their qualifications, the salaries they receive are higher. In a few cases, the interviewed beneficiaries of international protection enjoyed assistance from the governmental and non-governmental sectors in solving the problems of the recognition of their qualifications (or gaining new qualifications) in Poland. This allowed them to find relatively satisfactory jobs, with perspectives of further development.

Finally, our findings show that gender plays a significant role, and in the case of women it is an excluding factor in the labour market. Women, as culturally responsible for childcare, even if educated, are not used to work, and therefore they find it challenging to enter the labour market. If they are single mothers, childcare pushes them into dependence on social assistance.

Notes

1 The economic activity rate of the population aged 20–64 was 56.4% in 2018 (annual average). The employment rate of the population aged 20–64 was 73.6% in 2020 (annual average).
2 A governor of a voivodeship (province, region) in Poland.
3 The sum of actions that in total did not reach over 100 in the investigated time period. Zielona Linia, https://zielonalinia.gov.pl/.

References

Abdoulvakchabova, M., 2012. Problemy cudzoziemców w Polsce w świetle funkcjonowania Fundacji, Ocalenie, in: *Przestrzeganie Praw Cudzoziemców w Polsce, Biuletyn Rzecznika Praw Obywatelskich.* Warszawa, pp. 43–52.

AIDA, 2020. *Country Report: Poland.* AIDA Asylum Information Database.

Chrzanowska, A., 2007. Kulturowe uwarunkowania funkcjonowania migrantów przymusowych na polskim rynku pracy na przykładzie społeczności czeczeńskiej, in: Klaus, W. (Ed.), *Migranci Na Polskim Rynku Pracy Rzeczywistość, Problemy, Wyzwania.* SIP, Warszawa, pp. 113–128.

Górny, A., Kaczmarczyk, P., 2019. European Migration Transition in the Context of Post-Enlargement Migration from and into Central and Eastern Europe, in: Inglis, C., Li, W., Khadria, B. (Eds.), *The SAGE Handbook of International Migration.* SAGE, Los Angeles, London, New Delhi, Singapore, Washington, Melbourne.

Grzymała-Kozłowska, H., 2017. *Strategie adaptacji kulturowej w społeczeństwie polskim cudzoziemców starających się o ochronę i nią objętych, in: Uchodźcy w Polsce Sytuacja Prawna, Skala Napływu i Integracja w Społeczeństwie Polskim Oraz Rekomendacje, Ekspertyzy Komitetu Badań Nad Migracjami.* Komitet Badań nad Migracjami PAN, Kraków-Warszawa.

IOM, 2021. *Nostryfikacja dyplomu – Migrant* [WWW Document]. Migr. Infopl. www.migrant.info.pl/nostryfikacja-dyplomu.html (accessed 23 November 2021).

Kaczmarczyk, P., Aldaz-Carroll, E., Hołda, P., 2020. Migration and Socio-economic Transition: Lessons from the Polish Post-EU Accession Experience. *East European Political Society,* 34, 910–936. DOI: https://doi.org/10.1177/0888325420902238.

Kindler, M., Kordasiewicz, A., Szulecka, M., 2016. *Care needs and migration for domestic work – Ukraine-Poland: Global Action Programme on Migrant Domestic Workers and their Families, an ILO/UE project.* International Labour Organization, Geneva.

Klaus, W., 2007. *Migranci na polskim rynku pracy Rzeczywistość, problemy, wyzwania.* SIP, Warszawa.

Kosowicz, A., Maciejko, A., 2007. *Integracja uchodźców w Polsce w liczbach.* UNHCR, PFM, Warszawa.

MUW, 2014. *Sprawozdanie z realizacji indywidualnych programów integracji (IPI) w 2013 roku, na terenie województwa mazowieckiego [Report on the implementation of individual integration programs (IIP) in 2013, in the Mazowieckie Voivodeship].* Mazowiecki Urząd Wojewódzki Wydział Polityki Społecznej Oddział Programów i Analiz, Warszawa.

MUW, 2015. *Sprawozdanie z realizacji indywidualnych programów integracji (IPI) w 2014 r. na terenie województwa mazowieckiego.* Mazowiecki Urząd Wojewódzki Wydział Polityki Społecznej Oddział Programów i Analiz, Warszawa.

OECD, 2016. *Making Integration Work: Humanitarian Migrants.* OECD Publishing, Paris.

Pachocka, M., Sobczak Szelc, K., 2020. Refugee Protection Poland Country Report, Multilevel Governance of Mass Migration in Europe and Beyond Project (#770564, Horizon2020) Report Series. DOI: https://doi.org/10.5281/zenodo.3632827.

Pachocka, M., Pędziwiatr, K., Sobczak-Szelc, K., Szałańska, K., 2020. Reception Policies, Practices & Responses: POLAND Country Report, Multilevel Governance of Mass Migration in Europe and Beyond Project (#770564, Horizon2020) Report Series.

Pawlak, M., 2019. Kwalifikacje zawodowe, in: Górska, A., Koss-Goryszeska, M., Kucharczyk, J. (Eds.), *W stronę krajowego mechanizmu ewaluacji integracji. Diagnoza sytuacji beneficjentów ochrony międzynarodowej w Polsce.* Instytut Spraw Publicznych, Warszawa.

Peromingo, M., 2014. Work and refugee integration in Sweden. *Forced Migration Review, 48* 76–77.

PIP, 2019. *Info for foreigners* [WWW Document]. Państw. Insp. Pr. www.pip.gov.pl/en/legality-of-employment/64080,info-for-foreigners.html (accessed 5 August 2020).

Sobczak-Szelc, K., Pachocka, M., Pędziwiatr, K., Szałańska, J., 2020. *Integration Policies, Practices and Experiences – Poland Country Report (Working Paper No. 2020/60), Working Papers Global Migration Consequences and Responses.* Centre of Migration Research, University of Warsaw, Warszawa. DOI: https://doi.org/10.5281/zenodo.4008666.

Sobczak-Szelc, K., Szałańska, J., Pachocka, M., 2021. *The integration of asylum seekers and refugees in the field of education and labour market Comparative thematic report, Global Migration: Consequences and Responses – RESPOND Working Paper Series*. University of Warsaw, Uppsala.

Szałańska, J., 2019. *Uneasy Mission of NGOs in Protection and Reception of Asylum Seekers and Refugees in Poland. Reflections from Fieldwork*. RESPOND. www.respondmigration.com/blog-1/mission-ngos-protection-reception-asylum-seekers-refugees-poland (accessed 26 May 2020).

Wysieńska K., Karpiński Z., 2012. *Ekonomia imigracji – imigranci na polskim rynku pracy*. Warszawa: Stowarzyszenie Interwencji Prawnej. www.interwencjaprawna.pl/docs/ARE-611-ekonomia-migracji.pdf.

Ząbek, M., Łodziński, S., 2008. *Uchodźcy w Polsce Próba spojrzenia antropologicznego*. Oficyna Wydawnicza ASPRA-JR, Warsaw.

9

ACCESS TO HEALTHCARE BY ASYLUM SEEKERS AND BENEFICIARIES OF INTERNATIONAL PROTECTION

Introduction

One of the most important services provided to people seeking asylum or those granted some form of international protection is access to healthcare. According to the Refugee Convention of 1951, a person who has obtained international protection should have access to the same or similar healthcare as members of the host population. Numerous international organisations, including the UNHCR, work in close cooperation with national governments and other partner organisations so that refugees receive the health support and medical treatment they need in emergencies as well as in stabilised and protracted situations (UNHCR, 2021). Access to adequate healthcare and its quality is sometimes one of the most important factors determining the migration paths of people seeking asylum. As persons who are frequently victims of all kinds of violence endured either in their country of origin or while fleeing them in search of security and safety, the provision of adequate healthcare is of particular importance to refugees. As such they often require specialised medical treatment, not only with regards to their physical health but also mental health, with the provision of the latter sometimes even more salient. The easier access to such treatment may sometimes be the reason why refugees decide to stay in a given country. Conversely, limited access to some specialised treatments might be a key incentive that pushes people with international protection to leave a given country in search of better quality medical care or access to it.

The aim of this chapter is to describe and analyse asylum seeker and refugee access to medical services in Poland. As of November 2021, the situation of those who have applied for international protection differs significantly from that of those who have already been granted some form of protection. While asylum seekers are

DOI: 10.4324/9781003196327-9

provided with medical services by a healthcare provider selected by the Office for Foreigners (currently the private company Petra Medica) those whose application has already been assessed positively have access to healthcare through the National Health Fund (in Polish: *Narodowy Fundusz Zdrowia*, NFZ), which is financed by compulsory health insurance contributions[1].

The chapter sheds light on what the access to medical care both in the centres for foreigners and outside of them looks like. It provides some statistical information about this provision and evaluates the practice, its perception, as well as key problems linked with access to healthcare pointed out by interviewed asylum seekers. It also analyses the perceptions of the beneficiaries of international protection concerning their transition from medical care provided by the selected medical care institution during the asylum procedure to the coverage by the general healthcare system financed by the NFZ. It evaluates the experiences of the beneficiaries of international protection while accessing medical services provided by the NFZ with regard to their physical and mental health.

The chapter starts with a general overview of the institutional framework within which foreigners who have applied for international protection and those who have already received it can access medical services. Here also, statistical information about the number of asylum seekers entitled to healthcare provision and the cost of it are analysed. The following parts rely heavily on the fieldwork data and assess the perceptions and usage of healthcare services by asylum seekers and by those who have obtained some form of international protection in Poland. The chapter concludes by highlighting the key findings from the research as well as some brief information about the impact of the COVID-19 pandemic on the access of asylum seekers and refugees to healthcare in Poland.

The Institutional Framework of Healthcare Provision

As the legal regulations for access to healthcare for persons who are applying for international protection in Poland and those who have already obtained some form of protection are laid down in Chapter 4, we begin our analysis by shedding light only on the institutional framework of healthcare provision. Asylum seekers and those who have received some form of international protection in Poland have access to healthcare services through two separate paths: the healthcare provider selected by the Office for Foreigners and the National Health Fund. Up until 2015, asylum applicants were provided with healthcare services by the Central Clinical Hospital of the Ministry of Interior and Administration on Wołoska Street in Warsaw. One of our interviewees from the NGO sector described this old arrangement in the following way:

> (...) the beginnings were difficult. But I remember that in the last years of its functioning it significantly improved and, as for the Polish medical care conditions, it worked like a well-oiled mechanism. Of course, it was incomparable to what people have in Germany or Sweden, where the sickest

asylum seekers go. But for Polish conditions it worked really well and the asylum seekers were looked after very well.

PLMZSO1

In mid-2015, the contract between the Office for Foreigners and the Central Clinical Hospital ended and a new public tender led to the selection of a private company established in 1996, Petra Medica. This company also won a public tender in 2019, and its contract was renewed for the next four years. As the employees of the Office for Foreigners informed us, the main reason why this relatively small private company won against the large Clinical Hospital is that the public procurement law favoured "a better offer" (PLMZOF3/4), which most probably was also the cheapest offer. Petra Medica provides healthcare services in the centres for foreigners (basic treatment and diagnostics), as well as in specialist medical units outside the centres. In addition, asylum seekers receive psychological consultations and dental treatment. As will be shown below, the quality of the latter services is particularly strongly criticised by NGOs and some practitioners for not being adequate (e.g., no psychotherapy is offered, and the dental treatment in practice is limited to the possibility of teeth removals) (MGN2).

Before the asylum seekers are placed in one of the centres for foreigners, they must pass through one of the so-called "epidemiological filters" (Office for Foreigners, 2018). These facilities have also been used during the COVID-19 pandemic to quarantine asylum applicants after their arrival in Poland. They are located near Warsaw (Podkowa Leśna-Dębak) and the Belarusian border (Biała Podlaska), where most asylum seekers cross the Polish land border. They are aimed at providing medical assistance exclusively to foreigners who have just applied for protection in Poland and reducing epidemiological risks for the whole of Poland by prompt diagnosis of potential infectious diseases (AIDA, 2018).

Basic healthcare is organised in medical offices within each of the centres for foreigners. The medical doctor in the centres has six duty hours a week per 120 asylum seekers, while the nurse has 20 hours a week for the same number of persons. Both have 3 hours a week more for every additional 50 asylum seekers. Moreover, in every centre, duty hours for a paediatrician are organised (4 hours a week per 50 children), and these physicians are present in the centres at least two days a week (AIDA, 2020, p. 66).

As already mentioned, the provision of medical care for asylum seekers also includes treatment for those suffering from mental health problems. In 2018, psychologists worked in all the centres for at least 4 hours a week for every 120 asylum seekers. This was extended by 1 hour for every additional 50 asylum seekers. This assistance was limited to basic consultations; however, asylum seekers could also be directed to a psychiatrist or a psychiatric hospital (AIDA, 2018, pp. 56–57). When the COVID-19 pandemic started, the quality of the psychological assistance deteriorated further as it was provided not in person but by phone (AIDA, 2020, p. 66).

The Office for Foreigners spent on average 4,261 PLN for medical care for each foreigner applying for international protection in 2020. In 2015 when Petra Medica

TABLE 9.1 The number of asylum applicants covered by the medical care provided by the Office for Foreigners and the cost of medical services in the years 2015–2021

Year	*Number of applicants for international protection eligible for the medical care provided by the Office for Foreigners in the given year*	*The total cost of the medical care provided by the Office for Foreigners in the given year (in PLN)*	*Average yearly cost of medical care per foreigner (in PLN)*
2015	4,011	11,284,142	2,813
2016	4,171	10,307,245	2,471
2017	3,882	12,654,251	3,259
2018	3,117	10,537,122	3,380
2019	2,979	12,409,887	4,165
2020	3,063	13,050,472	4,261
2021*	3,450	7,348,021*	4,260

Note: * In the case of 2021, the data concern only the first half of the year.

Source: Own elaboration based on data received from the Office for Foreigners.

started to provide healthcare services to asylum seekers, the Office spent on average 2,813 PLN for each person. Although the number of foreigners applying for refugee status in Poland in the last six years (up until the second half of 2021) has been decreasing, the cost of medical coverage provided in and outside of the centres for foreigners to asylum seekers has been rising. As shown in Table 9.1, between 2015 and 2020, the highest total annual cost of medical care provided to asylum seekers in a given year was in 2020. In that year, the Office spent more than 13 million PLN for this purpose. In 2017, with more than 800 additional asylum seekers provided healthcare by Petra Medica, the overall cost was 12.65 million PLN. When the average cost of medical care provision per foreigner is taken into account, one may clearly see that the healthcare services offered to asylum seekers were most expensive in 2020. This has to do above all with the general rise in the cost of medical services in the country. Between 2015 and 2019 (a five-year period), more than 18,000 asylum seekers were eligible for medical care offered by the Office. Its expenses on healthcare services in and outside the centres for foreigners during this period amounted to 57 million PLN. The annual average spent by the Office for the provision of medical services per person during the five-year period (2015–2019) was 3,150 PLN. This cost has significantly risen in recent years. The latest data from the first half of the 2021 show that the overall cost of medical care provided by the Office for Foreigners will most probably be significantly higher than in 2020. This has to do not only with the higher number of foreigners applying for international protection (with Afghanis and Belarusians the new major groups) but also the rising cost of medical care (NFZ, 2015).

Neither the Office nor Petra Medica provided the authors with detailed information about the structure of expenses for providing medical services to asylum seekers. However, the officials from the Office informed us that the Office is paying Petra Medica a monthly fee for each foreigner. The interviewees argued that:

> A given foreigner may not use the medical services but he or she is covered by our services anyway [and] we transfer a monthly fee for him or her.
>
> *PLMZOF3/4*

It is important to mention that, in 2015, an amendment was introduced to the Law on Protection, placing on the asylum authority, that is, the Office for Foreigners, the responsibility for due examination if an asylum seeker is a person who requires special treatment and can be considered a vulnerable person (see Chapter 4). Some of the vulnerable groups covered by Article 68(1) of the Law on Protection include minors, disabled persons, elderly persons, pregnant women, single parents, victims of human trafficking, seriously ill persons, mentally disordered persons, and victims of torture (full list in Chapter 4). In the course of the asylum procedure, the Office for Foreigners is now obliged to examine whether the applicant should be considered vulnerable on one or more grounds and thus entitled to special treatment. As experts point out, this is an important improvement as prior to the amendment, the process of identification of vulnerable groups was based solely on ineffective self-identification mechanisms (Szczepanik, 2017). Identification of vulnerabilities implies the provision of medical and psychological treatment to vulnerable asylum applicants, as well as special procedural guarantees during the procedure, such as the presence of a psychologist during the interview or conducting the interview at the place of stay or residence of a vulnerable asylum applicant (e.g., hospital or private apartment).

As far as persons who have obtained some form of international protection are concerned, they have access to medical services covered by the compulsory health insurance managed by the National Health Fund and hence face the same challenges as Polish citizens. Low healthcare funding, insufficient and ageing medical manpower, and poor infrastructure are only some of the problems that are faced equally frequently by refugees and Polish citizens and residents using medical services covered by the NFZ. These major issues of healthcare provision in Poland frequently translate into difficult access to specialists, long waiting lists for specialised treatments, or the necessity to use private-sector entities and pay out of pocket for such services, to mention only some of the problems. In the case of beneficiaries of international protection, obstacles also include the language barrier and cultural differences. Unlike at the stage of applying for protection, the law does not distinguish between groups requiring special treatment that could be formally included in the healthcare services dedicated to this vulnerable group.

The transfer from the model of medical care provided by specially selected service providers (currently the private medical company Petra Medica), as in the case of the asylum seekers, to the general public national healthcare system, as in the case of beneficiaries of international protection, is frequently not an easy one and fraught with many uncertainties. That is why some of our interviewees from the non-governmental sector suggested that not only refugees but also persons seeking international protection should be treated like citizens when it comes to healthcare provision (PLMZSO1). According to them, there could be organisational and financial benefits to such an arrangement. At present, the cost of medical care for persons within the reception system can be either overestimated or underestimated, as it is the subject of agreement between the Office for Foreigners and the institution that wins the competition for the provision of medical services to asylum seekers. If the healthcare provisions for them were public and under supervision of the National Health Fund, such a situation should not occur. Another benefit of such a change could be a smooth transition in healthcare provision from the reception phase (applying for international protection) to the integration phase (benefitting from international protection), which at present remains highly problematic.

On the other hand, there are also some clear disadvantages of such a change of the current framework to bring the provision of medical services under the full umbrella of the National Health Fund. It seems that especially at the level of general medical healthcare services, the companies selected by the Office for Foreigners are better suited to provide such services because they pay more attention to the cultural and linguistic diversity of the asylum seekers and their specific needs. Also important is the possibility of faster access to general practitioners and the provision of some medications free of charge.

The payment of compulsory health insurance gives a person with international protection, like any citizen of Poland, a legal entitlement to access healthcare. As one of the practitioners pointed out:

> At the moment when they gain protection, they fall into the same NFZ system as we do. They must have their insurance paid either by their employer or labour office, or they can personally pay their insurance with the National Health Fund. They are similar patients to any other citizen of the country.
>
> *PLMZSO1*

Another social worker assisting beneficiaries of international protection explained to us that agencies providing social assistance would pay health insurance contributions only for those who cannot do it themselves:

> (…) for example, for people of post-production age (65 years old and older). Otherwise, if persons with international protection work, then we try to make sure that the employer pays for them. If someone does not work, then they should register at the labour office and obtain health insurance in this way.
>
> *PLMZSO2*

There is no public information about the number of beneficiaries of international protection who use medical services or the cost of it. There is only information about the total number of foreigners who are entitled to services covered by the National Health Found. In 2020, Polish Statistics published an exploratory report in which it revealed that 1,230,717 foreigners were registered by the National Health Fund at the end of 2019 (GUS, 2020). We know that only a small minority of them are beneficiaries of international protection but do not have information about the size of this group.

Perceptions and Usage of Healthcare Services by Asylum Seekers

After shedding light on the institutional framework of healthcare provision to asylum seekers and refugees in Poland, it is time to turn to their experiences and perceptions of medical care in the country. First, we shall elaborate on these issues with regard to asylum seekers, and in the next section with regard to beneficiaries of international protection. Their views on healthcare provision during this stage of the asylum procedure are also juxtaposed with those of practitioners working directly or indirectly on a daily basis with persons seeking asylum in Poland or those who have already obtained it.

One of the issues that concerns all those living in Poland who have access to medical care through the National Health Fund is that sometimes it is necessary to wait for an extended period of time before one sees a specialist. One of our expert interviewees stated:

> I think that our foreigners [asylum seekers], as a result of having their medical appointments booked commercially, have shorter waiting periods.
>
> *PLMZOF3/4*

We have not found confirmation of this hypothesis in interviews with persons concerned. One of the interviewed asylum seekers had the following observation about healthcare provision:

> I had a problem with my nasal septum and they told me that I would need to wait around two years. I decided not to do it and went on a paid visit.
>
> *PLMICh15*

As our fieldwork material shows, one of the interviewed asylum seekers was not even aware of the fact that persons in reception have the right to access specialised medical care. She claimed that:

> They were not referring us to specialists. We were maybe not entitled to such services in this period before the refugee decision. We started seeing doctors only when we obtained refugee status.
>
> *PLMIIr28*

On the whole, however, our migrant interviewees who were direct beneficiaries of healthcare provision spoke positively about it. Easier access to medical treatment might sometimes be the key reason why people in reception with family members requiring constant medical assistance decide to stay in the centres for foreigners or live in their vicinity. Sometimes, though, they may decide to leave such centres and be closer to more specialised medical care facilities outside of them. One of the interviewees who lived in the centre for foreigners pointed out that:

> The medical doctor was available every day. It was possible to come every day. There were no problems with drugs. When there was no possibility to do everything in the centre for foreigners, she gave us a referral to the hospital in Biała Podlaska [small city in eastern Poland close to the centre]. Once there was a situation when the kids got pneumonia, with fever and so on … So, we went to the hospital with them (…) and after a week everything was OK.
>
> *PLMIUk16*

Among the interviewees who spoke highly of the healthcare provision were two asylum seekers from Syria accommodated in the initial phase of their reception in one of the centres for foreigners. One of them said:

> In the camp there was an excellent doctor with great morals and his behaviour was very nice. He used to receive us very comfortably and provided us with the proper medication in the camp.
>
> *PLMISy24*

Another interviewee accounted for the specialised medical assistance he received from the ophthalmologist in the following way:

> You are sick. For example, you have a problem with your eye. The doctor sees it, tries to treat it …. Then she told me that next month she will come and see the eye, if it's not good then I would have to have an operation. Then I go, God willing.
>
> *PLMIIr27*

Some of our asylum-seeking interviewees who expressed appreciation for the medical care provision spoke highly of the assistance with regard to physical as well as mental health. One of the asylum seekers from the Middle East with whom we spoke in the course of the research pointed out that:

> At the beginning, when I arrived, I was in a very bad psychological state and then they brought me a doctor, and thank God, now I am under treatment of some psychiatrist.
>
> *PLMIJe29*

Here, it is also important to mention that prolonged uncertainty about the result of the asylum procedure may also negatively influence an asylum seeker's mental health condition. We were able to detect such a situation among, for instance, some of the interviewed Chechens. One of them pointed out:

> The only problem is that you live under constant pressure. If you receive a negative decision, a refusal, you can be deported back to Chechnya. So, people live in fear all the time. This is the worst thing. It can happen to you any time. I get up in the morning and I don't know what will happen today. I am always under pressure. I am afraid of being deported. This is how I feel. I went to see the psychologist. He sent me to a psychiatrist. I have problems with memory. I started to forget some events from my past. All the problems with my health are caused by constant stress that I have.
>
> *PLMICh06*

This issue, however, was not limited only to this group of asylum seekers. Two interviewees from Ukraine complained also about the effect of the prolonged uncertainty on their health condition. One of them claimed that she had been in good mental condition before being placed in the detention centre for foreigners. She said:

> My depression started when I was detained in the detention centre in Biała Podlaska.
>
> *PLMIUk20*

In addition, one of our male interviewees from Ukraine described the impact of the stress related to awaiting the decision on refugee status on the health of his partner in the following way:

> Whenever she is stressed, her skin gets red and, so to speak, she cannot get stressed.
>
> *PLMIUk16*

From the perspective of the Office for Foreigners' employees dealing with persons in reception, the healthcare provisions in Poland are sometimes of better quality than similar provisions in other countries of the EU. They argued, for instance, that:

> When it comes to medical care, we are probably at one of the highest levels. We have the same care as for citizens. In similar centres in Finland, they have ladies whose competences are between these of a nurse and a lifeguard. They only prescribe paracetamol to all the symptoms. If someone comes with toothache, then [they] get paracetamol for 2 weeks. If it does not help, then eventually [they] might be sent to specialists, but this is rare. Maybe for children healthcare it is not limited, but for adults for sure.
>
> *PLMZOF3/4*

This perspective was not shared by the interviewed practitioners from the NGO sector. In fact, the most critical assessment of healthcare provision to asylum seekers was collected during our expert interviews. One of the positive elements of the healthcare provision that they could see was slightly easier access to the general practitioners as compared to the same access among wider Polish society. They also believed that access to the basic type of medical assistance was assured for asylum seekers adequately. One of these interviewees, for example, pointed out:

> It is true that sometimes it is easier for asylum seekers to get to general practitioners, in the sense that there are shorter queues, because it goes through a different path, or that they receive medications free of charge. On the other hand, it's hard to expect that people who have no right to work will be able to pay for them.
>
> *PLMZSO1*

The most frequently raised criticism concerned limited access to specialised medical care. According to our interviewees from social organisations, this access has been increasingly restricted since the contract for medical services for persons in reception shifted from the Central Clinical Hospital to the private company Petra Medica. One of our interviewees pointed out:

> Since then [the moment when the contract was signed with the private company], we have been observing a deterioration of these medical services. People complain about lower availability, that they are often sent to semi-specialists who are not specialists in a given field.
>
> *PLMZSO1*

One interviewee from the NGO sector who remains in close contact with asylum seekers in Poland and assists them in various aspects of life, including healthcare, claimed that when medical services were provided to persons in the refugee procedure by the Clinical Hospital—that is, up to 2015—they had better access to specialists and specialised treatments. Our interviewee from one of the organisations assisting asylum seekers in accessing medical care argued that:

> There is a reluctance to perform medical operations that are not related to saving lives. We had the example of a child who had an eyesight defect. When this child came to Poland, probably 5 years ago, a medical diagnosis suggested that this eyesight defect could be operated on and that the surgery gave a 70% chance that the child would regain 100% vision. After 5 years, there would be a 30% or less chance of success because these defects deteriorate. In the end, the parents left the country with the child.
>
> *PLMZSO2*

Our interviewees from the social organisations also complained about deteriorating access to specialised therapies. One of them, for example, pointed out that:

> Now it works much worse on many levels but especially when it comes to providing such often life-saving treatment of a very specialised type of HIV or treatment of hepatitis C (...). We have patients who have been refused these treatments for some years. They are sent, but not to these specialised institutions, but to some others. Such mock steps are implemented (...). And the Office is also starting to force Petra Medica to comply with the contract.
> *PLMZSO1*

One group of vulnerable asylum seekers who face particular difficulties with adequate medical care in Poland are persons with disabilities. Some of our interviewees from the NGO sector observed that:

> As for people with disabilities, we often saw people from the Office for Foreigners who were doing their best to provide for such persons. For example, there is no clear path on how a person who is moving on a wheelchair or who needs crutches should be treated. How these crutches or wheelchairs should be arranged. In general, the system of rehabilitation and support for people with disabilities in Poland is weak and in the reception system is even weaker.
> *PLMZSO5/6*

For the aforementioned reason, the Office informed, on its website at the end of November 2019, that it is currently implementing a project of additional support for asylum seekers in Poland. It includes, among others, elements of material support. The Office purchased the following items with the intention of distributing them to asylum seekers: 10 wheelchairs and pairs of crutches, adaptive devices for disabled people, 225 prams, 225 vouchers for baby items (e.g., diapers, clothes, cosmetics, and hygiene items), 2,100 vouchers for school supplies (including stationery, backpacks, and sportswear), and 100 packages of medical and hygienic articles (Office for Foreigners, 2019).

Our interviewees from the NGO sector also pointed out several weaknesses in the current medical care provided to asylum seekers in regard to mental health. One of the basic problems linked with this provision has to do with the fact that psychologists, who may play an important role in the asylum procedure, are not necessarily viewed as neutral when they are being employed by the Office for Foreigners. This issue was mentioned, for instance, by the following interviewee who argued that:

> In theory, there are psychologists in all centres for foreigners but in practice it is usually one person who works in several centres. These psychologists travel between the centres. Let's say they are, on average, in the given centre once

> a week. They are employed by the Office for Foreigners, which means that not everyone in the centres will perceive them as neutral and independent persons.
>
> *PLMZSO1*

Another issue frequently mentioned in the expert interviews concerned the scope and frequency of psychological assistance. One representative of a social organisation said:

> This psychological help, especially such that is adequate to the needs of people with post-traumatic stress disorder (PTSD), was always totally insufficient.
>
> *PLMZSO1*

The NGO sector has been playing a crucial role in supporting the Office for Foreigners in providing specialised psychological care to asylum seekers. The social organisations help the Office for Foreigners address not only the frequency of psychological assistance but also the quality (PLMZSO5/6). One of the initiatives mentioned in this regard by our expert respondents was the project "Alter Camp". As part of it, one of the NGOs working with asylum applicants brought additional psychologists to one of the centres for foreigners (Czerwony Bór) three times a week, along with some volunteers, interpreters, and mentors. This project significantly improved this form of medical assistance in one of the centres for a short period of time (PLMZSO2).

Yet another problem linked to the provision of physical and mental health assistance for asylum seekers mentioned by one of our interviewees had to do with the lack of interpreters. Some of the NGO interviewees described it in the following way:

> There is no access to translators. If they are available, then one needs to wait for them for a very long time and they are provided with a maximum of 3 psychological consultations. We also refer to physical medical assistance because (…) there are no translations where they are crucial. Asylum seekers are often put out of the door. They come to a medical examination but because of lack of communication, the person who was waiting for his/her appointment with the doctor is asked to leave the medical office because there is no translation provided to the doctor. The doctor says that there is no way to communicate, so he/she will not carry out the examination.
>
> *PLMZSO5/6*

As far as vulnerable persons are concerned, experts point out that in spite of some improvements, including the elaboration of screening questionnaires to be used by psychologists in reception centres, even the identification of vulnerable persons remains a challenge. There is a lack of psychologists and therapists possessing the necessary qualifications and language skills to treat traumatised asylum seekers.

The assistance provided by specialists working for NGOs is not sufficient to fill the systemic gaps, for example, the lack of psychotherapy available under general healthcare provisions (AIDA, 2018; Szczepanik, 2017).

Perceptions and Usage of Healthcare Services by Beneficiaries of International Protection

Having shed light on the practice of the use of healthcare services by persons whose applications for international protection have not been processed yet, we now turn to those whose applications were assessed positively.

On the whole, most of our interviewees from this group were satisfied with the healthcare provision in Poland. For example, one of them said, "here, doctors treat [you] well" (PLMICh11). Another one who has had experience with medical treatment in a Polish hospital pointed out that, "in the hospital, everyone was paying attention to details"(PLMIUk16).

At the same time, a few of our interviewees with international protection formulated complaints about the long waiting time to see specialists, similar to the experience of many Polish citizens using the very same medical facilities financed by the National Health Found. One of them described the Polish medical system in the following way:

> If we are talking about paid private clinics, they are very fast and of good quality. If we are talking about the free[2] state medical system, the quality of it is good, but you have to wait a long time.
>
> *PLMICh11*

Some of our interviewees also recounted experiences of discrimination while accessing medical services, although sporadic. One of them recalled the following situation:

> I have experienced discrimination in the hospital. It was my first time in the Polish hospital and I didn't know what to do. So, I took a number from the machine and stood in the queue and waited in line for around 2 hours. When it was my turn one woman approached me and said: "You are a refugee, so for you entrance is prohibited. Go home and treat yourself there". It was a shocking experience.
>
> *PLMICh10*

Another interviewee who complained about the unjust treatment in access to medical treatment described the following situation:

> I experienced an incident when my blood pressure increased. I laid in bed for three days. (...) We called an ambulance, but it didn't come. They explained that 180 was not a high blood pressure, but I felt very bad that I couldn't

> move in order to walk to the hospital by myself. They said they don't send the ambulance to such cases. (...) I think that the true reason was that they heard a Ukrainian accent.
>
> *PLMIUk19*

As far as this case is concerned, there is the possibility that the medical personnel would react in a similar way to the description of symptoms by a person calling for an ambulance and speaking Polish without a foreign accent.

The beneficiaries of international protection interviewed in the course of our research also mentioned some linguistic barriers to access medical services. One of our interviewees pointed out that, for instance, the doctor he was seeing did not know English. He recalled:

> I was suffering because of the language, frankly, communicating with him was difficult because of the language.
>
> *PLMIIr28*

Another interviewee who had similar problems described the following coping strategy:

> If I don't understand what he is talking about, he knows it from the expression on my face and tries to explain it. But if I don't understand something completely, I look for the answers on the internet.
>
> *PLMIUk19*

If those with international protection do not want to or cannot wait too long to see a specialist, and have sufficient financial means, then they employ a similar strategy as Polish citizens, namely the use of the private medical sector. One person who did that was an interviewee who pointed out that:

> The only problem in Poland is the medical system. (...) I went to hospital in Brest in order to have an appointment with the endocrinologist because you had to wait for too long for such an appointment in Warsaw.
>
> *PLMICH04*

This interviewee also complained that, for such a visit with a specialist, she had to pay 80 PLN, which was not reimbursed to her as it was outside of the treatments covered by the National Health Fund.

The transition from the medical services provided by the private company Petra Medica to the public health system after the granting of international protection was also one of the changes that some of our interviewees found problematic.

These views were echoed by interviewed members of the host society working closely with people who have received international protection. Some of our expert interviewees argued that one of the problems seen in healthcare provision to those with international protection is that they lack knowledge about their rights in this respect. One of our respondents from a social organisation pointed out that:

> Many beneficiaries of international protection don't even know they have certain rights. In the project we now have, we have information sessions to which we invite people from the National Health Fund, from various institutions, to tell them what rights they have.
>
> *PLMZSO7*

On the other hand, one practitioner we interviewed in the course of the research argued that an important problem might be cultural barriers. Interestingly, this interviewee pointed out that:

> Chechens are unlikely to go to a psychologist because they still see it as "when I go to a psychologist, I am mentally ill. Never." But for example, I noticed that Syrians and Iraqis are aware that a psychologist is there to help me. (…) I also had people from that region who associated a psychologist with a psychiatrist. Meaning a person [who will] "give me pills to calm me down and let me forget".
>
> *PLMZP1*

One of the major issues, however, which has been repeated by numerous interviewees from the NGO sector as well as those working with refugees in the state institutions is the language barrier, or more broadly the lack of linguistic and intercultural competences of medical personnel. One of the strategies in addressing this challenge developed by some state organisations and many social organisations is the accompaniment of the refugee by a translator. One of the interviewed practitioners described it this way:

> If someone comes, has a problem and wants to go to a doctor and does not speak Polish, one of us goes to the doctor with such a person.
>
> *PLMZP2*

Some of the expert interviewees had acted as interpreters.

The linguistic competences of the medical staff are particularly important when it comes to the provision of psychological and psychiatric assistance. One of the interviewed practitioners very pertinently described a critical issue linked to the lack of specialists who are able to effectively communicate with the refugees:

> Psychological help is badly needed. (…) We have two psychologists in our institution who speak Russian [and] English, so we can provide this. What about people who speak Arabic? There is no one in Poland who could conduct such therapy (…), not even psychological consultations in Arabic. If it is done through an interpreter, then it is inefficient and many people back

> down, they don't want to do it. And in another language, you are not able to express all emotions, so it doesn't work.
>
> *PLMZP1*

Our interviewee also pointed out that the offer available in Warsaw in this regard is much richer than in other parts of the country.

Generally, however, the experts point out that specialised treatment for victims of torture or the traumatised is not available in practice in Poland because of the lack of qualified psychologists and therapists specialising in treating trauma, especially in an intercultural context (AIDA, 2018; Szczepanik, 2017).

Our expert interviewees also pointed out the important role played by the NGO sector in the provision of supplementary psychological assistance to persons with international protection. At the same time, some of the social actors argued that the provision of this type of psychological help has been strained by the financial difficulties of some of the organisations providing this type of assistance since 2015 and the redirection of funds from the Asylum, Migration and Integration Fund to state agencies and other types of organisations (PLMZSO1).

Conclusions

As shown above, the provision of basic healthcare to asylum seekers as well as beneficiaries of international protection in Poland is relatively adequately ensured. When it comes to people whose applications are being processed, they may even benefit from healthcare provision that in some ways is superior to what is available in other EU countries. One of the major issues linked with healthcare assistance to those in reception concerns psychological support and specialised medical support. Our empirical data shows that these types of healthcare provisions are seriously underdeveloped and, in view of the opinions of some of our interviewees, such services have not been improving, rather deteriorating recently. Some of our interviewees argued that the current quality of healthcare services (especially access to specialists) is lower than before 2015 when these services were provided by the Central Clinical Hospital of the Ministry of Interior and Administration. In addition, a deficiency was identified in terms of access to psychologists who provide support free of charge, either as part of guaranteed medical services or NGO assistance. This is connected to the general shortage of specialists who know foreign languages and are prepared to work with asylum seekers who may be affected by various trauma.

As far as the beneficiaries of international protection are concerned, they have the same rights of access to the public healthcare services as other citizens of Poland. Thus, from a legal point of view, this provision seems relatively adequately ensured. At the same time, for various reasons linked with insufficient economic, social, or cultural capital, they may be denied equal access to various types of medical treatments. One of the clear gaps in medical services identified by our interviewees was specialised treatment for victims of torture or traumatised refugees. There is a clear lack of qualified psychologists and therapists in the country who specialise in treating trauma and possess adequate cultural and linguistic skills. Our research has also identified barriers that refugees face when accessing medical services, including linguistic ones and others linked to stereotypes of people coming from a specific part of the world or belonging to a given ethnic or religious group. Similar to citizens of Poland, people with international protection who cannot wait to see a specialist are forced to find funding to receive adequate services in the private medical sector.

The access of asylum seekers and beneficiaries of international protection to healthcare has been additionally restricted by the COVID-19 pandemic. As medical services have switched in large proportion from on-site visits to telephone sessions (so-called medical "televisits", "tele-advice"), the quality of healthcare provision has seriously deteriorated for the whole society, but particularly for foreigners given the difficulties of communicating over the phone with medical staff in Polish or a third language. Like other health institutions in the country, the company Petra Medica introduced special procedures for asylum seekers living in the centres for foreigners and outside of them before they could see a doctor or a nurse. The on-site medical visit became possible only after a prior contact over the phone[3]. The pandemic has also seriously affected one of the centres for foreigners hosting asylum seekers. Media reports emerged in mid-2020 about a COVID-19 outbreak at the women and children's facility in Warsaw. The whole centre was quarantined and a few people were taken to hospital (Targowek.info, 2020). Clearly, the crowding in all centres analysed in the previous chapter makes them particularly vulnerable to virus outbreaks. While initially the government's communication about the vaccination programme did not specify asylum seekers as a group eligible for it, after the intervention of the Ombudsman, this issue was clarified with the Ministry of Health and access was granted (BRPO, 2021).

Notes

1 The planned amendments to the Law on Foreigners are supposed to change the institutional framework of healthcare provision for asylum seekers in Poland. From 2022, the healthcare provisions for asylum seekers are supposed to fall within the general system administered by the National Health Fund, according to a presentation by Agata Ewertyńska from the centre for foreigners during a special workshop for immigration officers (Zakopane 13.09.2021).

2 Here it is worth mentioning that these services are generally free of charge only for persons who are registered with National Health Fund (NFZ) and pay contributions to it.

3 More information is available on the website of Petra Medica: www.petramedica.pl/nasza-oferta/oferta-dla-pacjentow-indywidualnych/opieka-medyczna-dla-cudzoziemcow (accessed 11 November 2021).

References

AIDA, 2018. *Country Report: Poland – 2018 update.* AIDA Asylum Information Database.

AIDA, 2020. *Country Report: Poland – 2020 update.* Asylum Information Database (AIDA).

BRPO, 2021. *Co ze szczepieniami uchodźców i imigrantów – pyta Rzecznik*. Biuro Rzecznika Praw Obywatelskich, Warsaw.

GUS, 2020. *Populacja cudzoziemców w Polsce w czasie COVID-19*. Główny Urząd Statystyczny, Warsaw.

NFZ, 2015. *Prognoza kosztów świadczeń opieki zdrowotnej finansowanych przez Narodowy Fundusz Zdrowia w kontekście zmian demograficznych w Polsce*. Narodowy Fundusz Zdrowia, Warsaw.

Office for Foreigners, 2018. *Miesięczny raport z działalności urzędu – styczeń 2018* [WWW Document]. https://udsc.gov.pl/statystyki/raporty-okresowe/meldunek-miesieczny/2015-2/2018-2/ (accessed 29 December 2019).

Office for Foreigners, 2019. *Guidebook: Department for Social Services*. UDSC, Warsaw.

Szczepanik, M., 2017. Right to Healthcare and Access to Medical Services for Asylum Seekers and Beneficiaries of International Protection in Poland. Leg. Dialogue Top. Civ. Soc. https://legal-dialogue.org/right-healthcare-access-medical-services-asylum-seekers-beneficiaries-international-protection-poland (accessed 3 July 2020).

Targowek.info. 2020. *Już 63 Zarażenia Koronawirusem w Ośrodku Dla Uchodźców*. [WWW Document]. http://www.targowek.info/2020/06/juz-63-zarazenia-koronawirusem-w-osrodku-dla-uchodzcow/. (accessed 29 December 2021)..

UNHCR, 2021. *Access to Healthcare*. UNHCR.

10

UNTIL THEY BECOME CITIZENS

Refugees' Rights, Civic Participation, and Belonging

Introduction

The role of rights and citizenship is often considered fundamental to the successful integration of migrants in general and refugees in particular (Ager and Strang, 2008). This dimension of integration probably requires the most emphasis on the readiness of the host country's public institutions to engage in a two-way integration process[1] (see Introduction) since it is the state that grants rights to specific groups of people and enforces their observance.

Countries vary in regard to granting citizenship to beneficiaries of international protection. Signatories of the Geneva Convention of 1951, including Poland, are obliged to use either the principle of national treatment or the most-favoured-nation clause with respect to rights vested in recognised refugees. In addition, they are also obliged to facilitate the naturalisation of refugees, in particular to accelerate the naturalisation procedure and to limit the costs of the latter (Geneva Convention 1951, Article 34). However, the practice of refugees' naturalisation in Poland, in particular the number of refugees who were granted citizenship (176 people between 2012 and the first half of 2021)[2] and the time from arriving in Poland to being granted citizenship (at least seven to eight years), puts the facilitation obligation into question.

Among the possible explanations for the low naturalisation rate of refugees in Poland can be the citizenship law and the notions of citizenship and nationhood it explicitly or implicitly contains. Despite the lack of one common understanding of citizenship, almost all definitions point to the bond between an individual and a group (a community) or entity (state, institutions). Liberal theories of citizenship highlight the reciprocity in the relationship between individuals and the state. Republican theories focus on political communities (nations) as mediators between individuals and state institutions. The greatest emphasis on the rights and

DOI: 10.4324/9781003196327-10

responsibilities of individuals is put in communitarian theories, where citizenship is defined as the full membership of the community, with all its rights and responsibilities (Łucka, 2019; Marshall, 1950).

In Poland, it is not very clear what is the dominant notion of citizenship. The legal understanding of citizenship is twofold. On the one hand, the Law on Polish Citizenship 2009 allows foreigners to enter the community of citizens and have the same rights after fulfilling specific conditions. On the other hand, the Pole's Card (*Karta Polaka*)[3] mirrors the existence of status law[4] that grants special entitlements to Polish co-ethnics residing in other countries. In addition, in the public and media debates about either refugees or migrants (see Chapter 3), citizenship is often defined as synonymous with belonging to an ethnically bounded nation. Drawing on Brubaker's (1992, 1994) division between ethnic and civic nations and his ascertainment that the notion of citizenship is deeply rooted in a dominant vision of nationhood, the scale in Poland tilts towards the popular understanding of citizenship, namely the ethno-centric approach (Babakova, 2021).

Building on Ager and Strang's framework (2008), this chapter aims to present two important domains of integration, namely the fundamental principles of citizenship and rights, and belonging and civic participation as forms of social connection. It contains three parts. The first one describes the legal framework of access to citizenship and other rights for beneficiaries of international protection in Poland. The second one presents an overview of the refugee naturalisation statistics in Poland. The third part brings the findings of the RESPOND empirical research and sheds light on the experiences and perceptions of asylum seekers' and beneficiaries' of international protection towards acquiring citizenship, belonging, and their participation in the political, social, and cultural life of Poland.

Refugees' Rights and Access to Citizenship

To understand refugees' motivations in applying for Polish citizenship, it is indispensable to learn the differences in rights stemming from the different legal statuses. Beneficiaries of international protection have similar economic, social, and cultural rights as citizens of Poland (see Chapter 4). They also enjoy almost equal personal freedoms and rights, although some asymmetry exists. With respect to personal freedoms, the asymmetry in rights begins with the possibility of expulsion (even if treated as an exception by both the 1951 Geneva Convention and the law on granting protection in the territory of Poland of 13 June 2003) and impediments to travel abroad stemming from the fact that the Geneva passport or a national Travel Document is not universally recognised. However, the most substantial differences between citizens and non-citizens exist in the access to political rights.

In Poland, the possibilities for beneficiaries of international protection to participate in political life are very limited, and Polish law is one of the most restrictive in Europe in this respect. The MIPEX project (2020), assessing the possibilities of participation of foreigners in this aspect of life, confirmed this observation and classified Poland as the penultimate place (together with Serbia and the Czech

Republic) out of all examined European countries. Poland has neither signed nor ratified any of the chapters of the Council of Europe's Convention on the participation of foreigners in public life at the local level. The right to vote is vested only in citizens of Poland (in all elections and referendums) and of the European Union (only in local elections and local referendums). The possibility of establishing political parties and belonging to them is also an exclusive right of Polish citizens. In consequence, the parties rarely include issues important to immigrants in their programmes. Moreover, at present foreigners are not actively encouraged to participate in the political life of Poland. Until recently, foreigners themselves rarely publicly expressed their desire to have such rights. A herald of change was the protest action "Elections" (*Wybory*) organised by a Ukrainian artist, Marta Romankiv, in Gdansk, Lublin, Poznan, Szczecin, Bialystok, and Warsaw during the presidential elections in June 2020. Migrants living in Poland could symbolically vote by tossing invalid ballots into fictitious ballot boxes as a manifestation of their lack of political rights, including the right to vote in elections (Sudakowska, 2020). Currently, there is neither a public debate about granting political rights to migrants from non-EU countries nor a plan to include this issue in future migration policy. The document "Poland's migration policy—current state and postulated actions" of 2012, which emphasised the possibility of starting a debate on granting foreigners registered for permanent residence the right to vote at the local level in Poland, was revoked in 2016.

Given these barriers, for refugees who settled in Poland and wish to continue their life there, naturalisation is the obvious process aiming at obtaining full rights. Beneficiaries of international protection can obtain Polish citizenship through two procedures: by being citizenship granted by the Polish president (Law on Polish Citizenship, 2009, Article 18) or by being recognised as a Polish citizen (Law on Polish Citizenship, 2009, Article 30) (see Table 10.1).

The first path to acquiring citizenship stipulates that any foreigner can apply to the president to be granted Polish citizenship and there are no specific conditions or criteria for obtaining citizenship through this procedure. A foreigner only has to submit a form with information about himself/herself and justification as to why he/she should receive Polish citizenship to a voivode or consul,[5] who hands in the application to the president (Law on Polish Citizenship, 2009, Article 19–21). In this procedure, there is no criterion of knowledge of the Polish language; however, the application form is in Polish and should be filled out in Polish. Submission of the application to a voivode is free of charge, whereas in case of submitting it to a consul, there is an administrative fee of EUR 360 (MSWiA, 2019b). The cost of translating all documents into Polish has to be covered by the applicant. In this procedure, the president's refusal is a final decision and cannot be appealed.

The second option is that a foreigner can be recognised as a Polish citizen if he/she fulfils criteria specified in law (Law on Polish Citizenship, 2009, Article 30). Both refugees and subsidiary protection beneficiaries have to first obtain a permanent residence permit (*zezwolenie na pobyt stały*) or EU long-term residence permit in Poland. A permanent residence permit is granted to refugees and

TABLE 10.1 Differences in naturalisation procedures between refugees and beneficiaries of subsidiary protection

Naturalisation procedure	*Persons with refugee status*	*Beneficiary of subsidiary protection*
Recognition as a Polish citizen by a Voivode	Requirement of residency in Poland for 2 years after receiving a permanent residence permit. Requirement of knowledge of the Polish language. Possibility of appealing against the decision.	Requirement of residency in Poland for 3 years after receiving a permanent residence permit or long-term EU resident permit, or requirement of 10 years of continued residency in Poland and holding—upon applying for citizenship—a permanent residence permit or long-term EU resident permit.[a] Requirement of having a legal entitlement to stay in a residential property. Requirement of having a stable and regular source of income. Requirement of knowledge of the Polish language. Possibility of appealing against the decision.
Granting Polish citizenship by the president	No condition of residency in Poland for a specific time span. No requirement to submit evidence of loss or exemption from foreign citizenship (possibility of holding dual citizenship). Decision of the president is discretionary, there is no requirement for justification. Decision cannot be appealed.	

Note: [a]Except for children, to whom different regulations apply.

Source: own compilation based on the Law on Polish Citizenship, 2009.

subsidiary protection beneficiaries on their motion, based on whether they had continuously lived in Poland for at least five years before the submission of the application. The asylum procedure is taken into account in this calculation (Law on Foreigners, 2013, Article 195(1)(6) and Article 195(3)).

A refugee who has been granted a permanent residence permit and has been staying continuously on this basis in Poland for two additional years can be recognised as a Polish citizen (Law on Polish Citizenship, 2009, Article 30(1)(3)). There is no similar rule concerning subsidiary protection beneficiaries. To be recognised as Polish citizens, they have to fulfil the same criteria as any other foreigner who obtained a permanent residence permit or EU long-term residence permit in Poland (i.e., two to three years' stay in Poland on this basis or ten years of legal stay in Poland independently of the basis of the stay, stable and regular sources of income, legal entitlement to stay in a residential property) (Law on Polish Citizenship, 2009, Article 30(1)(1), (2), and (6)).

Applications for being recognised as a Polish citizen are submitted to the voivode who has jurisdiction over applicants' current place of stay (Law on Polish Citizenship, Article 36(1)). The fee for the decision of granting citizenship is PLN 219 (around EUR 50). The voivode's decision can be appealed to a minister competent for internal affairs (Law on Polish Citizenship, 2009, Article 10(4)). In theory, the procedure should last up to two months, but in practice it often lasts longer (AIDA, 2020).

For both refugees and subsidiary protection beneficiaries, to be recognised as a Polish citizen, they must prove that they know the Polish language (Law on Polish Citizenship, 2009, Article 30(2)). Foreigners should present a document confirming that they have either graduated from a Polish school, or a school with Polish as the language of lectures, or that they have passed the state exam for Polish as a foreign language (at least at a B1 level). Those examinations are held about three times a year (before 2018, the frequency was twice a year) in bigger cities in Poland, and in Ukraine, Belarus, France, and the United States. In 2021, they were scheduled to be held in several cities in different regions of Poland;[6] however, some of the scheduled exams were cancelled due to the COVID-19 pandemic. The fee for the exam is EUR 150, plus EUR 20 for issuing a certificate,[7] which is quite high, and when the costs of transportation to the city where the exam is held are added on top of this, it can be an obstacle to applying for naturalisation.

The open vision of Polish citizenship existing in law is the result of a long legislative debate about the need to revise the obsolete Act on Polish Citizenship (1962) after the fall of communism in Poland in 1989. Before the Law on Polish Citizenship of 2009 entered into force (in 2012), it was the president[8] who most often decided whether to grant citizenship and, in principle, could grant citizenship to a person who had lived in Poland for at least five years on the basis of a permanent residence permit (Law on Polish Citizenship of 1962, Article 8). The Law of 1962 also stipulated that the condition of permanent residence could be omitted in particularly justified cases. In practice, the decision of the president was discretionary, and citizenship could be granted to anyone the president wanted. In addition, the former law might require renouncing previous citizenship (Law on Polish Citizenship of 1962, Article 8 (3), Article 10(2), and Article 11(2)) since dual or multiple citizenships were not viewed well (Górny and Pudzianowska, 2009). A voivode was entitled to recognise as a Polish citizen only a stateless person or a person without a determined citizenship (Law on Polish Citizenship of 1962, Article 9). After adopting the new law in 2009, the procedure of a voivode recognising a Polish citizen started to be treated not as an exception but as an alternative to granting citizenship by the president. Also, since 2018, the voivode procedure has been the dominant way of obtaining Polish citizenship.

Naturalisation of Refugees: an Overview

The number of foreigners who have acquired Polish citizenship increased from 2,361 in 2011 to 7,159 in 2020 (Table 10.2). The gradual increase in the naturalisation statistics is the result of both an increase in immigration to Poland, especially since 2016, and changes in the law facilitating the naturalisation procedure for people of Polish origin. In 2019, Poland had a naturalisation rate[9] of 2%, which positioned the country in the middle among the EU Member States (Eurostat, 2021a). However, when comparing naturalisation statistics with the other states, Poland is positioned close to demographically much smaller countries like Romania (5,732 acquired citizenships in 2019), Ireland (5,791), or Luxembourg (5,657), far behind the more attractive destination countries like Germany (131,980), Spain (98,954), or Sweden (64,206) (Eurostat, 2021b).

The naturalisation statistics cannot be easily juxtaposed to the statistics of granting refugee status or other types of protection since acquiring citizenship by persons with the mentioned statuses takes at least seven years (for refugees) or eight years (for beneficiaries of subsidiary protection)[10] if they opt for the procedure of being recognised as a Polish citizen (Górny et al., 2017, p. 33).

There are no statistics depicting the actual numbers of beneficiaries of international protection who acquired Polish citizenship. The Central Registry of Data on the Acquisition and Loss of Polish Citizenship does not contain information on the legal basis of the applicant's stay on the territory of Poland (permit obtained) or information about whether the foreigner is covered by various forms of international protection (refugee status, person under subsidiary protection, or temporary protection). However, it was possible to obtain data about the number of persons with refugee status recognised as Polish citizens by a voivode on the basis of the procedure stipulated in Article 30(1)(3) of the Law on Polish Citizenship since 2012, that is, the year the law entered into force (see Table 10.3).

Since the procedure stipulated by Article 30(1)(3) of the Law on Polish Citizenship is intended for persons granted refugee status, the above-presented data do not include persons with other types of protection who acquired citizenship. In addition, it only shows the number of refugees who were granted Polish citizenship by a voivode and does not include the number of those who were granted citizenship by the president. Our empirical research showed that the latter form is preferred by the beneficiaries of international protection because it does not require the language certificate and paying for the language exam.

Another source of data, the Office for Foreigners, can be helpful to determine the number of persons granted international protection status (either refugee status or subsidiary protection) who acquired Polish citizenship. According to the Office, between 2011 and 2019 50 people were deprived of international protection status (or the decision of granting the status had expired) with relation to obtaining Polish citizenship. However, the given statistics do not match those obtained from the Ministry of the Interior and Administration. As explained by an employee of the Office for Foreigners, the Office receives information about changes in the legal

TABLE 10.2 Acquisition of Polish citizenship in 2011–2021

Naturalisation Procedure	*2011*	*2012*	*2013*	*2014*	*2015*	*2016*	*2017*	*2018*	*2019*	*2020*	*2021 (as of 30 June)*	*Total 2011–2021*
Recognised as Polish citizens by a voivode	37	339	1,832	1,881	1,639	1,390	2,656	3,257	4,293	5,114	2,738	**25,176**
Being granted Polish citizenship by the president	2,324	2,456	2,418	2,637	2,413	2,739	1,637	1,972	2,157	2,045	1,064	**23,862**
Total	**2,361**	**2,795**	**4,250**	**4,518**	**4,052**	**4,129**	**4,293**	**5,229**	**6,450**	**7,159**	**3,802**	**49,038**

Source: Data received from the Ministry of the Interior and Administration, 2021.

TABLE 10.3 Number of refugees who were recognised as Polish citizens in 2012–2021

Year	*2012*	*2013*	*2014*	*2015*	*2016*	*2017*	*2018*	*2019*	*2020*	*2021 (as of 30 June)*	*Total 2012–2021*
Number of persons	0	0	16	18	31	18	59	20	10	4	**176**

Source: Data received from the Ministry of the Interior and Administration, 2021.

status of a person with a delay of a couple of months or even years after acquiring Polish citizenship.

Attitudes towards Acquiring Citizenship

None of our respondents had applied for Polish citizenship as of the time of the study, although the majority of them expressed their willingness to do so in the future, which proves that naturalisation in Poland is a long process, even for beneficiaries of international protection. A grant of citizenship by the president is perceived by them as a more accessible way of acquiring citizenship due to the lack of specific requirements present in the procedure of recognition as a Polish citizen (i.e., a minimum period of residency in Poland or knowledge of Polish language at least at a B1 level). Other obstacles to naturalisation through recognition as a Polish citizen include difficulties with providing in writing a legal entitlement to stay in a residential property (e.g., owners often do not want to sign a rental agreement and prefer oral agreements) and difficulties with obtaining civil registration documents from a country of origin (Kaźmierkiewicz, 2019a, p. 25). In addition, there is no fee for the procedure of the president granting citizenship, which is also not without significance.

As pointed out by a practitioner from a social organisation, every year an increasing number of beneficiaries of international protection apply for citizenship while preferring the presidential procedure:

> Many are interested in this path by the president because you don't have to wait until all these years have passed—that you have to acquire permanent residence [permit], you can submit an application to the president at any time. The only problem is that the president can reject the application and there is no possibility of appeal against his decision. And people often want to apply for citizenship.
>
> *PLMZSO1*

The strongest motivations for applying for citizenship by refugees are the freedom of movement and equality of rights not available for them in Poland without having citizenship. Our institutional respondents spoke about the two dimensions of freedom of movement that influence the decision to apply for citizenship: first is the possibility to leave Poland and settle in another EU country after acquiring Polish and, simultaneously, European Union citizenship and, second, the ability to travel occasionally to the country of origin. It turned out that the latter motivation is very frequent for refugees, since the status of a Polish citizen would be a guaranty that after visiting their families in the countries of origin they would be allowed to return to Poland:

> Some people apply for citizenship in order to go home safer. Because if you are a refugee and you go home, you can be deprived of this form of protection. And this is not a situation that is a very direct threat to life, but they also have put together their whole lives here and do not think about returning permanently to their countries of origin. But they want to go, for instance, to visit family. And then, if they have Polish citizenship, it allows them to leave and come back.
>
> *PLMZSO1*

Another practitioner from a social organisation reiterated the importance of obtaining citizenship in Poland to have equal rights with the members of the host society:

> It is very important [to get citizenship]. It's really much easier. If you are a citizen and if you are a refugee, they treat you differently. If you have citizenship, you are a Pole.
>
> *PLMZSO7*

Because the law enables any person to apply for citizenship to the president without determining the legal status of the applicant, this way of acquiring citizenship is also considered by asylum seekers whose asylum procedure will last a couple of years or longer. One of the interviewed subjects from Ukraine—an asylum applicant—raised the issue of the inability to travel as a nuisance:

> I can't see other countries. A lot of my friends are leaving, and they are touring Europe. "Oh, I'm leaving for Holland in two days". And I say, "I can't leave". I don't like explaining because then there are questions, "oh, why so?"
>
> *PLMIUk18*

The latter factor, apart from his prolonged asylum procedure and lack of possibility to go back to Ukraine, made him consider applying for Polish citizenship:

> Well, I would like to write right away, because there is such a chance to obtain citizenship, one may try to write to the president of the country. And this is one chance, either yes or no. Write a request to the president, and immediately go through all the offices.
>
> *PLMIUk18*

Despite the importance of naturalisation for the integration of a migrant in the host country and society, not all beneficiaries of international protection are interested in obtaining citizenship. A practitioner who works with them suggested that this attitude could be related to the identity of a refugee stemming from an actual lack of belonging:

> [...] sometimes it seems to them that it is not profitable for them to acquire citizenship. Maybe they think it is not profitable because it is contradictory to their perception of themselves: "I'm a refugee and I feel worse, you never understand me here because I'm not at home". Indeed, somehow someone may not be at home, and I don't know if acquiring citizenship would make it different. I find a lot of people who can already get citizenship, who participated in IIP, but they are not interested.
>
> *PLMZP2*

Lack of belonging can explain the attitude of our respondent with subsidiary protection who showed no interest in applying for citizenship. He argued that he was not capable of voting in the election because he is not interested in politics in Poland, which he referred to as "this country". He said:

> Maybe if I would be 60 years old then, maybe, I could vote. But now [i.e.] after the next four years, I'd have to choose who's good for this country? No, I don't think so.
>
> *PLMIUk16*

Another factor hindering naturalisation of beneficiaries of international protection is a lack of information about the naturalisation procedures provided by the administration offices; having that information would allow an immigrant to plan their stay in Poland appropriately (Kaźmierkiewicz and Frelak, 2011, p. 19). In fact, as confirmed by our research, no consulting is offered by the public institutions in terms of long-term residence planning.

As proved by the interviews, although obtaining citizenship is an important step in the integration process, it does not protect people of different origins against discrimination on the basis of "a different skin colour or a different accent" (PLMZSO2). Discriminatory incidents against Polish citizens having "not-Polish-looking" physiognomy illustrate the ethno-centric understanding of citizenship and nationhood rooted in a large part of Polish society.

Civic Participation of Refugees

Civic participation in a broad meaning can be defined as any individual or group activity addressing issues of public concern (Anheier and Toepler, 2010). A basic division has been drawn between political activity (Parry et al., 1992) and more private forms, such as participation in associations and social life (Putnam, 2000, 1993).

Although there is no distinct boundary between these forms, political activity is often reserved for citizens and treated as their privilege. In its broad meaning, civic participation can be readily linked with the existential agency, understood as the fundamental capacity of all humans to be self-reflective, initiate their own actions, and consequently influence their own lives (Hitlin and Elder, 2007, 2006). In this sense, forced migrants' civic participation in host countries comprises all the mentioned steps: self-reflection on their situation, taking independent action through involvement in associations, or showing interest in public life, and, eventually, influencing their own lives through political or social activity (Cetrez, Petrogianis, and Szalanska, 2021).

For the purpose of this chapter, based on the interviews with beneficiaries of international protection, we indicated the following forms of civic participation of refugees: involvement in associational life, engagement in social organisations' activities, and showing interest in news in Poland and in the country of origin.

With regard to refugees' involvement in associational life in Poland, it turned out that the refugees or beneficiaries of subsidiary protection whom we talked to, if they worked for an NGO, mostly did it as part of voluntary service. But such involvement cannot be perceived as common practice. Out of our 16 respondents with international protection, only one man, a Chechen, was engaged in volunteering for an NGO. In general, the level of public activity of migrants or their level of involvement in associations in Poland is low. Beneficiaries of international protection are members of just a couple of social organisations: Association of Refugees in Poland, Ocalenie Foundation, Foundation Free Syria, Foundation for Somalia, Foundation Multiocalenie, Foundation Sintar of Issa Adayev, and Chechen Diaspora in Poland (Kaźmierkiewicz, 2019b, p. 60).

With respect to migrants' self-organisation in Poland, it has been expanding recently, as stated by one of our respondents from a social organisation:

> As we speak about integration, we can actually say that we have an increasingly strong migrant environment; typically migrant, identity-related non-governmental organisations have emerged. They are not only organisations that support migrants, but they are identity organisations, just like organisations where people with disabilities organise themselves, [as well as] LGBTQ people, women, independent parents. The same here for migrants and refugees, they have started organising themselves.
>
> *PLMZSO5*

This self-organisation or active participation in social organisations is a feature of long-term residing, or better, of settled migrants:

> Those who actively contribute are people who have been in Poland for a long time. It can be said that they are integrated. As for new migrants, they are often people from Ukraine. It's just that they appear and disappear. I don't know the reason for this.
>
> *PLMZLG2*

The latter observation is a good explanation of the relatively weak self-organisation or participation in social organisations of forced migrants interviewed by the researchers. All of them arrived in Poland after 2011, and the vast majority of them came after 2014, so a period of six years or shorter is probably too soon for them to start a social activity. The other, better explanation is that beneficiaries of international protection in Poland struggle with daily life difficulties, like finding a job, earning enough money to survive, finding accommodation they can afford, and so on, and self-organisation or social activity is not on their lists of primary needs. Another reason can be individual psychological factors behind their eagerness to be involved in civic participation.

Nevertheless, self-organisation of beneficiaries of international protection can be facilitated by existing NGOs. An example of such facilitation is a Refugee Self-Help Centre (SINTAR) established by refugees of Chechen origin and the Other Space Foundation in cooperation with the Institute of Culture of Caucasian Nations. The aim of the centre is to increase refugees' levels of self-reliance in order to facilitate their integration. The centre focuses on cultural and civic education: organising Polish and Chechen language and history classes, English language courses, *vainakh* dance, drama and art workshops, computer classes, and so on (Stefańska, 2015, pp. 23–24). Another example is the Foundation for Somalia, established and run by refugees. It provides a space for assistance and information exchange for asylum seekers and refugees who try to navigate their new Polish reality.

The empirical data showed that beneficiaries of international protection occasionally participate in cultural activities offered by NGOs or other institutions focused on integration. An example of such an institution that attracts both migrants and Poles is the Multicultural Centre in Warsaw, which offers a social space for intercultural exchange, such as joint cooking, a multicultural Christmas Eve, and similar events.

Although none of the refugees with whom we talked was a member of a social organisation, some of them stated that they participate in NGO social activities, but rather as guests than organisers (PLMISy23, PLMISy24, and PLMISy25). The common characteristic of the mentioned respondents is that they all came from Syria and they have already received a refugee or other type of international protection status, and the latter seems to encourage them to participate in social activity in Poland.

Another form of political and social participation in the host country is engagement in consultative bodies. In the Polish institutional system, there is no official consultative body or dialogue platform at the national level that is made up of representatives of migrant associations or Polish NGOs dealing with immigrant issues. However, such bodies are present at the local level in some Polish cities: Warsaw, Gdańsk, Kraków, Lublin, and Wrocław. A particularly interesting case is the City of Gdańsk, which in 2016 appointed Poland's first local Immigrant Council. Twelve residents of foreign origin in Gdańsk (Chechnya, Colombia, Germany, Kazakhstan, Palestine, Russia, Syria, Ukraine, the United Kingdom,

Uzbekistan, and Tunisia) advise the mayor and other local authorities on issues and policies related to migrant and refugee integration. To represent the immigrant population in its variety, the selected volunteers have different backgrounds, education levels, and religious beliefs, and include four women. Professionally, the group counts a doctor, a PhD student, an activist, a social worker, a journalist, an entrepreneur, and others. What they have in common is their willingness to live, work, and raise their children in Gdańsk (European Commission, 2016).

What is significant is the inclusion of migrants in consultancy in local governance could not be possible without lobbying for such a solution by social organisations. Whereas bigger Polish cities empower migrant organisations with the possibility of consultancy, only Gdańsk included the actual migrants (and refugees) on the advisory board. As a practitioner from a social organisation told us, the lack of migrants in consultative bodies can stem from the migrant organisations considering themselves the representation of migrants' interests and, as such, acting on behalf of migrants:

> Certainly it is a bit that through the participation of refugees in NGOs, through the fact that they are employed as mentors or in other positions, these people are often mediators [of refugees' interests] but it is not formalised in any way that we comprise some board consisting of representatives of these communities. I think sometimes we talk about it. At the organisational level, it is quite obvious that migrants should be included in these discussions about issues, which concern them. But this is not obvious for decision-makers at all. It's not like we know better what's best for them.
>
> *PLMZSO1*

Although the respondents in our study were not involved in political activity in Poland, the majority of them expressed interest in the political, social, and economic situation of the host country, which they performed by following the news. In addition, the interest in developments in Poland was much stronger and more frequent than in the countries of origin. With regard to the news in the host country, the respondents seemed to be interested particularly in news related to the situation of foreigners. For instance, one of the respondents, while being asked whether he was interested in what the politicians say in Poland, replied: "Yes, I wonder, what they say about foreigners" (PLMICh02). The interest of other Chechen respondents in the news in Poland, where expressed, resulted from their expectations of staying and living in Poland, whereas following the news in Russia and Chechnya was related to their bonding with their homeland (PLMICh10, PLMICh15, and PLMICh03). The following statement presents a good example of the mentioned observation:

> As long as I live here, I'm interested in the future of this country. I don't want something wrong or bad to happen in this country. Naturally, I want people to live here well and in peace. I'm not so much interested in politics, mostly

> I read something related to refugee issues. You can't be ignorant about those issues, which directly concern us. I also watch and read news from Russia, [though] I can't say I follow on daily basis, but nevertheless it is my homeland.
>
> *PLMICh10*

All four Ukrainians with whom we talked declared an interest in political and economic issues in Poland to a far greater extent than in developments in Ukraine. Presumably, they link their future with staying and living in Poland, and they do not anticipate the possibility of going back to Ukraine ever. The following words of one of the Ukrainian interviewees present a good example of this approach:

> About Poland, yes, [I check] on various websites, because it occurred to me, that to know what is going on with the body, you need to know its temperature. I live here and I need to look, to understand what is going on.
>
> *PLMIUk18*

With regard to the Syrian respondents, almost all of them declared interest in the news in Poland, which can be related to their already obtained refugee status and plans to stay and live in the country.

We also interviewed people who were not interested in the news at all because of its negative overtone. Another repeated reason for expressing a lack of interest in developments in Poland was the limited knowledge of Polish, which makes understanding all the intricacies of the political scene in Poland difficult.

The majority of our respondents were more interested in the news in Poland than in their countries of origin. Some of our respondents admitted they had stopped following the news in their countries of origin due to a loosening bond with their homelands and treating the latter as part of the past, which can also be their method for coping with traumatic experiences:

> I'm losing connection already. I'm not really interested. Of course, I'm following, that's not step-by-step or anything, but I'm interested in Poland much more than that. Like what is happening in Europe and in the European Union much more than I'm interested in what's happening there.
>
> *PLMISy23*

The expressed interest in the news in Poland also can be a marker of forced migrants' agency and their efforts to adaptation to the new reality. We can only guess whether this interest will be transformed into a form of active citizenship such as voting in elections or involvement in associational life once they acquire citizenship. Nevertheless, comparative research shows a correlation between refugees' access to political rights and their actual civic participation in the host country (Cetrez, Petrogianis, and Szalanska, 2021).

Refugees' Belonging in the Host Community

Refugees' feeling of belonging in the host country, society, or community is another aspect of integration. Belonging is about emotional attachment, about feeling "at home" and about feeling "safe" (Yuval-Davis, 2006, p. 197). Previous research has pointed out different levels of belonging. For Yuval-Davies (2006) there are: social locations related to a social position of an individual, individuals' identifications, and emotional attachments to various collectives and groupings, and ethical and political value systems with which people judge their own and others' belongings (Yuval-Davies, 2006, p. 199). The researcher Guest focused on neighbourhood belonging, in which he distinguished social ties among residents and place attachment as two features of social embeddedness (Guest et al., 2006). While place attachment describes a sense of belonging and a feeling of home through emotional bonds towards places and local areas, social ties describe behavioural aspects of embeddedness and the connectedness to the locale (Guest et al., 2006). The focus on social ties evaluates knowledge of one's neighbours by name and place of living, the number of small talks on the street, occasional visits, and the number of close friends in the neighbourhood (Hipp and Perrin, 2006).

To fully understand the social integration opportunities in Poland, one needs to realise the impact of securitisation of refugees on public attitudes towards admission of asylum seekers (see Chapter 3). Despite the dominant negative attitudes of Polish society towards refugees,[11] our migrant respondents did not recall any incident at the level of neighbourly ties. Quite the opposite, beneficiaries of international protection and asylum seekers who lived outside the centres for foreigners felt welcomed by their neighbours, and they managed to establish good relationships with their neighbourhood, even if the latter is based on occasional visits or pure courtesy:

> We build relationships with our neighbours. From time to time we invite them on our holidays, sharing with them our traditional dishes and so on.
>
> *PLMICh09*

As a Ukrainian woman told us, having a dog opened good opportunities for getting to know her neighbours better, especially for her husband who usually walked with the dog:

> For example, my husband goes out with the dog and he knows everyone, who lives on which floor. Unlike me, I know only neighbours from my floor and also a guy by sight. But only a little. And my husband knows everyone.
>
> *PLMIUk19*

She also regretted that her Polish is not good enough, according to her opinion, to socialise more with her neighbours:

> We only say hello to each other. We don't invite one another. I am keen to do so, but I feel ashamed that I cannot speak with them normally. But if they knocked on my door, I would invite them.
>
> *PLMIUk19*

Apart from their neighbours, our respondents listed also Polish acquaintances from work and peers from studies with whom they had established relations. One Ukrainian man told us about going on holidays to his close friends, although did not reveal whether they were Ukrainians or Poles:

> I met a lot of people at work, or on a walk on the boulevards. For several years, we have been going to our close friends' for the holidays, in the fourth or fifth generation. It was just such a moment, I do not know how it happened. And that's mostly positive. Sometimes there are misunderstandings, but there always are.
>
> *PLMIUk18*

The other respondent, a Syrian man, was positively surprised by the support he received in the first months of his living in Poland:

> I didn't have any idea about the Polish language or the assistance during these first six months, but it is okay. Why? Because I have very nice neighbours. We often meet in some bars near my home and they are really very nice people. I was so happy that during these six months, I got my first Polish classes not by the legal offices like this. It was just with my friends, neighbours, and Polish people, because I live in this region and there are just Polish in this place.
>
> *PLMISy25*

Later during the interview, the mentioned Syrian respondent admitted that owing to his knowledge of Polish he had more Polish friends than of other nationalities:

> I use Polish with my friends and I told you that I have Polish friends more than other nationalities or Arabs, for example. This is why if you have contact, you can use and keep practicing for sure.
>
> *PLMISy25*

His example only proves that knowledge of the language is not only a means of integration but also a means to establish bonds with the locals of the host country.

Some respondents admitted they felt a difference between the bonds they used to have in their countries of origin and those they have established in Poland:

> Here [in Poland] we are all just knowing each other. Yes, we help each other when we need help, but still you keep a distance and [you are] not willing to open up to another person because you don't feel that much trust.
>
> *PLMICh10*

As presented above, in general, our respondents had positive relations with their neighbours and they managed to establish some bonds with the host society, even if these bonds were often limited to their neighbourhood, work, or studies. However, in many cases, the new bonds seem to be superficial and could not compete with well-established social networks of the respondents in their countries of origin.

Conclusions

It turns out that the declarative vision of open citizenship in Poland is not the case for the beneficiaries of international protection. Since having equal rights with the citizens of the host country is fundamental to successful integration, and acquiring citizenship is a prerequisite for refugees to achieve this equality in Poland, the low naturalisation rate of beneficiaries of international protection in Poland is a serious obstacle in the integration process. The biggest differences in rights between refugees and citizens have been ascertained in the area of political rights. Refugees do not have voting rights, either in national or in local elections and referendums. They cannot establish or join political parties, and therefore their voice is hardly heard in political debates.

With respect to access to Polish citizenship, among all beneficiaries of international and national protection, only refugees (persons with refugee status) are listed in the Law on Polish Citizenship as ones to be given some facilitations in the procedure of recognition as a Polish citizen (i.e., shorter period of residing in Poland after receiving a permanent residence permit). However, the statistics show that not many refugees use this facilitated procedure, since only 176 refugees were recognised as Polish citizens between 2012 and 2021, although the number of those who could potentially apply for it was 10 times higher.[12] Another explanation for this low number could be that they might prefer the procedure of granting citizenship by the Polish president because it does not have as many requirements as the administrative procedure and is faster than applying to the voivode. Since an accurate number of refugees who were granted Polish citizenship by the president is not available, we can only guess, based on expert opinions, whether the latter procedure is more preferable to them or not.

Our interviews with forced migrants demonstrated that after receiving a status of international protection most refugees are willing to stay and live in Poland, although some of them believe in the possibility of returning to their countries of origin. Despite the anticipation of living in Poland, during the first years after receiving this status (which as well can be two to three years after arriving in Poland), they rarely think of applying for Polish citizenship. In their perception, the whole process is not easy, which is reflected in the low naturalisation statistics of refugees. Another thing is beneficiaries of international protection must reside in Poland at least for seven years (in terms of refugees) or eight years (in terms of beneficiaries of subsidiary protection) in order to apply to a voivode for being recognised as Polish citizens.

With respect to bonds with the host country, the majority of refugees whom we talked to followed the news in Poland and were interested in political developments, particularly those concerning policies and attitudes towards migrants. In relation to ties with their countries of origin, some of the respondents admitted they maintained them, but the ties were limited to contact with their families living in the countries of origin. They declared they have established friendly relationships with their neighbours, although it seems that the majority of these relationships were based on superficial politeness. None of our respondents was a member of an association, a foundation, or a trade union, which shows that joining such organisations by refugees is not common practice. However, they expressed their openness to participate in integrative activities organised by migrant NGOs.

Notes

1 The UNHCR defines the integration of refugees as "a dynamic and multifaceted two-way process which requires efforts by all parties concerned, including preparedness on the part of refugees to adapt to the host society without having to forego their own cultural identity, and a corresponding readiness on the part of host communities and public institutions to welcome refugees and meet the needs of a diverse population. The process of integration is complex and gradual, comprising distinct but inter-related legal, economic, social and cultural dimensions, all of which are important for refugees' ability to integrate successfully as fully included members of the host society" (UNHCR, 2014).
2 Ministry of the Interior and Administration, 2021.
3 Pole's Card (in Polish: Karta Polaka) is a document confirming belonging to the Polish nation. The Pole's Card may be given to individuals who declare their belonging to the Polish nation and prove their attachment to Polish culture and traditions, and who do not have prior Polish citizenship or permission to reside in Poland. Law on the Pole's Card of 7 September 2007 (Law of 7 September 2007 on the Pole's Card (Ustawa z dnia 7 września 2007 r. o Karcie Polaka (t.j. Dz. U. z 2019 r. poz. 1598).
4 Based on ethno-cultural affinity with the kin state, a status law grants special entitlements to co-ethnics residing in other countries. Such privileges do not embrace all citizenship rights but include social, economic, and cultural prerogatives, and constitute a form of semi-citizenship. Status laws exist in numerous countries in Eastern Europe (such as Bulgaria, Hungary, Poland, Romania, Slovakia, and Slovenia) (Łucka 2019, p. 339).
5 Applies to those living abroad.
6 In Warsaw, Kraków, Gdańsk, Wrocław, Poznań, Katowice, Lublin, Łódź, Rzeszów, Opole, Bielsko-Biała, Białystok, Bydgoszcz, Chełm, Przemyśl, and Słupsk..
7 Egzaminy certyfikatowe z języka polskiego jako obcego, http://certyfikatpolski.pl/.
8 Before 1989, the Council of State of the Republic of Poland (Rada Państwa) was an organ of executive power.
9 Naturalisation rate is calculated as the share of foreign citizens acquiring citizenship of a state in relation to the total number of foreign citizens resident in the same state.
10 Persons who were granted refugee status or subsidiary protection can apply for a permanent residence permit after five years of uninterrupted stay in Poland. The time they spent in Poland during the asylum procedure is included in the mentioned period. Then, after obtaining a permanent residence permit, two (for refugees) or three more years (for beneficiaries of international protection) must pass in order to apply for recognition as Polish citizens (Law on Polish Citizenship, Article 30 (1) (1) and (3)).

11 The prevailing negative attitudes towards foreigners or towards admitting refugees were reflected in the following surveys: CBOS (2018, 2017, 2016) and IPSOS (2016, 2015). See more in Chapter 3.

12 Between 1992 and 2012, the average number of asylum applicants who were granted refugee status each year was 195 (Górny et al., p. 40).

References

Ager, A., Strang, A., 2008. Understanding Integration: A Conceptual Framework. *Journal of Refugee Studies,* 21, 166–191. DOI: https://doi.org/10.1093/jrs/fen016.

AIDA, 2020. *Country Report: Poland – 2020 update.* Asylum Information Database (AIDA).

Anheier, H.K., Toepler, S. (Eds.), 2010. *International Encyclopedia of Civil Society.* Springer-Verlag, New York.

Babakova, O., 2021. *Sprawdzian polskości. Wersja hard dla migrantów,* Wp.pl, https://wiadomosci.wp.pl/sprawdzian-polskosci-wersja-hard-dla-imigrantow-6715601239137120a?nil=&src01=f1e45&src02=isgf (accessed 14 December 2021).

Brubaker, R., 1992. *Citizenship and Nationhood in France and Germany.* Cambridge, Mass.: Harvard University Press.

Brubaker, R., 1994. Nationhood and the national question in the Soviet Union and post-Soviet Eurasia: An institutionalist account. *Theory & Society,* 23, 47–78. DOI: https://doi.org/10.1007/BF00993673.

Cetrez, Ö, Petrogianis, V., Szalanska, J. (reviewed and accepted). Constraints and Agency: The Refugee Experiences in the Context of the Journey, Civic Participation, and Health, in: Barthoma, S., Cetrez, Ö. (eds.), *RESPONDing on migration: A holistic perspective to migration governance. Acta Series: Studies in Global Migration: Societal Challenges.* ISBN-number: 978-91-513-1250-7, pp. 313–334.

European Commission, 2016. *Poland: The country's first Immigrant Council appointed in Gdańsk* [WWW Document]. European Web Site on Integration. https://ec.europa.eu/migrant-integration/news/poland-the-countrys-first-immigrant-council-appointed-in-gdask (accessed 23 June 2020).

Eurostat, 2021a. *Residents who acquired citizenship as a share of resident non-citizens by former citizenship and sex,* Eurostat Database. https://ec.europa.eu/eurostat/en/web/products-datasets/-/MIGR_ACQS (accessed 14 December 2021).

Eurostat, 2021b. *Acquisition of citizenship by age group, sex and former citizenship,* Eurostat Database. https://ec.europa.eu/eurostat/databrowser/view/migr_acq/default/table?lang=en (accessed 14 December 2021).

Geneva Convention, 1951. The Convention Relating to the Status of Refugees of 28 July 1951.

Górny, A., Pudzianowska, D., 2009. *Poland Country Report.* EUDO Citizenship Observatory. https://cadmus.eui.eu/bitstream/handle/1814/19631/Poland2010.pdf?sequence=1 (accessed 14 December 2021).

Górny, A., Grzymała-Moszczyńska, H., Klaus, W., Łodziński, S., 2017. "Uchodźcy w Polsce. Sytuacja prawna, skala napływu i integracja w społeczeństwie polskim oraz rekomendacje", *Ekspertyzy Komitetu Badań nad Migracjami PAN.* Polska Akademia Nauk, Warsaw.

Guest, A.M., Cover, J.K., Matsueda, R.L., Kubrin, C.E., 2006. Neighbourhood Context and Neighboring Ties. *City & Community,* 5, 363–385. DOI: https://doi.org/10.1111/j.1540-6040.2006.00189.x.

Hipp, J.R., Perrin, A., 2006. Nested Loyalties: Local Networks' Effects on Neighbourhood and Community Cohesion. *Urban Studies,* 43, 2503–2523. DOI: https://doi.org/10.1080/00420980600970706.

Hitlin, S., Elder, G.H.J., 2006. Agency: An Empirical Model of an Abstract Concept. *Advances in Life Course Research,* 11, 33–67.

Hitlin, S., Elder, G.H.J., 2007. Time, Self, and the Curiously Abstract Concept of Agency. *Sociological Theory* , 25, 170–191.

Kaźmierkiewicz, P., 2019a. Obywatelstwo, in: Górska, A., Koss-Goryszeska, M., Kucharczyk, J. (Eds.), *W stronę krajowego mechanizmu ewaluacji integracji. Diagnoza sytuacji beneficjentów ochrony międzynarodowej w Polsce.* Instytut Spraw Publicznych, Warsaw, pp. 49–52.

Kaźmierkiewicz, P., 2019b. Budowanie mostów między społeczeństwem przyjmującym a beneficjentami ochrony międzynarodowej, in: Górska, A., Koss-Goryszeska, M., Kucharczyk, J. (Eds.), *W stronę krajowego mechanizmu ewaluacji integracji. Diagnoza sytuacji beneficjentów ochrony międzynarodowej w Polsce.* Instytut Spraw Publicznych, Warsaw, pp. 49–52.

Kaźmierkiewicz, P., Frelak, J., 2011. *Political participation of third country nationals on a national and local level.* Instytut Spraw Publicznych, Warsaw.

Law on Foreigners, 2013. Law of 12 December 2013 on foreigners (consolidated text, Journal of Laws 2020, item 35 with amendments). In Polish: Ustawa z dnia 12 grudnia 2013 r. o cudzoziemcach (t.j. Dz.U. z 2020 r. poz. 35).

Law on Polish Citizenship, 1962. In Polish: Ustawa z dnia 15 lutego 1962 r. o obywatelstwie polskim (Dz.U. 1962 nr 10 poz. 49 z późn. zm.).

Law on Polish Citizenship, 2009. Law of 2 April 2009 on Polish citizenship (consolidated text, Journal of Laws 2020, item 347), in Polish: Ustawa z dnia 2 kwietnia 2009 r. o obywatelstwie polskim (t.j. Dz.U. z 2020 r. poz. 347) (hereinafter: Law on Polish citizenship).

Law on the Pole's Card, 2007. In Polish: Ustawa z dnia 7 września 2007 r. o Karcie Polaka (t.j. Dz. U. z 2019 r. poz. 1598).

Łucka, D., 2019. Between Alien and Citizen: Denizenship in the 'Old' and 'New' Europe. *Polish Sociological Review,* 207, 337–354.

Marshall, T.H., 1950. *Citizenship and Social Class and Other Essays.* Cambridge University Press, New York.

Parry, G., Moyser, G., Day, N., 1992. *Political Participation and Democracy in Britain.* Cambridge University Press, Cambridge.

Putnam, R.D., 1993. *Making Democracy Work: Civic Traditions in Modern Italy.* Princeton University Press, Princeton, NJ.

Putnam, R.D., 2000. *Bowling Alone: The Collapse and Revival of American Community.* Simon and Schuster, New York.

Stefańska, R., 2015. *Integration policy and activities in Poland (Technical Report No. 2015/07), INTERACT Research Report.* Migration Policy Centre. DOI: https://doi.org/10.2870/938460.

Sudakowska, J., 2020. "Kogo to obchodzi, że cudzoziemcy nie zagłosują w wyborach?", Krytyka Polityczna, 26.06.2020. Available at: https://krytykapolityczna.pl/kultura/biennale-imigranci-wybory-prezydenckie/ (accessed 14 December 2021).

UNHCR, 2014. *Integration of Refugees.* Rationale for Discussion. Nicosia, July 2014.

Yuval-Davis, N., 2006. Belonging and the politics of belonging. *Patterns of Prejudice,* 40, 197–214. DOI: https://doi.org/10.1080/00313220600769331.

11
CONCLUSIONS

This book is the result of a joint effort of several years of research focused on the admission, reception, and integration of forced migrants in the context of Poland.[1] The research was conducted within the RESPOND project, implemented by an international consortium aiming to study the possible and optimal responses to mass migration to the EU since 2015 using various methods and theoretical perspectives. The uniqueness of the analysis based on the outcomes of this project lies not only in the fact that it comprehensively deals with the important topic of forced migration governance in the Central and Eastern Europe (CEE) region in recent years, with the example of Poland, but it gives new insights, so far absent in the literature, on reception and integration policies from the perspective of asylum seekers and beneficiaries of international protection.

After the completion of our field research in 2018–2020, the reality has brought numerous new national, regional, and global challenges that have had a severe impact both on the migration situation in Europe and Poland and on the law, policies, and practices regarding the management of migration processes, also in relation to forced migration. However, every endeavour must end at some point. The scope of our book does not include detailed considerations of the COVID-19 pandemic, which has had a substantial impact on the decline in mobility and migration on a global scale and has been associated with the introduction of restrictions not only on crossing international borders (including external and internal EU borders) but also on the daily movement within the territory of states both for citizens and foreigners. From the point of view of governance measures, the pandemic in Poland began in March 2020. At that time, the government introduced a state of epidemic emergency and the first full lockdown, with borders almost closed to foreigners, the evacuation of Polish citizens from abroad, international passenger air and rail connections suspended, and most offices and public places, including those providing services to forced migrants, closed. Even at the end of 2021, Poland was

DOI: 10.4324/9781003196327-11

still struggling with the 4th wave of the coronavirus and the beginnings of a 5th wave. This, in turn, affected access to healthcare services, also for forced migrants (Pędziwiatr et al. 2022a).

The second half of 2021 brought a new crisis—most often referred to as humanitarian—on the eastern border of Poland, which is part of the EU's external border. This crisis was connected with the attempts by the Belarusian regime of Alexander Lukashenka to exert migration pressure on the EU, on the border with Poland, Lithuania, and Latvia. Belarus acted as an intermediary in bringing migrants from Middle Eastern countries to its territory and then encouraged or even forced them to cross—often illegally—the Belarusian border with neighbouring EU countries. Unfortunately, Poland has not worked out an effective way to defuse this tension, putting border security first instead of the safety of migrants and respect for fundamental human rights and national, European, and international law relating to refugees. The practice of pushbacks, previously associated only with checkpoints at the eastern border, in mid-2021, became common practice, supported by controversial new laws dealing with forced migrants attempting to enter Polish territory through the "green border" with Belarus.

In September 2021, a state of emergency[2] in 115 localities in Podlaskie Voivodeship and 68 localities in Lubelskie Voivodeship was introduced, which limited the ability of journalists and independent observers to monitor the situation at the border and holding back civil society and humanitarian organisations from providing aid to migrants stuck in the border areas (often big forests or swamps). At the border with Belarus, migrants who had already experienced multiple pushbacks to Belarus were then pushed back to Polish territory. Numerous reports of violent practices applied by border services in Belarus (but also in Poland) towards forced migrants, documented infringements of human rights, such as the right to ask for asylum and the right to life and safety, as well as infringements of children's rights were released by civil society[3] or local communities[4] involved in providing humanitarian or legal aid to forced migrants. The government's response to the higher migration pressure at the border with Belarus remained, however, characterised by militarisation and even more intensive practices of deterring migrants from Polish territory, as well as restricting the possibility to provide support to people in need. Furthermore, Poland did not ask the EU institutions, including Frontex, for support, demonstrating independence and sovereignty towards the EU, despite the knowledge that the crisis on the eastern border has a deeper context of an international political conflict and a power struggle between Belarus, supported by the Russian Federation, and the European Union.

International attention driven by the crisis at the EU border with Belarus (shared by Poland, Lithuania, and Latvia) in the second half of 2021, on 24 February 2022 turned to Ukraine after it was invaded by Russia. The scale and severity of the Russian military aggression have forced millions of Ukraine's residents to flee their houses or even the country. In just the first days after the invasion of Ukraine, the authorities of Poland, by then the main receiving country for Ukrainian refugees, and of other EU states, realised that the consequences of the war in Ukraine are the greatest humanitarian challenge since the end of Second World War. It is also a great challenge for the research community involved in studying forced displacement, as well as all grassroots and top-down initiatives responding to the crisis on all levels—local, state, regional, and global (see e.g., Pędziwiatr et al. 2022b).

In this book, we have tried to show that although Poland was not the main host country for asylum seekers in the European Union, and the migration and refugee management crisis of 2015–2016 was not revolutionary for its migration situation in terms of numbers, it is a country that requires attention for several reasons. The first reason stems from its migration past after 1989 and the opening of borders and inclusion in international cooperation in the field of migration governance only in the early 1990s, and from the changing migration status in the 21st century from a mainly emigration to an emigration-immigration country. Second, it is a country whose relations with the EU in the area of migration management plunged dramatically after 2015, despite the previous strong Europeanisation of Polish migration and asylum policies. Third, the current external geopolitical conditions are less and less favourable, and this applies to the situation in the three non-EU countries neighbouring the east with Poland: Russia—which is politically and militarily unpredictable in the international arena—followed by Belarus—which is politically and economically dependent on Russia—and finally, Ukraine, first plunged into the internal political and economic crisis caused by the Russian aggression in 2014 and then invaded through a full-scale attack by its eastern neighbour in 2022, which already has led to large-scale forced migration to Poland.

Regarding Poland's migration governance, it is necessary to state that despite the increasing role of migration processes in the social and economic structures, there is no agreed-upon migration doctrine. Political documents regarding migration policy include some objectives of the state in relation to the arrivals of foreign nationals and their integration into Polish society. In general, they do not reflect a long-term strategy, called for by experts in migration governance and even by the politicians themselves. Only one of the proposed documents referring to Polish migration policy (Zespół do Spraw Migracji, Ministerstwo Spraw Wewnętrznych, 2012) was officially accepted in 2012 and served as a point of reference for further planning in the area of receiving migrants and describing the rights and obligations of different actors in the migration field. This document was, however, revoked in 2016, as declared by the authorities (the Law and Justice party), due to the changed migration situation and purported need to respond to new "threats" posed by migration movement across EU borders. Despite attempts to elaborate new migration policy (Departament Analiz i Polityki Migracyjnej MSWiA, 2020; Zespół do Spraw Migracji MSWiA, 2021), as of the end of 2021, no official strategic document had been elaborated or accepted by the government. Notably, both the drafts and officially accepted documents relating to migration governance included associations of asylum seekers reaching Polish territory with irregular economic migrants, which resulted in a focus on proposing solutions aimed at tackling abuses rather than addressing the vulnerabilities of forced migrants.

Similar to migration policy, national integration policy does not exist "on paper" and, unlike migration policy, it has never been agreed upon in written form, apart from very general statements regarding the integration of migrants included in both the accepted and draft official documents regarding migration policy. Nevertheless, integration policy is implemented by various state and non-state actors according to the legal stipulations scattered in several legal acts in Poland (regarding, among other issues, granting international protection in Poland, access to the labour market, social assistance, education, and healthcare). This differentiates integration policy from asylum and reception policies, for which the list of legal documents is quite precise (Sobczak-Szelc et al., 2020, p. 25). In practice, the legal basis (and thus also legal obligations on the side of the state) related to integration are narrowed to very specific categories of migrants—repatriates and beneficiaries of international protection. The latter, together with their family members, are covered by narrowly defined state integration policy through what are called individual integration programmes (IIPs). These IIPs are financed from the central budget, but they are implemented by local authorities (family support centres, which are local social policy units) (Sobczak-Szelc et al., 2021, p. 280).

Poland is at the same time a country with a growing interest among the local government authorities in shaping their own migration policy in the vacuum of such policy at the central level and in implementing integration activities aimed also at forced migrants, and with a strong and active role of NGOs and other social actors providing support to migrants. Such a picture means that in the case of Poland one can talk not so much about a model multi-level governance in the area of international migration management, including supranational, national, and subnational levels, but rather about decoupled and disjointed governance (Pachocka and Wach, 2019), where the key role, at least in the integration policy addressed to forced migrants, is played by subnational actors (local governments, NGOs, etc.) with the support of international organisations, in particular the European Union, through various funding schemes and cooperation platforms.

Regarding access to the territory and the labour market, state actors still play the crucial role, which is understandable when we take into account the high level of formalisation and institutionalisation in this area. Thus, applying domestic and EU or international law, state institutions control the arrivals of newcomers (be they voluntary or forced migrants), determine the conditions of their stay in Poland (including stay under protection status), and decide about the obligation to leave Polish territory. Based on the outcomes of empirical studies, we may claim that in the post-2015 period, Poland's application of admission policy towards forced migrants has been characterised by various deterring practices (constituting "push back" and "push out" factors; for more, see Klaus, 2017; Klaus and Pachocka, 2019) and politicised to an extent biasing a just assessment of the scale of real needs and observed abuses in the context of accessing the asylum procedure in Poland.

***

Our book is intended as a publication with a wide range of possible applications in teaching, research, and dissemination of evidence-based knowledge among diversified target groups, including scholars, lecturers, students of different faculties (such as migration studies, European studies, political science, social policy, international relations, sociology, law and administration, etc.), decision-makers at the national and international level, representatives and experts from international organisations, NGOs and think tanks, practitioners working with migrants, and anyone interested in migration, asylum, reception, and integration issues in Europe/the EU. We hope it is a useful tool for transferring reliable academic knowledge based on our own interdisciplinary research results in an accessible way to different audiences in Europe and beyond.

Notes

1 Conducted by the team of the Centre of Migration Research, University of Warsaw.
2 The state of emergency was revoked and replaced with provisions banning access to the border zone from 1 December 2021 (as mentioned in Chapter 4).
3 The humanitarian crisis at the Polish-Belarussian border led to the establishment of an umbrella initiative—the Border Group (Grupa Granica)—for organisations and independent activists involved in monitoring the situation at the Polish-Belarussian border, providing various kinds of aid, from humanitarian through psychological to legal. However, there were also other civil society actors and *ad hoc* groups of activists involved in responding to the humanitarian needs at the border with Belarus, acting outside of the Border Group or in cooperation with it.
4 The involvement of residents of the border zones inaccessible to non-inhabitants during the state of emergency or other laws restricting entrance to these zones for actors providing humanitarian support to migrants was crucial during the crisis at the Polish-Belarussian border.

References

Departament Analiz i Polityki Migracyjnej MSWiA, 2020. *Polityka migracyjna Polski – diagnoza stanu wyjściowego*, www.gov.pl/web/mswia/polityka-migracyjna-polski--diagnoza-stanu-wyjsciowego.

Klaus, W., Pachocka, M., 2019. Examining the Global North Migration Policies: A "Push Out – Push Back" Approach to Forced Migration. *International Migration* 57, 280–293. DOI: https://doi.org/10.1111/imig.12575.

Pachocka, M., Wach, D., 2019. Działania m.st. Warszawy na rzecz integracji beneficjentów ochrony międzynarodowej w Polsce – model wielopoziomowego zarządzania czy chaotyczne zarządzanie (disjointed governance), VIII Konferencja Komitetu Badań nad Migracjami Polskiej Akademii Nauk, Wrocław, 11.09.2019 r. Unpublished.

Pędziwiatr, K., Brzozowski, J., Wiktor-Mach, D., Stonawski, M., Trzeszczyńska, P., Kaczorowski, K., 2022a. *Migracje i Covid-19. Transformacje wielokulturowego Krakowa*. Nomos: Kraków.

Pędziwiatr, K., Brzozowski, J., Nahorniuk, O., 2022b. *Refugees from Ukraine in Kraków*. Multiculturalism and Migration Observatory: Kraków.

Sobczak-Szelc, K., Pachocka, M., Pędziwiatr, K., Szałańska, J., 2020. *Integration Policies, Practices and Experiences – Poland Country Report.* Zenodo. DOI: https://doi.org/10.5281/zenodo.4008666.

Sobczak-Szelc, K., Pachocka, M., Pędziwiatr, K.,; Szałańska, J. 2021. Integration of Asylum Seekers and Refugees in Poland: Policies and Practices. In: Studies in Global Migration. Vol.1. *RESPONDing to Migration: A Holistic Perspective on Migration Governance* (1st ed., pp. 277–298).

Zespół do Spraw Migracji, Ministerstwo Spraw Wewnętrznych, 2012. *Polityka Migracyjna Polski – stan obecny i postulowane działania,* https://ec.europa.eu/migrant-integration/sites/default/files/2019-07/PMP_przyjeta_przez_Rade_Ministrow_31_lipca_2012__2_.pdf.

Zespół do spraw Migracji MSWiA, 2021. *Polityka migracyjna Polski – kierunki działań 2021–2022,* www.gov.pl/web/mswia/projekt-uchwaly-rady-ministrow-w-sprawie-przyjecia-dokumentu-polityka-migracyjna-polski--kierunki-dzialan-2021-2022-id179.

INDEX

Note: Page numbers in *italics* indicate a figure and page numbers in **bold** indicate a table on the corresponding page. Page numbers followed by 'n' indicate a note.